THE GIFTING GOD

THE GIFTING GOD
A Trinitarian Ethics of Excess

Stephen H. Webb

New York   Oxford
OXFORD UNIVERSITY PRESS
1996

Oxford University Press

Oxford   New York
Athens   Auckland   Bangkok
Calcutta   Cape Town   Dar es Salaam   Delhi
Florence   Hong Kong   Istanbul   Karachi
Kuala Lumpur   Madras   Madrid   Melbourne
Mexico City   Nairobi   Paris   Singapore
Taipei   Tokyo   Toronto

and associated companies in
Berlin   Ibadan

Published by Oxford University Press, Inc.
198 Madison Avenue, New York, New York 10016

Library of Congress Cataloging-in-Publication Data
Webb, Stephen H., 1961–
The gifting God : A trinitarian ethics of excess /
Stephen H. Webb.
p. cm.
ISBN 0-19-510255-X
1. Generosity – Religious aspects – Christianity.   2. Trinity.
I. Title.
BV4647.G45W43   1996
248.4 – dc20   95-26480

1 3 5 7 9 8 6 4 2

Printed in the United States of America
on acid-free paper

Acknowledgments

The ideas presented here took shape over the course of the last four years. Thus, many people were helpful in various, indeterminate ways. If I cannot specify or name all of the gifts I have received during this period, it is not because this help has been vague but because it has been pervasive, and my gratitude is not lessened by the practical difficulties of an equally comprehensive expression.

Many of the people I thanked in earlier works should be thanked again. Indeed, this project builds on my previous books, *Blessed Excess; Religion and the Hyperbolic Imagination* (Albany: SUNY Press, 1993) and *Re-Figuring Theology; The Rhetoric of Karl Barth* (Albany: SUNY Press, 1991), in which I examined the rhetoric of excess from a formal, structural perspective, showing the isomorphic relationship between certain religious works and ideas and the trope of exaggeration. In those books I was content to play the role of the literary critic, culling examples of a neglected figure of speech from both texts and arguments and hoping to show that the importance of hyperbole is not limited to single statements or the flourish of an occasional embellishment.

Although in both books some substantive theological reflections emerged from my interest in rhetoric, once I achieved some distance from them I became dissatisfied with their limited focus. It is too easy, as many postmodernists demonstrate, to brandish the category of excess without reflecting on the problems of social structure and moral duty. In fact, postmodernism does have a moral edge; it can be defined as an obsession with excess to the extent that excess upsets our metaphysical desires for control and disables our personal quests for domination. Excess decenters the subject and thus makes room for new kinds of otherness. Frequently, however, postmodernism has been accused of practicing a negative theology that resists substituting a constructive position for the celebration of hermeneutical ambiguity and pluralism. By focusing on the phenomenon of gift giving, I have tried to find that place where excess and ethics intersect, where, that is, excess, taken to its own extremes, contains a corresponding ethics, one that is congruent both with postmodernist fascinations with incompletion and otherness and with communitarian concerns for virtue and tradition. (I further explore the intersection of ethics and excess in a forthcoming book on theology and compassion for animals.)

William C. Placher was the most important contributor to my project. Bill continues to be my first (and best) reader, as well as a theologian whose praxis of giving has influenced more than the words on these pages. I already regret the few places in this book where I have not followed his advice. Steve Smith, Brad Stull, and Larry Bouchard gave me some wonderful suggestions and advice when I was revising this manuscript, just when I needed them most. Many of their comments made me realize how much more work I still want to do on these issues. The thrust of this project began as an essay, "A Hyperbolic Imagination: Theology and the Rhetoric of Excess," in *Theology Today* 50 (April 1993):56–67, and some of the paragraphs and phrases of that essay have been included in modified forms in this book.

The first draft of this book was written during the weekends of the spring of 1993 and a daily schedule of writing during that summer in Bloomington, Indiana, where my wife, Diane Timmerman, was completing her M.F.A. in theater. Her theater friends became my own, and their giving sustained my writing. Diane has taught me more about giving than any book simply by being the kind of person that I would like to become. In a way, this book is a result of taking her giving and trying to give it back in another form. This book is the gratitude that her giving has made. This book is also dedicated to the memory of Erik Tomusk (1959–1993), for whose life I am grateful and from whose death I learned that giving also means letting go.

Contents

THE GIFTING GOD

Introduction:
Giving and Thinking

Everybody in the United States seems to be involved in a great debate about gift giving that has inestimable political ramifications. Now more than ever before, we need theological clarification about what generosity is and how giving should be formulated and practiced. Although private acts of donation are widely lauded as crucial for the health of our country, public acts of giving are coming under increasing scrutiny. On one side of the current debate, giving is the problem, and the solution demands an honest reconceptualization of generosity. To simplify an ongoing conversation, conservatives are arguing that giving must be connected to merit, that gifts should be earned. Generosity should be careful, calculated, measured by what it produces. The language of giving, in other words, should reflect the language of business and economics. A gift should be an investment. Otherwise, gifts are wasted, squandered; they create disorder and dependence, and thus giving threatens to become, ironically, immoral.

On the other side of the debate, giving is still presented as the solution to many problems, even though the pressure to articulate how giving works makes the supporters of generosity uncomfortable and hesitant. The liberal tradition persists in defending a giving without strings attached, without, that is, an explicit expectation of a return. Liberals are rightly guided by the insight that if generosity is not at least a bit disinterested (that is, uninterested in the repayment of the gift), then it is hardly generosity at all. Yet even liberal theoreticians of generosity acknowledge that giving must be connected to the common good—or at least constrained by a responsible community—in order for giving to achieve its ends.

These debates have not only theological analogues but also theological roots. How we think about God's giving will shape how we give to others, and how we think about giving in general will inform our theological reflections. This book sets out to put into dialogue various theories about giving and various portraits of God's benevolence. I hope to show that the two sides of this debate can be reconceived (perhaps even reconciled) if we think about giving from the proper (that is, trinitarian) theological perspective.

I first became aware of the fundamental problems associated with giving when, in an informal conversation with a few students at Wabash College several years ago, my attempt to defend the palpable reality of generosity was repeatedly rebuffed. These students took it for granted (that is, as a given) that any apparent act of giving was really (and obviously) driven by self-interest. Later, in a lecture I gave to the Wabash community, when I tried to develop the case for giving more formally, I encountered a similar resistance. Everybody seems to know that giving is calculated, not spontaneous, and structured (and thereby canceled) by the expectation of an equivalent return. The very pervasiveness of this assumption makes me suspicious. On the one hand, I wanted to congratulate and encourage my students for seeing the deeper reality hidden beneath mere appearances. After all, the distinction between reality and appearance is the primary methodological maneuver of any philosophy, the very foundation of critical reflection. On the other hand, this totalizing insight into the epiphenomenal structure of generosity was just too easy. It smacked more of cynicism than wisdom. The idea that exchange is the foundation of generosity is a quick or premature judgment, assumed and not earned, disconnected from lived experiences of successful or failed acts of giving.

Indeed, I am convinced that a great reversal has taken place in our thinking about giving: what was once hidden is now flaunted, and what was once accepted (given) is now always questioned (returned). The theoretical triumph of reimagining the motivation for generosity has led to a new orthodoxy with its own troubling consequences. Certainly, gift giving can be a sentimental and token gesture, a cloak for naked self-interest and a deceptive instrument of control and manipulation. Think, for example, about how the word *charity* has taken on so many negative connotations today. Doing good in our culture is getting harder, so perhaps it is comforting to believe that good cannot be done at all. Nevertheless, it is time to challenge the all-too-easy critiques of generosity in the name of something more troubling and demanding than cynicism alone.

Is it possible to conceptualize all of our acts of giving solely on the slim basis of self-centered agency? In a recent work, Walter Lowe has called such insights "ready-made Enlightenment" claims that have the form of critical thought but actually embody new myths and dogmas, claims that rationalize rather than disturb the status quo.[1] Likewise, Paul Piccone speaks of an "artificial negativity," an opposition that is created by the dominant order as a way of generating a creativity that only perpetuates that order.[2] Any critique, too easily accepted and propagated, can become a hindrance to further thought and action. Criticism can function to limit the imagination and legitimate the present situation, as well as to alter and challenge that which is taken for granted. The deep truth of self-promotion that lies beneath the allegedly superficial surface of other-regard has become so conspicuous in our day that it is now crucial to ask what reality it, in turn, is concealing.

The most critical contemporary thinking, I believe, needs to recover the giving that our culture obscures behind a painfully barren monologue on self-interest. To accomplish this task, I have not endeavored to "save the appearances" (as Aristotle describes his method in the *Nicomachean Ethics*) of generosity but rather to investigate the possibility of that which has come to be seen as increasingly and plainly impossible. Here theology can play a helpful role. It is time for theology to question the questions of contemporary culture. Although theologians have a long tradition—linked with discussions of sin—of criticizing and limiting any individual's claim to have acted generously, theology is essentially a responsive discipline, so the theologian must in the end resist the temptation to absolutize the critique of generosity, no matter how much that critique is dependent on (usually unacknowledged) theological resources. Theology, like any form of critical thought, refuses the appearance of self-sufficiency in the world, but it discounts appearances, running the risk of being ungrateful for all that is, only in order to awaken us to a greater magnitude of debt, a more original and amazing donation, and hence a higher order of gratitude. Theology, which narrows our perceptions of what is as a way to widen our imaginations of what might yet be, discovers the persistence of generosity and envisions the novelty of excessive giving even where the status quo of self-interest and exchange seems perpetually to prevail. Theology lures us into an unsuspecting abundance that liberates and transforms, freeing us from the incessant struggle for recognition and the duplicity of self-admiration.

A theologian writing about giving is thus always aware of a first giver, the givenness of all things, and the responsibility for returning the gift. Indeed, to write about giving is itself an act caught up in the structure of donation and indebtedness, priority and dependence, so that how one writes—one's style—reflects what one wants to say. My desire is to respond to the problem of gift giving in a way that is receptive and grateful but not passive and idle. In fact, I want to render uncertain that which is usually taken for granted, which in this case is not the reality but the illusion of generosity. Yet, I do not want to idealize giving as something that is pure and untainted by self-interested motivation. To transvalue self-interested acts so that giving appears as the radical opposite of exchange is to disconnect the theological imagination from quotidian reality and to empty theological rhetoric of any referential content. Giving necessarily takes place in a context, so that it is never completely free of economics. Indeed, I want to show that giving has its own kind of economy by arguing that giving can create relationships of expectation and commitment without becoming another form of buying and selling. Giving does not need to be conceptualized as a solitary act; one can add to the gift without thereby subtracting from it. Thus, part of my argument will be that a gift accrues more giving, and the exemplification of this thesis requires me to try to give something back to giving by showing not only the complexity and difficulty but also the beauty and necessity of this seemingly simple act.

More specifically, this book is divided into two equal parts. The analytical part (which comprises the first two chapters) attempts to sort out, both sociologically and philosophically, the various problems that distort our culture's understanding of gift giving. Giving is an act that joins (at least) two people, and the dichotomy of two basic orientations—self and other—governs the debates about generosity. The result is a genuine dilemma or puzzle. Can the gift be for the other without being against the self, and can the gift that does not subtract from the self really add to the other? In other words, is there a way of relating the self to the other that escapes the polarity between selfishness and self-sacrifice? Are the self-interest and other-concern orientations mutually contradictory? The constructive task (which comprises chapters 3 and 4) is to affirm a giving that is other-oriented without being self-destructive. The true gift should speak of self and other together, in a single discourse or action that nevertheless accounts for the irreducible doubleness of this pair. The issue of the gift is the possibility of glimpsing an opening in which the other is present to the self, by an act that nonetheless begins with the self. Through the gift, the giver lets go of something in order to let the other be, and thus the self finds itself elsewhere, in an event in which something different happens to the ordinary and everyday.

Part of the problem with my conversations with students pertained to vocabulary. Traditionally, the issue of giving was framed in psychological terms by the possibility of altruism and, conversely, the limits to egoism. This psychology has theological roots. Altruism is the secular equivalent to the religious category of sacrifice, just as egoism is another name for the sin of selfishness. Modern Western culture has undertaken a prolonged and massive rehabilitation of the terms *egoism* and *selfishness*, while the very purity of the ideas of altruism and sacrifice has become the easy target of ridicule and rejection. In this linguistic climate, the very grammar of giving is threatened. How can we speak about giving without invoking the theological vocabulary of sacrifice? Moreover, what is the plausibility of theology if *giving*—a term so closely related to grace—is illusory?

When I decided to write about these issues, I realized a new set of terms was needed. The framework for the problem of giving is, it seems to me, increasingly economic, not psychological. The logic of economics has successfully colonized and thus presently regulates what can and cannot be said about giving. Simply put, economic realists (or cynics) defend an economy of the self in which every expenditure is balanced by an equivalent appropriation. I give to you if, and only if, you give to me. Throughout my book, I call this perspective, which I introduce and analyze in chapter 1, the *model of exchange*. Although the circularity of this model (what is given always returns) can highlight the values of equality, responsibility, and reciprocity, this model more likely permits the cunning of self-interest to dominate every social interaction. Although I think giving should take place in a milieu of mutuality, I resist the idea that calculation cannot be displaced by spontaneity and generosity. Ontologizing exchange can be reassuring; exchange is, after all, the principal category of understanding operative in the modern Western world. To suspect all relationships of harboring exchange is to prove our own presuppositions final and universal. To think the other of exchange, we must bracket our own convenient expectations and prejudices.

Exchange has a place in giving, I decided, but only if it is contextualized by something else. The best opposition to the dominant model of exchange is not the old language of altruism and sacrifice but a discourse—what I call the *model of excess*—that is very contemporary and capable of disrupting the reduction of generosity to economics. Indeed, it is important to reflect on not only the rhetoric about giving but also the rhetoric that *is* giving. At its best, gift giving signifies both a challenge to and a continuation of the model of exchange because it is an act of communication that both embellishes (in a trivial sense) and profoundly alters the ordinary and expected trading of goods and information. The rhetoric of the gift is the rhetoric of excess, the (im)possibility of saying more, doing more, and giving more than exchange encourages or permits. Our culture understands and values acts of excess as moments of rebellion against the predominance of economic exchange. The gift is exchange hyperbolized; it is, in fact, one of the basic forms of the trope of hyperbole. Excessive giving, understood theologically, has the potential to interrupt and disorient the training all of us receive in economizing our resources that ensures that what we give is equal to what we take.

This potential is not, of course, always realized. Whereas exchange seeks balance and equality at the price of calculating the good of the other only in terms of the good for the self, excessive giving stems from a strong self-affirmation that also risks overlooking the good of the other. I argue in the first two chapters that the attempt to circumvent the economics of giving by emphasizing excess inevitably trivializes and deflates the act of generosity; in fact, squandering (what I call excess that is not theologically shaped) is dependent on the economics it seeks to overcome. As some critics argue, gift giving is merely a way of embellishing or enhancing (in a way that repeats and reinforces) the unbreakable logic of barter and trade. Squandering attempts to negate the economics of the modern soul without affirming a constructive alternative. Excess provides a holiday from the rigor of exchange; conversely, exchange needs the release of excess in order to maintain itself as the primary model of agency in the modern, industrialized West. The question persists: Is the rhetoric of the gift mere rhetoric (form without content), or does it point to possibilities usually suppressed and ignored? Does giving give us something different or more of the same? Is excess merely another (no doubt more seductive) form of exchange, a different logo for the logos of calculation and reciprocity, or is there something *more* to giving? If so, what is the *more* on which giving depends?

Perhaps the cynicism of our culture can help us be more clear about the origin, shape, and future of gift giving. The first two chapters press the point that giving is usually either marginalized as an extravagant act that has value for the self alone or reduced to a surreptitious form of exchange in which the self receives as much as the other is given. The second two chapters engage this perplexity with a theological strategy. Indeed, the problem of conceptualizing and practicing an excessive generosity that is constructively related to the constraints of exchange warrants a careful examination of religious theories of giving. A gift that is not excessive is hardly a gift at all; giving without exchange leaves little room for the return of the gift, a relationship of solidarity and mutuality. Are these elements in giving necessarily mutually exclusive, and, if not, how are they to be ordered? The question is whether giving can embody elements of both excess and exchange at the same time. The more I tried to answer this question, the more I needed theological language about grace and community to illuminate the dynamic of giving. The element of excess assigns the power of giving to the initial act, regardless of consequences, and the perspective of exchange puts the accent of power on the outcome of the act, denying spontaneity and freedom. Only a giving that begins with an original and abundant gift and aims at a community of mutual givers can be both extravagant and reciprocal. Thus, my analysis of theories of giving in the first two chapters already draws on and assumes my theological reconstruction of giving in the last two chapters, just as my theology of giving depends on the framework I establish in the first two chapters. (Indeed, readers more interested in theology can read the last two chapters before the first two.) The result, I hope, is a genuine give-and-take conversation, a revisionary theology that correlates tradition and situation in mutually critical and generous ways.

Against the false alternative between excess and exchange, then, I develop a third option in chapters 3 and 4, a theo-economics of giving, in which generosity is funded by an excessive God, who nonetheless promotes reciprocity and mutuality. I use the word *theo-economics* hesitantly in the body of this text because it can signal a premature synthesis of theology and economics. What I offer is not a theological interpretation of economics or an economic reduction of theology but a model of religious agency that brings together excess and exchange in a manner that keeps them separate and yet joined. Theology, I wager, provides a model of antieconomic behavior that goes further than the negations of squandering. The Christian God squanders, but not as an exercise of blind self-affirmation or sovereign freedom; instead, God gives abundantly, in order to create more giving, the goal of which is a mutuality born of excess but directed toward equality and justice. Christianity affirms both excess and mutuality by taking them to the extreme point—located through hope on an eschatological horizon—where they meet, one leading to the other.

The connection of excess and exchange in theology, however, is not so easily accomplished. In fact, I argue in chapter 3 that the same dualism that governs philosophical conceptions of generosity also regulates many theological doctrines of God. God is usually portrayed either as an excessive giver who does not need exchange, to the point of controlling our own giving, or as giving reciprocally, so that God's giving imitates rather than transforms our own. Can theologians conceptualize a divine excess that nonetheless leaves room for some kind of exchange? The attribution of benevolence to God is one of the most common ways of identifying the divine. God is good. Why? Because God gives. What does God give? Everything, from who we are to what we have and need. But how does God give, and how does that giving relate to our own attempts at generosity? That is, can we give as God gives? Can excess be exchanged? The more I relied on the theological notions of grace and community (church) in order to understand giving, the more I realized that thinking about giving also helps us think better about theology. The category of the gift, properly understood, helps us think more clearly about how God's grace is neither utterly irrelevant to human actions nor tied too closely to them. The theory of giving helps us understand how grace works by creating its own kind of economy, quite different from the economics of exchange that pervades the modern spirit.

The question of the relationship between God's giving and our own has fascinated and troubled philosophers and theologians at least since Plato's *Euthyphro*, in which Socrates' opponent defines *holiness* as the commerce between the divine and the human. Does God give to us in a balanced and proportional manner, rewarding our efforts according to the logic of desert? Does religion merely reproduce the dynamic of exchange? E. B. Tylor's *Primitive Culture* (1871) was one of the earliest and most influential anthropological theories tracing the origin of sacrificial rituals to the human attempt to bribe, pay tribute to, and trade with hidden supernatural forces. Religion thus economizes (organizes and makes a profit from) our relationship with the unknown. Religion is embellishment that perpetuates the order of the same (that is, the self) rather than inaugurates something different (the other). Religion is exchange taken to a higher, more fanciful (but still repetitive) level.

Such theories presuppose the dominance of exchange over excess, to the point where religion merely imitates the economics of the everyday. As a Christian theologian, responsive to the intrusive reality of grace, I could not accept these attenuations of God's presence/presents in the world. The alternative is to portray God's grace as pure excess, a unique, abundant, and sovereign initiative unrelated to our response, but I did not want to isolate and compartmentalize God's grace from the practical realm of material culture, the patterns of appropriation, production, and consumption that circumscribe and define quotidian reality. Hence, throughout this book, I argue that, to make sense and to be relevant, God's giving must be correlated to our own practices of exchange and reciprocity, yet this correlation cannot be strict or exact. For the Christian theologian, there can be neither absolute similarity nor pure dissimilarity between God's giving and our own. If God's giving is sui generis, an excess purified of the mutuality of exchange, then God is removed from human concerns and activities, yet a God who gives just as we do, trading this for that, cannot be the source of an abundance that enables us to give extravagantly. Drawing on the trinitarian doctrine of God in chapter 4, I argue that God is both excessive and reciprocal, and I call this theological model of generosity *gifting*. Indeed, the range and breadth of God's giving serve to draw together excess and exchange, joining them in a constructive manner.

The theology of chapter 4 is thus a direct response to the philosophical problems I develop in chapters 1 and 2. Gifting combines excess and exchange without obliterating their differences. My goal is not to retreat from critical discourse in order to arrive at a protective place where the purity of giving can be defended from the stain of self-interest. Sentimentalism aside, all gifts combine, at some level, power and care. After all, our very birth is a gift, symbolized by one's name, which is unsolicited, both bestowed and imposed, a sign of the fact that we are recipients, whether we like it or not, and that every gift comes as both surprise and demand, grace and task. The point is to find a force in giving that is not intrusive alone but compels the gift along as an affirmation of our individuality and freedom. The power of the gift should reside in the process as a whole and not just in its beginning or end. The gifts of God determine who we are by enabling us to give to others. In the trinitarian pattern of giving, the excessive gift endows a mutual exchange, simultaneously making the excessive productive and the reciprocal unpredictable. Thus, Christianity offers the possibility of a gift that is not bound by the dilemma of self and other but rather emerges from and returns to a community of givers, all empowered by an original abundance capable of accelerating the gift even as it is exchanged.

1

The Return of the Gift

Man's chief difference from the brutes lies in the exuberant excess of his subjective propensities, — his pre-eminence over them simply and solely in the number and in the fantastic and unnecessary character of his wants, physical, moral, aesthetic, and intellectual. Had his whole life not been a quest for the superfluous, he would never have established himself as inexpungably as he has done in the necessary. And from the consciousness of this he should draw the lesson that his wants are to be trusted; that even when their gratification seems farthest off, the uneasiness they occasion is still the best guide of his life, and will lead him to issues entirely beyond his present powers of reckoning. Prune down his extravagance, sober him, and you undo him.

William James, "Reflex Action and Theism"

Gravity is from the fall, and is to be defied; deliver us from the pull of the fundamental. Practice levity, and levitation. Oh for the wings of a dove, the spirit; the winged words that soar, the hyperbole or ascension.

Norman O. Brown, *Love's Body*

Someone gives something to somebody. These three elements constitute what we commonly call gift giving, an apparently simple structure that, when closely examined, opens onto a multitude of complex questions. Even a partial list of these questions would serve only to raise countless issues that cannot be rendered clearly or completely. Such issues, however, can be grouped around the three basic aspects of giving that my initial sentence outlines. *First, someone gives.* What is generosity? Why should someone give something to somebody else? How is generosity motivated and maintained? *Second, something is given.* What is a good gift? What distinguishes a gift from other objects, and how is the gift presented in order to verify this distinction? To whom should the gift be given? *Third, someone receives.* What happens to the gift? How is it to be received, and how is it to be returned, if at all? What relationship is now secured between the giver and the givee?

13

These three sets of questions, ranging from the origin of giving through its mediation in the object given to the gift's final destination, can be reduced to a more fundamental one. Simply put, is generosity in the form of gift giving possible, and, if so, what conditions make it possible? These questions are usually approached under the rubrics of sacrifice and altruism, but they can also be approached in terms of the different shapes and contrasting rhetorics of gift giving and economic exchange. How does gift giving differ from the economic activity of buying and selling? What kind of difference does this difference make?

These obviously broad and complex questions can be approached in many different ways. I do not intend to survey the history of various theories about giving or develop a comprehensive account of all of the moral issues raised by generosity.[1] Instead, in the first section of this chapter, I outline two basic forms of gift giving—what I call excess and exchange—that dominate most discussions of this phenomenon. These forms are differentiated by competing rhetorics, but they are also determined by broad social structures, so in the second section I provide an overview of gift giving as a social institution that raises philosophical problems. I offer a reading of gift giving in our contemporary situation that highlights certain difficulties with that practice, difficulties (both rhetorical and practical) that are reflected in theoretical articulation. I then turn to an analysis of specific theories of gift giving—Marcel Mauss, Marshall Sahlins, Pierre Bourdieu, Richard Titmus, and Lewis Hyde—and show how these difficulties resist resolution and point to the need for a broader framework.

Between Excess and Exchange

Because the practice of giving, referring to a variety of activities ranging from simple generosity and neighborliness to heroic and mythic deeds of self-sacrifice and martyrdom, has always been central to Christianity and Western culture as well, it might seem more commonplace than problematic. Nevertheless, the very range of this practice makes it so crucial yet cumbersome to discuss. My central claim in this chapter is that theories of gift giving tend to take one of two antithetical positions. At one extreme, they stress (even exaggerate) the excessive nature of the generous act. Gift giving is portrayed as the exact opposite of the economic activity of bartering, trading, and exchanging. It is a spontaneous and extravagant gesture that violates the laws of economics by surpassing the measurement of this for that. Borrowing a term much used by Nietzsche, I call this kind of giving *squandering*, a glorified discharge of energy that resists not only economic but also thermodynamic conservation—the forces that convert every output into something productive and useful.

Squandering is, in fact, an exaggerated word: to hear it pronounced is to think of excess, to be drawn in by the extravagant. To squander is to waste, to give against the metaphysical aesthetics of balance and proportionality, and to act recklessly, disregarding the calm, cool voice of reason. We squander when we do not care what the systems that be will do to our gifts, when we defy all of the efforts to make our giving reasonable and prudent. This approach, which I examine in much more detail in chapter 2, can either advocate gift giving as a welcome alternative to the predominance of the economic sphere or marginalize gift giving as a kind of afterthought or shadowside to the pervasive nature of economic thinking and activity. Squandering, I argue, is a dominant motif in modern discussions of gift giving, but it is also tensely related to an inimical formulation.

At the other extreme, gift giving can be reduced to economics proper. In this minimizing perspective, generosity is always secretly ruled by the rules of economics. Giving is really a form of exchange, although it pretends to be something more. This perspective is theory laden because it denies appearances for the sake of an underlying reality accessible only to critical thought. Naming the given object a gift masks and distorts the "fact" that a commodity has been exchanged, that is, that what is given must be equivalently returned. Generosity as such is thus thought to be impossible, although ideologically it can be a useful even if imaginary idea. This approach appeals to modern sensibilities that are suspicious of any claims for generosity above and beyond the actual give-and-take of reciprocity. If the first model of giving is dependent on the trope of hyperbole, this model is dependent on the reversal of irony: what proceeds as the gift is soon shown to be something else and returns as the commodity. The hyperbole of the gift is merely decorative and thus deceptive.

My goal is to show how, in our modern period, these two approaches to giving, excess (or squandering) and exchange (or reciprocity), have become increasingly polarized, so that any coherent account of generosity is severely strained. Briefly stated, I argue that, in most theoretical accounts of giving, excess and exchange are either insufficiently distinguished or completely compartmentalized from each other. Excess is either really just another name for exchange, or it is so disconnected from exchange that it becomes irrelevant and thus unable to challenge the dominance of exchange. In other words, giving is viewed either as an illusory way of talking about the reality of calculation-driven exchange or as an extravagant act that has little social value. Indeed, I want to argue that no current theory satisfies *both* our desire to give and our need to receive gifts *and* our suspicions of gift giving as an activity that demands careful formulation and practice in order to distinguish it from exchange proper. Although I am more sympathetic to the theory of squandering than to the theory of economics or exchange, in the next chapter I discuss some of the limitations of squandering, in the context of the denial of gratitude and with reference to its most significant representatives, Emerson, Nietzsche, and (more ambiguously) Derrida. Indeed, in this and the next chapter, I argue that the theory of excess, taken to an extreme, ironically gives gift giving over to the cunning of calculation that it tries to escape.

The first two chapters, then, should serve to make my Christian account of giving all the more warranted and all the more plausible. Indeed, in chapters 3 and 4, I argue that an adequate theory of gift giving finds support and completion in a theological account of God as the paradigmatic gift giver and the church as the community of givers. This theo-economics brings together excess and exchange as aspects of a single process of generosity and mutuality, in order to preserve squandering from its most self-defeating expressions. Hence, the task of theology is to show how God enables an excessive giving that promotes equality and reciprocity without thereby diminishing the power of excess.[2]

Style and Function

Gift giving is at least in part a cultural artifact, a socially created institution, embedded in specific rituals and particular languages of rules and customs. What giving does is what it says, so that language and act are fused together. Style and function are thus the two interrelated features of the form of the gift. Gift giving, after all, is not only a physical act but also rhetorical; it is a form of self-expression and a way of communicating with others, as well as a means of distributing goods outside the usual operations of the market. What we say about giving, then, is significantly determined by the actual practices and arrangements of generosity, even as language retains the power to shape and change social possibilities.

In Western culture, gift giving seems to be a rather modest activity with little potential to transform general social structures or particular self-understandings. Many anthropologists have argued, following the classic work of Marcel Mauss and the more recent work of Marshall Sahlins, that gift giving was a central activity in primordial cultures, the basic mechanism by which both goods were exchanged and relationships of obligation and affection established. However, the growth of the purely economic sphere has marginalized gift giving in most modern Western countries. Moreover, the mediation of governmental redistribution programs has further complicated the role of giving in contemporary society. Both trends problematize not only the function and value of the gift but also the ways in which we talk about generosity. More particularly, the economic displacement of the gift disputes the origin of giving, whether giving is different from exchange, and the governmental mediation of the gift challenges the destination of the gift, whether the gift can create a community and contribute to the common good. In both cases, the sociological issue of the place of the gift is related to the rhetorical issue of the language of the gift. What can we say about giving that actually corresponds to why and how we give? Moreover, how does our talk about giving shape the ways in which we give?

Michael Walzer explores the subordination of the gift to economics in "Money and Commodities," a chapter in his *Spheres of Justice* arguing that "the gift is determined by the commodity." It thus presupposes the interplay between possession and dispossession. "What can be owned can also be given away."[3] Walzer wants to suggest that private property makes gift giving both specialized and special; that is, gift giving in its modern guise now becomes a function of the freedom of disposal, unconstrained by social rules or cultural rituals. The gift is ultimately a personal expression of private ownership, not social solidarity or individual virtue. It serves to redistribute goods in a way unrelated to the demands of justice, and yet gift giving for Walzer is itself just, because it exercises the power implicit in the fundamental feature of modern economies — the right to own. Giving is a privilege granted by the rights of private property.

For Walzer, economic exchange is the very foundation for gift giving. Although the gift is itself not exactly exchanged, giving is made possible by exchange. Only because objects are first exchanged can they also be given. What is missing from this account is an appreciation of the distinct language and power of giving and thus its potential social significance. To put the problem in overly general terms, when all objects of value are exchanged, giving is reserved for objects with trivial or sentimental value alone. Giving is a way of personalizing or privatizing exchange, but it is not a form different in kind from exchange. Even commodities, after all, are attractively packaged, so that an object exchanged seems nearly indistinguishable from a gift. At most, giving creates local economies that draw together friends, family, or clan by circulating objects that do not have significance outside the specific group. The gift belongs to the home, to circles of intimacy and affection, not to the public, where objects are valued according to more general criteria. Giving supplements exchange with warmth and privacy, but it does not significantly differ from or call into question the dominance of exchange as the primary pattern of interaction. Consequently, gift giving is merely one among many arenas of social activity, all of which are subordinated to the rules and the power of the marketplace. The gift makes no difference.

If one aspect of gift giving in our culture is its economic reduction to a particular modality of private ownership—what we can call its com-modification—a related feature is the way in which public, social acts of giving have been co-opted by the government, what we can call the bureaucratization of giving. In the modern welfare state, for example, the government mediates many of our responsibilities for others. The government, theoretically, satisfies some of the basic needs of its citizens, and this uniform implementation of a minimal redistribution of wealth can be a great advance over reliance on private and therefore haphazard generosity. The improvement is more than one of efficiency and convenience. As Michael Ignatieff has argued, gift relationships can be enslaving: "In many Western welfare states, entitlements are still perceived both by the giver and the receiver as gifts. To be in need, to be in receipt of welfare, is still understood as a source of shame."[4] If welfare is treated as a gift relationship, then it can be humiliating, not helpful. By making giving impersonal and systematic, government regulation can free givers and givees alike from many cumbersome situations. Nevertheless, transferring the gift to a third and neutral party solves the problem of what a gift exacts only at the cost of curtailing the giving process. Gifts create obligations that are more nebulous than the precise exchange of buying and selling, but that makes it all the more important to inquire into what gifts actually do. One of the most demanding aspects of the gift is the imposing and sometimes uncomfortable question it raises of how, if at all, it should be returned. Giving not only involves the giver in the life of the givee but also requires something of the givee, so that the course of the gift compels an active participation. Is it possible that the return of the gift is not only an encumbrance but also an exercise in freedom and responsibility?

Givers also lose when giving is abbreviated. Although bureaucratizing gift giving enables the disadvantaged to feel free from shame, it does nothing for a society's needs for solidarity. If needs are correlated to rights, then satisfying a need can hardly be construed as offering a gift; generosity and justice thus become radically severed, and the consequences are disastrous.[5] Giving is no longer connected to the notions of community and the public good. The displacement of generosity from the public realm constitutes a troubling loss. Everyone is treated (theoretically) equally, which does not imply that each person will be treated individually. The result is that we all treat each other as strangers, and compassion loses its human face. Compassion becomes supplemental and thus trivial. Indeed, in an era of bureaucratized giving, generosity serves an increasingly personal, psychological function, so that the bureaucratization and commodification of giving go hand in hand. Giving comes to dramatize our search for self-identity in an increasingly complex and mobile society. As Barry Schwartz notes: "It is clear that the presentation of a gift is an imposition of identity."[6] What we give is who we wish to be—how we want to be perceived and how we perceive others—and not what others need in order to become givers in turn.

Bureaucracy redistributes goods to satisfy some minimal level of need, but that cannot satisfy our own basic need to help others. As Ignatieff suggests, "The deepest motivational springs of political involvement are to be located in this human capacity to feel needs for others."[7] To distribute goods on the basis of needs alone is just, but it cannot do justice to the community-creating power of giving. To meet the need for generosity is the purpose of what is commonly called the *third sector*, those independent, nonprofit, voluntary associations that are concerned with charity and the common good, as opposed to the government (the first sector, concerned primarily with order) and the market (the second sector, concerned mainly with profit). Susan A. Ostrander and Paul G. Schervish have argued that the three sectors can be thought of as forms of social relations rather than specific places or institutions.[8] Whereas the first sector relies on the medium of votes and the relation of the second sector is money, the third sector must appeal to norms, values, and morals in order to accomplish its tasks. What the third sector offers is a form of exchange based on "giving and getting," giving people what they cannot buy while at the same time expecting them to contribute to particular causes and sustaining their contributions by enabling them to participate in communities based on shared values.

Ostrander and Schervish characterize the third sector as constituting relationships of reciprocity, and this description demonstrates that the problem of exchange is not so easily defeated. In capitalist society, it goes without saying, all needs are exploited for the purposes of profit, so that even the need to be generous in ways not satisfied by governmental bureaucracy becomes the object of political and economic activity. Ronald Reagan's hope was that less government would translate into an increase in the power of charity. Scholars like Teresa Odendahl, however, claim that "Charity has become a rhetorical device by which to justify this dramatic political development,"[9] the shift from statism to the privatization of the redistribution of wealth. The need for generosity is thus politically manipulated and utilized to dismantle governmental distribution programs that promote justice, while nonprofit groups are not supported by the public gifts that make private giving possible. The result only exacerbates the lack of social significance for generosity.

Without serious attention to the relationship of excess and exchange, then, even public displays of giving serve only to advance private interests. Indeed, Odendahl argues that organized charity frequently functions to meet the needs of the wealthy more than the poor. The wealthy do not try to attack intractable social problems but rather give to elite institutions that provide ways of organizing and rewarding their own capacity for luxury. Institutionalized charity thus transforms the need for generosity into a means of investment and profit. Disconnected from the demands of justice and the common good, third-sector institutions can increasingly pursue their own private agendas, without worrying about those who are not effectively vocal and organized. On a psychological level, giving becomes a way of denying one's wealth and status; modest living and proportional philanthropy assuage guilt and prove merit. On a social level, giving creates protective circles for retreat and refuge from the rigors of the market. In any case, giving does not challenge, let alone transform, the pervasive reality of exchange. It is no wonder that cynicism about disinterested giving prevails. It seems apparent to many people that generosity can never circumvent the machinations of exchange.

Yet, it is too easy to complain about the lack of generosity in our culture. Robert Wuthnow has argued that even though most Americans think that their fellow citizens are becoming more self-interested and less altruistic, a tremendous number of people, three fourths of those he surveyed, stated that it is absolutely essential or very important to help others.[10] Clearly, people still think of giving as a basic prerequisite for human flourishing. The most distinctive aspect of Wuthnow's survey is that he found no contradiction between individualism and altruism. People who give to others can articulate that activity only in the language of self-interests and satisfaction. We use the language of therapy and reward in order to synthesize the disparate orders of desire and compassion. Wuthnow even goes so far as to suggest that the most altruistic persons in his survey are the most individualistic. These people portray voluntarism as a creative solution to personal problems. One way to look at Wuthnow's data is to think of this coincidence of interests and compassion as a cunning way of rationalizing a mode of behavior that does not have the public support of a shared discourse. Certainly, luck or circumstances sometimes provide situations in which self-interest coincides with care for others. We also can learn how to combine these drives into one occupational or vocational pursuit in which they become no longer distinguishable: certain professions help us synthesize duty and sacrifice, occupation and supererogation. Associating caring with the roles we play is perhaps the simplest way of explaining why and how we care. Nonetheless, it is fascinating that Wuthnow's survey found so many people who felt compelled to talk about how they get the most out of their compassion, how they maximize the benefits that the expenditure of other-regard entails. The genre within which most people personalize their accounts of compassion remains oddly contrary to the main thrust of compassion itself.

Actually, Wuthnow isolates two different narrative structures that people use to account for generosity. Both use the language of fulfillment, but in one the gift is exchanged for fulfillment, whereas in the other fulfillment is the precondition for giving. The first strategy implies that caring is motivated by a sense of emptiness or lack. In this model, giving is born from need — a need that originates in the self, not a desire for the benefit of the other. By giving to the other, this need is met, and thus the gift of generosity is returned to the giver. Here the accent is on reciprocity, the completion of the giving process. By ending the story of the gift with an emphasis on the satisfaction of the giving, this narrative strategy brings generosity to an acceptable but predictable closure. As Wuthnow explains:

> Having set the story up as a gift transaction, the speaker seems compelled by the narrative itself to bring the relationship described into a state of equilibrium at the end. Rather than simply letting us understand the event as altruism, the speaker completes the transaction by claiming to have enjoyed it. Thus we run no risk of concluding that the gift was given

grudgingly or for an ulterior motive; the giving was made worthy by the receiving. (p. 95)

Without a credible public discourse on generosity, stories of giving must come full circle by denying their starting point, the generosity of the gift. Indeed, the story itself can stand for the fulfillment that the gift intends; one of the functions of giving, then, can be the permission to tell stories about it, stories that show the giving to be not really giving at all. The story becomes the return of the gift, thus negating (or recouping) what it feigns (or offers) to represent (give).

The second narrative structure puts fulfillment at the beginning, not at the end of the giving. In this model, giving occurs at the level of leftover or surplus energy. It is not prompted by need but by an abundance. Here the emphasis is on excess, the extravagance of the generous act. The more you have, the more you can afford to give. Gift giving is the by-product of a closed system, which creates more energy than it consumes. Giving is not sacrificial but incidental. How the individual giver achieves the autonomy sufficient for such abundance is problematic, but that is a problem anterior to the acts of care and compassion. A modified version of this model, according to Wuthnow, still emphasizes the plenitude that precedes generosity, but it also admits that caring adds to that initial abundance. In this less static version, self-worth is still a prerequisite for giving, but now generosity has a pedagogical value; it challenges, educates, and expands the already centered self. Caring is a way of exercising one's moral capacity, of staying in human shape. In the language of economics, short-term losses can be accepted because they contribute to future gains.

These two narrative structures correspond to what I am calling the paradigms of exchange and excess, and in both versions the story of the gift ends where it began: with the giver alone. The closure of the stories that giving creates (the resolution or meaning that giving receives in the end) seems to negate the very possibility of giving beginning. Gift stories become confessions or explanations, first-person narratives that never move beyond the self. Both of Wuthnow's narratives interiorize giving so that it is no longer shaped by or contributes to a community that precedes and receives the gift. Indeed, whether fulfillment comes at the end or the beginning of generosity, compassion becomes a matter of individual attitude and style. As Wuthnow explains, "Fulfillment is the strength, the identity, the self-esteem needed for the individual to care. Fulfillment is also the handle on caring that fits most comfortably in our cultural grip" (pp. 114–15). Today, we are most encouraged to give to ourselves rather than to others; we need to constantly reward ourselves for working hard or promise ourselves future pleasures for present sacrifices. As a result, almost anything can be counted as compassionate, and thus it is difficult to know when somebody is *not* acting compassionately.

The triumph of the language of fulfillment over that of altruism and sacrifice represents a gain in honesty and self-scrutiny. If compassion is difficult and rare, then claims about acting compassionately should be modest and self-critical. Yet the narrowing of public discourse can also have a devastating effect on individual agency. As Wuthnow observes, "The possibility of compassion depends as much on having an appropriate discourse to interpret it as it does on having a free afternoon to do it" (p. 45). The lack of an appropriate correlation between discourse and deed results in a cynical tendency to dismiss any language that attributes generosity to anything but the realm of self-interest.[11] "The fulfillment I receive," Wuthnow concludes, "is thus a transaction with myself. It is indeed the perfect kind of relationship to cultivate in a society as individualistic as ours."[12] The result is that cynicism is our most public discourse on issues of generosity, and speaking about giving as other-oriented is forced to sound naive, innocent, and reactive. Indeed, in our post-Freudian situation, we have grown comfortable with the idea, best argued by Pierre Bourdieu, whom I discuss later, that all of our givings are secretly controlled by ulterior motives that undermine even our best intentions. Consequently, the discourse on giving—what we say to each other about this common practice, which, in turn, shapes what we think about how we give, and even whether we give at all—is in danger, not for altogether superficial reasons, of becoming undone.

To be more precise, today the language of economics, not psychology, has invaded and colonized the traditional discourse of generosity. It seems obvious, almost trivial, to say that we have become too inclined to allow the vocabulary of our givings to be supplanted by economic metaphors that reflect the encroachment of a calculative mentality on all areas of our existence. We talk about generosity in terms of the utilitarian trinity of investment, profit, and interest, and we resolutely believe that the circulation of all of our acts constitutes a complex but ultimately circular network of interconnections aimed only at self-enhancement. Although other-regarding narratives probably rarely correspond to reality in a precise way, cynicism denies the disruptive, rather than descriptive, power of compassionate discourses, the way in which the language of giving can interrupt, even if it does not represent, the behavior we all too often take for granted. We have given up the elevated language of love for the easier but demoting discourse of economics; the result is an anorexic constriction of generosity from excess to irony. According to the frugal economics of the modern soul, the gift always ironically returns—in fact, it is never really meant to be given at all—with an accumulation of value. It is today accepted as a cynical truism—it goes without saying, no matter how often we say it—that we give only in order to receive.[13] Irony is revealed as the not-so-hidden trope of cynicism.

Unlike irony, which subtracts, negates, and takes away (as Socrates in *The Clouds* is able to talk Strepsiades out of the coat on his back), hyperbole extends, amplifies, and *gives;* it is thus fruitful to think of giving as the praxis of the figure of exaggeration. Indeed, our culture today utilizes hyperbole and its innocence and naivete as a counterpart to and a complement of the excesses of irony's cynicism; in the midst of a corrosive skepticism, giving must become increasingly excessive, even random, in order to demonstrate its independence from the conscious and unconscious drives of economizing desire and manipulation. Consequently, generosity becomes conflated with excess for its own sake, a squandering that denotes, at worst, the merely frivolous, the promiscuous, and the luxurious or, at best, the intoxicating and ecstatic.[14] Excessive acts are useful in an overly technologized culture only as an inebriated interruption of the everyday by the extraordinary, a transitory and compensatory experience of release and relaxation. Excess is thus reduced to hype, to hyperbole understood as mere ornamentation or embellishment; excess is that moment when language normally used as an instrument of labor gets to go on a holiday. Such hyperbole is related to language as the weekend is related to the workweek. In a culture that utilizes hyperbole to heighten the unsurprising, gift giving is in danger of becoming another conspicuous commodity, an emblem of the excessive only in the sense of the superfluous and irrelevant. In this case, giving, which does indeed surpass the boundaries of the quotidian imagination, can be indicted for offering a "something more" that is in actuality only "just enough" to stimulate the boredom of an unrestrained rationalism and to supplement the confinement of an oppressive functionalism. Excess and cynicism, then, require and encourage each other.

In this debate between excess (hyperbole) and exchange (cynicism/irony), the purpose and future of religion is at stake. If religions once served to promote, shape, and direct excessive acts of generosity and self-donation, for many people today religious activity seems to be connected to excess in a pejorative sense alone. The religious praxis of giving, which traditionally contrasts the strenuous nature of the sacrifice against the ease and pleasure of generosity, risks being irrelevant to the actual practices of exchange that dominate our lives. For Christianity, the theological discourse on giving as sacrifice has been shaped by the spiritualization and internalization of the crucifixion, and so the theologian cannot completely abandon the idea of sacrifice. Unfortunately or not, though, the word *sacrifice* today has lost all of its innocence. It can no longer be employed without a very disturbing recognition of its high costs. In Wuthnow's survey, when the language of giving was replaced by the language of sacrifice ("I want to give of myself for the benefit of others" to "I want to sacrifice myself for the benefit of others"), the number of positive responses dropped from 42 to 15 percent.[15] This is regrettable because caring does involve sacrifice, yet it is clear that the language of sacrifice is in trouble in our culture for sound reasons. Part of the problem is that it entails an intensification of the economy of the gift that involves the double and excessive move of heightening and masking the two dangerous sides of generosity. The image repertoire of sacrifice, which retains vestiges of victimization in the service of a rigid social structure, helps perpetuate the myth that giving must entail the will to suffer, even to do violence to oneself,[16] and does nothing to expose or resist the reality that generosity is always usurped by those who position themselves to be recipients without being subjected to the same values as the givers. Indeed, the very vocabulary of sacrifice is taught most to those who have the least to give but the most to gain from the generosity of others.

Moreover, it is no accident that in many Western texts on sacrifice the figure of the feminine is held to be the ideal instance of self-donation. In the traditional division of gender labor, women are assigned the task of giving and the rhetoric of excess, and men control the labor of commerce and exchange. Both genders lose something valuable in this exchange; men are alienated from the practice of mutuality and the joys of noncompetitive sharing, but women lose in ways that are even more degrading. Woman, tradition teaches, is the being for the other, but, we now respond, in such a way that she is denied being for herself.[17] The ideology of sacrifice not only promotes a self-violence that is only incidentally related to the dynamism of generosity but also magically mystifies the actual exchange of expenditure and recuperation by encouraging extravagant behavior that is reinvested in the maintenance of a dominant hierarchy. Sacrifice, then, also has its economy, one that turns the other's loss into the self's gain while rectifying this imbalance with a cunning language that reverses this unilateral flow by compensating the giver with the word of praise that covers the expropriation of the gift. To speak of sacrifice, therefore, is to draw on the luxury of a tradition that has conceptualized giving at the expense of the marginalized and oppressed. In sum, sacrifice promotes the negative aspects of excess ("give until it hurts") and simultaneously supports the worst kinds of reciprocity (giving is a mask for an exchange in which the winners exploit the ideology and the losers do all of the giving).

If the language of sacrifice does not appear to play a constructive role in our culture, then a second Christian discourse on giving—what we can call the language of generosity—is nearly indistinguishable from secular discourses, so that it also risks making religion superfluous. The language of Christian generosity can best be examined by comparing it to the language of sacrifice in terms of the dynamic of excess and reciprocity.[18] The language of sacrifice, popular mainly in conservative theological circles, suggests that selfishness is natural, and thus gift giving is possible only in terms of strenuous obedience to transcendent demands or as the product of the external force of grace. The language of generosity, an opposite discourse more popular in liberal theological circles, suggests that giving is natural, indicating that giving is the way in which people best discover themselves, others, and even the divine.[19] Sacrificial language would seem to admit that almost all acts not subjected to divine intervention are ruled by reciprocity. Giving must be almost excessively violent to disrupt this basic human condition. Moreover, giving understood as sacrifice is a way of forgoing a present good for a future reward. Only by an eschatological promise of the return of the gift can the bonds of reciprocity be broken and generosity compelled.[20] Then again, the liberal notion of generosity also accepts the prevalence of reciprocity. Giving is viewed as a natural form of excessive energy that engenders relationships of mutuality and support. If the language of sacrifice naturalizes reciprocity, then the language of generosity naturalizes excess. Taking the conservative position to an extreme would lead to cynicism about the possibilities of giving in all but the most divinely charged cases. Taking the liberal position to an extreme would glorify giving without counting the cost that generosity often entails. In both positions, excess and reciprocity are oddly disconnected from each other. In sacrificial language, the excess must come from a divine source that is not, in turn, reciprocally related to the givee; moreover, the sacrificial act of the human giver is done in spite of reciprocity, not for it. In the liberal language of generosity, excess is an aspect of the autonomous individual, a by-product of strength and energy, and thus it is not itself subjected to the bonds of reciprocity. Excess in the liberal notion of generosity is for itself; it intends its own satisfaction.

For all of its limitations, the notion of sacrifice captures something about giving that the framework of generosity cannot encapsulate. Indeed, some of the most powerful modern accounts of giving emphasize its excess, what I explore further in Nietzsche's theory of squandering. If an act of giving merely fulfills a sense of duty or office, then it can hardly be deemed generous. Giving, to deserve the name, must be supererogatory. The idea of supererogation preserves the excess that the term *sacrifice* stresses without promoting the self-violence or ideological abuses of that term. The term *supererogation*, which means to overspend or spend in addition to what is required, derives from the Latin *supererogare*. Note the use of this term in the Vulgate account of the Good Samaritan parable in Luke 10:35: "And on the next day he took out two denarii and gave them to the innkeeper, and said: 'Take care of that man, and whatever you supererogate, when I return I will give back to you'" (my translation). Interestingly, the term is used in reference to the innkeeper's activities, not the Samaritan's. Moreover, the excessive acts of the innkeeper are encouraged by a promise of repayment, with a small subsidy or downpayment offered in advance. So, although the Samaritan is traditionally identified as the paragon of generosity, the innkeeper, too, is magnanimous; the innkeeper must trust that his expenditures will be reimbursed, and in the meantime what he spends is more than the situation requires. The message of this story is ambiguous: Is it possible to overspend without expecting some compensation in the end? Can excess ever be completely disconnected from reciprocity? Is giving more like squandering (which implies waste, surplus) or investment (an expenditure that intends an equal or greater return)?

The history of the term *supererogation* raises similar ambiguities. In the Middle Ages, supererogatory acts provided the opportunity to purchase the means for the alleviation of guilt and punishment. Jesus Christ and the saints, the argument went, through their exemplary lives, built up a treasury of good works by obeying not only the commandments of God (which all are to obey) but also the voluntary counsels of perfection (the optional commands of poverty, chastity, and obedience). Extreme renunciation, then, created a surplus of moral wealth that could be drawn on with the right intention and for the right purpose. Moral funds could be transferred from one account, where they were excessive, to another account, where there was a deficit. God is interested in the ultimate balance of the entire ledger of all acts performed, and so God permits this creative accounting. The church is the accountant, and the methods used are nothing less than good business practice: funds are manipulated in such a way as to equalize their distribution without depleting the endowment. A profit—the brimming treasury of moral merit generated by the parsimony of the saints—is reinvested in the system as a whole in order to subsidize less efficient parts of the operation. The result is that an initial excess, the heroic deeds of the saints, is utilized to create a situation of reciprocity, in which all can profit from the labor of the few. Excess is subordinated to exchange.

The same problems arise in purely philosophical accounts of supererogation. David Heyd has distinguished a variety of forms of supererogation: in addition to saintliness and heroism, there are beneficence, doing favors, volunteering, forbearing to do what is within one's rights, and forgiveness.[21] According to Gregory Mellema, all of these acts have two things in common: first, they are morally praiseworthy, but their omission is not morally blameworthy; second, the performance of the act fulfills no moral duty or obligation.[22] The problem with these definitions is that we live in a society in which our vocational range of duties is increasingly narrow, so that almost any act can seem to be supererogatory. Indeed, just as the Protestant Reformers rejected the notion of a two-tiered set of moral responsibilities, obligations and counsels, it is difficult to understand how an act can be clearly moral but not obligatory. The temptation in such a system is to relegate to the category of the supererogatory acts that are unpopular, difficult, or unpleasant. The alternative is to demand a level of morality for all that appears to be unachievable. Does everyone have a basic duty to strive toward perfection? If so-called second-mile acts are universally required as part of a communal moral code, why do we consider them extravagant and heroic? Conversely, if the supererogatory is risky, spontaneous, and extravagant, how can it be defended as moral with regard to either a utilitarian or a duty-based ethic? Moral theory finds itself in a dilemma: it seeks to promote the maximal good, but it speaks the minimal language of requirement, duty, and obligation. Yet, even the most basic goods have an infinite dimension that renders them immune to the language of requirement. The good to be done is always greater than what we imagine our duties to be. Thus, we must either inflate the language of duty to cover acts that clearly transcend that category, or we must delegate a whole range of moral acts—acts that prompt self-examination by setting the standards by which we measure our potential for good—to a nonmoral category. At this point, the language of morality is in need of a supplemental discourse, a theological understanding of the importance of excessive acts of generosity.

The problem is that we do not have a language that is appropriate to the complexity of the excessive nature of generosity. The intention of the generous act, according to the logic of supererogation, must be free from the ordinary obligations and responsibilities of social discourse, which is why many authors connect gift giving to excess. It must also be free from the notion of desert or justice; if someone deserves what we give to them, then what we give is not a gift. Generosity is thus related to tolerance and mercy, as well as to the theological category of grace. The question immediately arises whether generosity complements or violates the standards of justice. This question becomes more pointed the further one pushes the excessive dimension of gift giving, but even in the most careless squandering there cannot be an absolute disregard for the other. The nature of gift giving requires that a benefit to the other must be intended. As Lester Hunt notes: "In the case of generous acts, there is no such 'because' or 'in order to' beyond the intention of benefitting someone: we do not do *that* in order to do something else. That is, the intention in generous acts is gratuitous."[23] If the generous act is reckless for the sake of irrationality rather than otherness, then it becomes gratuitous in a pejorative sense, and such private profligacy can hardly be considered generous. A vocabulary is needed that would do justice to the excessive nature of some moral acts, yet also locate those acts in the social realm of the everyday, the realm of interpersonal relationships circumscribed by obligation, duty, need, desire, and affection.

Many treatments of giving emphasize its social, interpersonal function. Indeed, if gift giving captures something of the excess of sacrifice, it also resonates with exchange, mutuality, and reciprocity. After all, we not infrequently want to decline a gift, which demonstrates the potentially restrictive side of the gift relationship. To give is to obligate, and to receive a gift is to enter into a relationship that cannot be easily exited. For this reason, theorists have often connected gift giving not to extravagance but to equivalence. Aristotle, for example, thought that being wealthy aided in the development of the virtue of generosity or liberality, not because one must give a lot of money in order to be generous but because giving without a sense of pain or sacrifice is the essence of generosity.[24] Gift giving is best practiced, then, between friends; it is an expression of equality, respect, and admiration. It is the opposite of charity, which often implies a sense of pity for the givee as well as a sense of duty or obligation to act. It is not impulsive or spontaneous but thoughtful and prudent, even regular and habitual. Indeed, Aristotle thought that the generous man, the *eleutheros*, requires *phronesis*, or sound judgment, because the giver must find the mean between the extremities of niggardly (deficient) and profligate (excessive) behavior.[25] The wise gift giver knows when and how best to give, and this requires careful reflection, attention, and calculation. Even magnificent spending for noble causes must be judged according to whether it fits the occasion and reflects the proper motive and judgment. Aristotle's approach to gift giving is still relevant, even arguably dominant, in our culture, and yet the idea that giving is best practiced between equals according to the rules of moderation and exchange fails to do justice to the Christian notion of sacrifice or its secular counterpart, squandering. Nietzsche and Aristotle, then, represent two sides of an issue that do not easily fit together.

My goal is to go beyond the polarization of excess and exchange—indeed, to establish a relationship between these terms that does not collapse one into the other—and, to accomplish this task, I draw from the full range of resources, both Nietzschean and Aristotelian, of the language of gift giving. Ideally, giving a gift should be both an aggressive gesture of extravagance and a modest expression of solidarity. It should be both sacrifice and exchange, without being merely one or the other. I have already argued that gift giving recapitulates the excessive divestiture that sacrifice seeks to name. Indeed, to give is to "give up" something of value. Nevertheless, giving is not about self-control or discipline. Although gift giving can imitate the dynamics of sacrifice, we ordinarily do not think of it in the terms of asceticism alone. Gift giving connotes something less dramatic and more intimate than what the image of sacrifice suggests. It shifts the focus from the rigor of self-denial to the joy of attending to the other. We give gifts because we want to and because we are attracted to the good of the givee. Gifts are drawn from us, in a seductive manner; even when we ask, awkwardly, what somebody wants for a gift, or when somebody during the holiday season draws up a list of gifts they need, gifts cannot be demanded or required. They are born of joy, not pain. We give in order to belong, to enjoy together an unsought abundance. It is possible to understand the gift, then, as simultaneously excessive and reciprocal. Gift giving is not an obligation, required by the rules of exchange—it is almost by definition not the fulfillment of a duty—and yet it is a practice that we consider essential to our humanity as well as to social solidarity.

Nonetheless, naming—and constructively conjoining—both of these dimensions of giving at the same time can be extremely difficult. In fact, I want to argue that the task of doing justice to both excess and reciprocity demands a framework that modern theories do not provide. As a result, the modern discourse on gift giving oscillates between extravagance and exchange. Excess serves to compensate or supplement exchange; exchange functions as the inescapable framework for excess. The further excess is pushed to transgress the dominance of exchange, the less relevant and demanding it is, to the point where exchange is all that is left. Excess and reciprocity are the two weights between which the discourse on giving uncertainly seesaws, seemingly incapable of finding the right balance. If I am right, then any discourse on giving wobbles at the moment it tries to do justice to both of these opposite positions. What is missing in these precarious theories is a way in which both excess and reciprocity can be preserved in a mutually critical and reinforcing manner. It seems that in our human situation we must either give recklessly (even anonymously), without regard for purpose or consequences, or we must give in a calculating fashion, either in the exchange of commerce or in the exchange between friends. To escape this binary logic, we need to find a pivot for excess and reciprocity by placing giving in a larger (and religious) context, demonstrating that giving is a response to a prior giving, empowered by an initial excess that nonetheless leads to mutuality and reciprocity by directing our giving toward a harmonious horizon. We need not only a broader language about giving but also an institutional setting in which the gift can function as both provocation and demand, initiating gratitude and encouraging reciprocity. Without the appropriate institutional setting, the rhetoric of giving, no matter how broad, will continue to be excessive in the pejorative sense (wasteful, irrelevant). That is the argument of chapters 3 and 4, which provide a framework—a rhetoric with ecclesiastical implications—that brings together the best elements of giving as sacrifice-squandering-excess and giving as generosity-liberality-reciprocity.

I now turn to a close reading of several of the most influential modern theories of gift giving. I argue that the oscillation between excess and exchange produces theories of giving that make gift giving an increasingly difficult activity to understand, let alone practice. I first examine the anthropologist whose work on giving is the classic statement of the issues that are currently being debated in the revival of interest in this topic. Marcel Mauss argues for the priority of giving over exchange, but he does so in such a way as to leave the relationship between excess and reciprocity unclear. Indeed, any attempt to retrieve generosity must face the critique that the very act of appropriation demonstrates the inescapability of the logic of exchange. Marshall Sahlins is an anthropologist who is more clearly committed to the idea of excess, yet he locates excess in certain primordial cultures as a state of abundance prior to economic development; by doing so, he does not aid in the development of a theory of abundance and giving appropriate to the modern world. Pierre Bourdieu is, in many ways, the opposite of both Mauss and Sahlins. He finds exchange wherever others find giving. His critique of the possibilities of giving is the most extreme instance of the exchangist mentality itself. Bourdieu raises the question of whether gift giving can ever be anything more than another form of economics proper. Richard Titmus is one of the first scholars to try to argue that gift giving is an aspect of modern culture that needs to be cultivated and encouraged. He leaves open the question of whether gift giving is something that should be planned as an aspect of the broader economy or whether the gift can create an alternative community.

Finally, more than any other writer, Lewis Hyde has tried to imagine what the communal life of gift giving might look like. Even though he, too, mixes and confuses the discourses of excess and exchange, I have learned a lot from his work, and in chapter 4 I return to a version of Hyde's gifting community in my own reflections about God and the church. To the extent that modern theories are unable to correlate excess and exchange, the theory of squandering becomes more attractive as a way of affirming giving while discounting and abridging the problem of the return of the gift, which is the problem of the community embodied by the gift. In the next chapter, I deal more fully with the theory of squandering, while keeping in mind the community that Hyde ultimately envisions. This chapter and the next point to the following conclusion: to have both excess and reciprocity, we need an endless narrative (one that does not end where it begins), a theo-economic structure that preserves their tensile relationship and yet brings them together in a constructive fashion.

The Gift of Marcel Mauss

The difficulty of understanding what gift giving might mean in our culture has attracted many to anthropological studies of gift giving in primordial cultures. Marcel Mauss's *The Gift* is itself a gift, one that has invited many responses and yet still circulates in the academic world with much profit.[26] More than any other book, it has motivated the current interest in gift-giving practices, both in other cultures and in our own. In a study of traditional cultures, Mauss calls giving a total social event because it is the primary means of articulating social relations. In gift giving, the objects exchanged are the vehicles of a complex network of relations in which prestige, status, sympathy, kinship, obligation, and wealth are conveyed. Each gift reflects society as a whole, and giving defines and sustains the relationships upon which society is built.

In a strategy of great originality, Mauss conceptualizes economics on the basis of the gift, a reversal of the contemporary assumption. Exchange, for Mauss, is an attenuated and diminished form of giving. Today, however, we must struggle to imagine gift giving as anything but exchange. Note how we try to separate the gift from the commodity by giving only "useless" objects or by presenting gift objects in such a way (such as through wrapping) that they are clearly distinguished from commodities. In primordial and traditional societies, such subterfuge is not needed because the gift is the form that all exchange takes. Such a gift can shatter the binary opposition of economics and generosity. It is not gratuitous, though neither is it a matter of pure exchange. It is at once an expression of both generosity and power, affection and manipulation, fluidity and stability, solidarity and rivalry. Purely economic exchange, impersonal and self-centered, is the calcification of a process that was once sweeping in its social implications and consequences.

One of the key terms in Mauss's study is the indigenous Maori concept of *hau*, the spirit of an object that in Mauss's understanding is the force of the gift that compels its return. For Mauss, the *hau* is the aspect of the gift that involves the giver, making the gift an extension of the giver's personal being, thus obligating the givee to respect and return the gift.[27] The gift dynamic itself, then, without any external compulsion, both extends outward toward the givee and returns to the giver, forming a unique social bond. Mauss has been criticized for exaggerating the voluntary dimension of reciprocal giving in primordial cultures,[28] but the capacity of the gift to form free relationships of obligation is a crucial claim because it supports the overarching agenda of his project. He is interested in the question of not just how best to read primordial gift-giving practices but also how to revalue gift giving today. Indeed, Mauss wants the return of gift giving in order to moderate the rigors of capitalism in a way that is neither leftist nor rightist.

"Once again," he prophesies, "we shall discover those motives of action still remembered by many societies and classes: the joy of giving in public, the delight in generous artistic expenditure, the pleasure of hospitality in the public or private feast" (p. 67). The hope he extends is slight but significant. As Blake Leland notes: "He calls for a return to the 'morality' of the archaic institution, to a world in which humanity is not alienated from its products, in which distribution is more important than accumulation of wealth, and the group more important than the individual."[29] Giving, prudently recovered as a counterbalance to the dominance of the *homo oeconomicus* type, can create social solidarity without displacing individual initiative or freedom.

Though prior to and more encompassing than exchange, giving thus has a distinctly calculable utility. Indeed, any attempt to envision giving at the center of a society will burden it with conservative social functions, thus trading excess for reciprocity. Excess apparently never escapes the logic of intention, and since excess is connected to surplus, it is also a privilege only the few can afford. Mauss, for example, is drawn to the potlatch rituals of the Native Americans of the Northwest Pacific coast, people with a genius for generosity in the way that they intensify giving by uniting it with destruction. A potlatch is a public demonstration of wealth, which, through "the violence, rivalry and antagonism aroused," summons similar acts of wanton wastefulness; "the rich man who shows his wealth by spending recklessly is the man who wins prestige."[30] Such squandering is a sign of power and honor. This connection of expenditure to violence is a crucial motif repeated in several modern theories, from Nietzsche to Georges Bataille and N. O. Brown. Lévi-Strauss argues that the potlatch continues today on a more mundane level, through the activity of gambling as well as the emphasis on giving gifts that are functionally useless and thus wasteful. Lévi-Strauss suggests that as the explicitly reciprocal function of primordial giving rituals declines in modern culture, their excessive aspect must be exaggerated if gifts are to have any meaning at all.[31] Waste and destruction are thus modern forms of ritualizing exchange. Lévi-Strauss forces the issue of whether even the most spectacular giving secretly serves a fairly specific social function. He criticizes Mauss for being mystified by native explanations and constructs. However, Mauss also wants to assign giving a social value, and he sees no conflict between the violence of the potlatch and the intimacy of mutual sharing. Mauss wants to recover the gratuity and recklessness of giving as a more genial form of exchange. The question remains: Can gifts really be both extravagant and useful?

In his discussion of the reciprocity of giving, Mauss borrows from the work of Bronislaw Malinowski, who examines the giving practices of the Melanesian islanders in *Argonauts of the Western Pacific*.[32] Malinowski focuses on the *kula* practice, a form of intertribal exchange that unites the various tribes by keeping articles constantly moving in opposite directions (in such a way that the two flows of goods balance each other) along a circular route. Although Mauss interprets the *kula* as a form of potlatch, Malinowski is more sensitive to its reciprocal function. Indeed, the *kula* raises the central question about all communal gift-giving rituals: Does giving always return to itself, creating and maintaining an enclosed group rather than opening outward toward the other? Is the circle formed by giving a closed circuit? If so, can such giving really be considered voluntary and free? For Malinowski, there are no pure gifts; giving in Melanesian societies always serves a social function rather than an individual need. "It must be remembered that accidental or spontaneous gifts, such as alms or charities, do not exist, since everybody in need would be maintained by his or her family" (p. 177). The function of the *kula* is to make lifelong partners and thus to encourage other kinds of trade in addition to gift giving. Articles passed are simple ornaments that form bonds of allegiance.[33] The participants in the *kula*, then, are aware of the utility of excess. Proper *kula* gifts are "a kind of economic monstrosity, too good, too big, too frail, or too overcharged with ornament to be used, yet just because of that, highly valued" (p. 173). These gifts are never to be kept for any length of time; they must keep moving. Generosity is privileged[34] but only as a means to tribal alliances. Indeed, Malinowski admits that generosity is rewarded: "A man who is fair and generous in kula will attract a larger stream to himself than a mean one" (p. 98). The result is not the destruction of private property; on the contrary, "the distinction between mine and thine is not obliterated but enhanced" (p. 174). Giving supplements and supports the aboriginality of exchange.

For Mauss, the *kula* and the potlatch are nearly indistinguishable, but, in Malinowski's description of the *kula*, the excess of potlatch gives way to the exchange of commerce and the maintenance of social obligations. Mauss's goal is admirable, and I take it up in chapters 3 and 4. For now, though, the limitations of his project are important. He tries to recover a past where generosity and commerce are indistinguishable in order to imagine a future in which giving can again invigorate exchange with warmth and solidarity. Unfortunately, by collapsing the two activities into each other, he does justice neither to the implacable dominance of exchange nor to the disturbing marginality of excess. When Mauss talks about the return of the gift, then, it is not clear how he thinks the gift can preserve the individual's independence and autonomy, so prized in modern culture, and at the same time create social bonds of reciprocity. It is not clear, in other words, how excess (potlatch) can create exchange *(kula)* while still being excessive. For Mauss, in the end, excess and exchange are not only compatible but also the same, so that the return of the gift does not radically threaten the authority of economic utility and calculation.

Marshall Sahlins and the Recovery of Abundance

If Mauss does not distinguish (in order to constructively join them) between the poles of excess and reciprocity, another famous text on giving in traditional cultures argues explicitly in favor of excess. Marshall Sahlins, in *Stone Age Economics,* combines the disciplines of anthropology and economics to criticize the notion that paleolithic hunting societies were thermodynamically regressive, operating on a subsistence level.[35] Instead, he claims that these societies were affluent in a way that has not been matched since. In fact, wealth is a burden to nomadic tribes. For Sahlins, it is axiomatic that mobility contradicts property. As a result, these tribes want not, so they lack not. "This modesty of material requirements is institutionalized: it becomes a positive cultural fact, expressed in a variety of economic arrangements" (p. 12). Sahlins seems to be saying that the problem of the economic utilization of scarce resources can be solved by minimizing wants in proportion to means. However, he is not advocating a renunciatory or ascetic lifestyle. The tribes he studies, he insists, are not poor. Indeed, they are free. They have no anxiety about the future and no food storage systems. Compared to the joyless way in which we worry today about making means meet ends,[36] these people are characterized by economic confidence, not panic. In this argument, Sahlins is clearly seeking paradox and provocation: "The evolution of economy has known, then, two contradictory movements: enriching but at the same time impoverishing, appropriating in relation to nature but expropriating in relation to man."[37] He wants to defend the thesis that poverty is not constituted by some objectively established set of goods; instead, it is a variable relationship between means and ends. Poverty is a social, historical, and dynamic term. Even more generally, "Every exchange, as it embodies some coefficient of sociability, cannot be understood in its material terms apart from its social terms" (p. 183). Economics is a function of history and sociology.

Although Sahlins envisions an economy based on surplus, not scarcity, his theory of gift giving actually reduces it to a form of exchange, not excess. Giving for Sahlins is a matter of organizing, or making a profit from, surplus value, and thus it serves a stabilizing political function. Giving is made possible by the presupposition that all goods are mobile. Once put into circulation, the gift symbolizes (and accumulates even more) extra value or profit. For Sahlins, the power of the gift in primordial cultures, what Mauss found in the *hau*, is the moral sense that the surplus a gift accrues is owed to the original giver. This becomes evident not in the original giving, but when a third party enters the arrangement. When a gift is given *on*, its surplus value should be passed *back*. Furthermore, this moral dimension coincides with the political. The giver is the author of the relationship, and authority is always profitable.

Sahlins explicitly defends gift giving as a form of exchange that serves the social function of solidarity: in this, he thinks he finds himself in agreement with Mauss: "For the war of every man against every man, Mauss substitutes the exchange of everything between everybody" (p. 168). For Sahlins, Mauss's work deserves a place in the history of political philosophy: gift exchange sublimates the aggressive drives that can lead to war. The result is a kind of peace that is voluntary but also culturally controlled: "Except for the honor accorded to generosity, the gift is no sacrifice of equality and never of liberty. The groups allied by exchange each retain their strength, if not the inclination to use it" (p. 170). To counterbalance the fear and hostility that exchange defers, generosity must be ritualized and exaggerated, but Sahlins finds little excess in such giving. He suggests that for Mauss, as well as in his own analysis: "The gift is Reason. It is the triumph of human rationality over the folly of war" (p. 175). The gift is an intermediary form of stability between war and commonwealth. It is not a natural, spontaneous human gesture but an advanced stage of social progress. By contrast, the modern struggle to make exchange exact and equivalent is a poor substitute for the mutual sharing of surplus goods that is made possible by the minimalization of needs. "Equivalence becomes compulsory in proportion to kinship distance lest relations break off entirely, for with distance there can be little tolerance of gain and loss even as there is little inclination to extend oneself" (p. 196). Equivalence is born at the outer limits of kindness and generosity.

Sahlins realizes that something ideological is at stake, in addition to factual and methodological debates about how best to describe prehistorical humanity. Sahlins blames scarcity on capitalism, rather than seeing capitalism as the necessary response to scarcity: "Where production and distribution are arranged through the behavior of prices, and all livelihoods depend on getting and spending, insufficiency of material means becomes the explicit, calculable starting point of all economic activity" (p. 4). More profoundly, he challenges the notion that scarcity is a human constant, the root cause of human anxiety and hardship: "To assert that the hunters are affluent is to deny then that the human condition is an ordained tragedy, with man the prisoner at hard labor of a perpetual disparity between his unlimited wants and his insufficient means" (p. 1).[38] The question immediately arises as to whether he idealizes the past. What is more important, for my purposes, is how he can help us envision the future. We consumption-hungry moderns appear to be driven by infinite need, so it is true that scarcity is, at least in part, what we make of it. Likewise, Sahlins treats abundance as a state of mind, something that is given if we could only recognize it. Sahlins seems to be saying that we can satisfy our wants by either producing much or desiring little, the latter being the better strategy for a successful accommodation to serious constraints.

The irony is that North Americans have long operated out of a theory of abundance, denying the reality of limits to growth and prosperity.[39] This theory of abundance, however, does not presuppose minimal needs and mobile goods; it assumes instead that natural resources are infinitely exploitable. Most recently, we people of plenty have become frustrated by a plethora of wants disproportionate to available means. We are driven to accept Sahlins's alternative—that is, either endlessly increase productivity or stoically accept lower standards of living. The problem is that we do confront real scarcity, and we cannot simply wish abundance into being by changing our attitudes. For Sahlins, giving is merely a way of structuring the nomadic mobility of goods; generosity, which is possible only because minimal needs produce abundance, buys political and moral obligations. Giving serves to redistribute surplus for the purposes of maintaining loyalty and legitimating authority. Sahlins thus disconnects giving from the pursuit of social justice and economic welfare. I argue in chapters 3 and 4 that what we need is a way of producing abundance and thereby destabilizing social structures, through new strategies of giving. By changing both our imaginations and our practices, giving can lead to an economy of abundance, as well as originate from it.

Pierre Bourdieu and the Total Critique of Giving

In a comprehensive critique of all gift-giving practices—brilliantly ex-emplifying the prevalent cynicism on this issue—Pierre Bourdieu ar-gues that gift economies are inherently self-deceptive.[40] Bourdieu's argument can be read as a rejection of the theatrical aspects of giving. All social structures need to be dramatized, he admits, but since any single cultural activity is not necessary for the existence of the group (although some such activity is), such dramatizations must conceal their own essential randomness by acts of complexity and specializa-tion that mimic the dynamic of production and labor. Drama and ritual are thus forms of unproductive but nonetheless rigorous labor:

> In the work of reproducing established relations—through feasts, cere-monies, exchanges of gifts, visits or courtesies, and, above all, marriages—which is no less vital to the existence of the group than the reproduction of the economic base of its existence, the labour required to conceal the function of the exchanges is as important an element as the labour needed to carry out the function. (p. 171)

Bourdieu extends this analysis to gift giving by arguing that it is merely a way of prolonging, manipulating, and concealing economic ex-change. "A rational contract would telescope into an instant a transac-tion which gift exchange disguises by stretching it out in time" (p. 171). Archaic societies are unable or unwilling to grasp the economy in itself, as it really is. Their economies, then, must be for something else; that is, they must be disguised. Economic transactions must be reproduced on a ritualized and dramatic level. Moreover, the act of concealing eco-nomics itself becomes a primary economic activity; embellishment and deception are labor intensive. In sum, for Bourdieu, the gift is, on a psychological level, an act of repression and, on the social level, an act of symbolic subterfuge. Bourdieu's Platonic critique attacks the very foundation of theater itself: dramatization is necessary not as a way of probing the depths of otherwise disconnected and disorganized social activities but as a way of concealing through artistic rendering the reality buried beneath the ritual.

The melodrama of the gift obscures the reality of exchange by blur-ring the categories of ownership, production, and profit to the benefit of the status quo. The chief point of the gift is to waste time in an organized manner, thus denying the distinction between productive and unproductive labor. "In a world in which time is so plentiful and goods are so scarce, his [the peasant's] best and indeed only course is to spend his time without counting it, to squander the one thing which exists in abundance" (p. 176). In primordial cultures, the most profitable activities are the useless ones. "Measured by the yardstick of monetary profit, the most sacred activities find themselves constituted negatively, as *symbolic*, i.e., in a sense the word sometimes receives, as lacking concrete material effect, in short, *gratuitous*, i.e., disinterested but also useless" (pp. 176–77). Giving is the trick of distributing material but accruing symbolic capital in such a way that these two opposite activities are magically disconnected. "Wastage of money, energy, time, and ingenuity is the very essence of the social alchemy through which an interested relationship is transmuted into a disinterested, gratuitous relationship, overt domination into misrecognized, 'socially recognized' domination, in other words, *legitimate authority*" (p. 192). Gift economies are a gentle, friendly form of exploitation. Authority depends on vague, diffuse generosity, and that very generosity masks the authority. In the absence of other juridical or political bonding systems, giving creates obligation without overt coercion. Dispossession is the only official, recognized form of possession in cultures that privilege the group over the individual. Symbolic capital is more important than economic capital; wealth is created by distributing goods, which produces respect, obligations, and loyalty—the very preconditions for maintaining and expanding power. In the end, the basic labor of gift giving is the strenuous work of denial. What we give hides what we hoard. Drama enacts psychological repression on a social level.

What distinguishes the gift from mere exchange, then, is the very labor required for the form of the presentation, the manner of the giving, which exceeds the bare essentials of exchange. Gift giving, in fact, is the very form that ritual and custom take in a given society; it is the form of form itself. Form is that aspect of an exchange that serves to qualify or disguise the interests that brought the parties together in the first place. Aesthetics, theater, rhetoric, ritual, and religion are all initiated by (and implicated in) attempts to cover up the (unpleasant?) dynamic of negotiated power relationships. In fact, one could say that religion still attempts to perpetuate and profit from those aspects of ancient economies that have remained resistant to disenchantment: the ideology of selflessness and sacrifice. Bourdieu thinks that in modern economies the world of art, more than religion, continues the obfuscations of gift giving:

> The world of art, a sacred island systematically and ostentatiously opposed to the profane, everyday world of production, a sanctuary for

gratuitous, disinterested activity in a universe given over to money and self-interest, offers, like theology in a past epoch, an imaginary anthropology obtained by denial of all the negations really brought about by the economy. (p. 197)

Bourdieu wants to embrace a heroic disenchantment that would see exchange as the basis of all giving. If Sahlins naturalizes the idea of abundance, finding in native economies an attitude that creates surplus, without the need of giving, Bourdieu naturalizes the economic sphere, where only exchange is given, finding in all social interaction creative ways of covering up the stubborn fact of scarcity.

Of course, Bourdieu has presupposed what he set out to prove, that the only real economy is the material one. He maintains from the start the controversial assumption that "practice never ceases to conform to economic calculation" (p. 177). Even symbolic capital and nonmaterial interests yield themselves to economic modeling. Bourdieu's method is utterly comprehensive, but it verges on a naive economism. Such a totalizing critique not only appeals to the contemporary sentiment of cynicism but also further contributes to the marginalization of giving as a wasteful, redundant act with little or no positive social relevance. For Bourdieu, the exaggerated rhetoric of giving must be diminished and deflated in order to uncover the substance it conceals. That which is more is really less. The ruse of excess must yield, under the pressure of a massive philosophical reduction, to the frugality of irony. Rhetorical embellishment must give way to economic productivity. Bourdieu has succeeded in perpetuating the oldest philosophical polarization: style and substance, form and function, rhetoric and truth.

Richard Titmus and the Social Utility of Giving

In *The Gift Relationship,* a book about the commodification (procurement, processing, and distribution) of blood, Richard Titmus tries to distinguish the social from the economic in public policy making in order to reinstate the importance of the former against the latter.[41] More specifically, Titmus wants to reinfuse the modern welfare system with the sensibility of giving. He tries to answer the question that Mauss begs and Sahlins disregards, namely, How can individual giving sustain mutuality and transform social institutions? For Titmus, welfare is not about helping those who cannot help themselves. It is, or should be, about helping all of us learn how to give, as well as receive. Titmus thinks modern society needs to increase opportunities for giving, which he equates with both freedom and power. Those unable, for whatever reason, to give must be empowered to do so. "To abolish the moral choice of giving to strangers could lead to an ideology to end all ideologies" (p. 12). Not only is the act of giving a good in itself, but it also enhances social solidarity. "The social relations set up by gift-exchange are among the most powerful forces which bind a social group together" (p. 73). Every gift is a message: a signal for the initiation of a social dynamic or an index of a broad set of relationships and expectations. Giving creates a system based on trust, in which the giver sees no immediate reward for his gift, yet gives anyway, for the good of the other and the eventual good of the giver. Humanitarian social giving is a virtue that must be allotted specific arenas of practice in order to create a more humane social order.

Because giving blood causes some pain and procures no palpable benefit for the giver, it is an ideal forum for the study of gift giving. Indeed, historically, blood has been mystified as an entity of great power and mystery, but even today it is an important commodity because it is so intimately connected to oneself. Titmus argues that blood is an ideal example of an object that should be given, not sold, because it relies on and encourages social trust. Blood testing can minimize the significance of that trust, but it does not eliminate it; the system (at the time of Titmus's work and, even with safeguards, to some extent today) must trust donors to be honest about their medical histories, and the patients must trust the blood in the system. The private market increases these risks because it both destroys social solidarity and creates incentives for dishonesty. Giving should be a personal decision, encouraged but not rewarded. In donating blood, people can give to strangers in a direct, simple, and deliberate manner.

Titmus's presupposition is admirable: the need to give should be treated as a basic right. Whether the market system is empirically inferior, both economically and morally, in the distribution of blood is a debatable issue. The more difficult question is how giving can be both a right that the government should protect, an exercise in freedom and autonomy, and a virtue that the government should encourage, a necessary component of social stability. How can the government support giving without providing incentives that would thereby supplant generosity? Titmus knows that the free market insidiously restricts the freedom to give. "It is indeed little understood how modern society, technical, professional, large-scale, organized society, allows few opportunities for ordinary people to articulate giving in morally practical terms outside their own network of family and personal relationships"

(p. 226). He also knows that the modern welfare system replicates the adverse consequences of the market by mediating giving so that an enormous distance exists between the giver and the recipient. This is unfortunate: "It is the responsibility of the state, acting sometimes through the processes we have called 'social policy,' to reduce or eliminate or control the forces of market coercions which place men in situations in which they have less freedom or little freedom to make moral choices and to behave altruistically if they so will" (p. 242). Titmus wants a giving that is beneficial but not strictly profitable, and such opportunities must be carefully planned in order to preserve spontaneity.

Ironically, the kind of giving that Titmus wants the government to encourage is only vaguely connected to everyday expressions of social solidarity and support. He wants people to be able to sacrifice for the whole as a way of verifying social confidence. As one critic notes:

> He is especially interested in the expression of impersonal altruism. It is not the richness of family relationships or the close ties of a small community that he wishes to promote. It is rather a diffuse expression of confidence by individuals in the workings of a society as a whole. But such an expression of impersonal altruism is as far removed from the feelings of personal interaction as any marketplace.[42]

Titmus succeeds in making room for giving only as a means of personalizing and supporting the status quo. Each act of giving is a modest vote of confidence in the vague entity called society. The excess of generosity does not transform social structures but enables exchange to go on as before, even if more smoothly, kindly, and gently. Giving allows the giver to feel connected to a system that is still impersonally regulated by the law of exchange.

Lewis Hyde and the Community of the Gifted

By emphasizing the mobility of the gift, the way in which the gift is always moving, making new connections, and metaphorically drawing together that which is separated, Lewis Hyde does more than any of the other authors examined here to synthesize the excessive and the reciprocal in the community of those who give. Beginning with the assumption that "a gift is a thing we do not get by our own efforts," Hyde's *The Gift* is addressed to the contemporary artist frustrated by the constraints of a market economy.[43] Hyde seeks to recover the gift value of art, both to the artist, who receives it in an inspired state, and to the audience, which never really possesses it and thus must pass it along. Like Titmus, Hyde is trying to protect one area of society from the dominance of market logic. He is most influenced by Mauss's interpretation of *hau*, the idea that the gift is self-propelled. For Hyde, "a gift that cannot be given away ceases to be a gift" (p. xiv). In explicating this claim, he is especially drawn toward Native American culture, noting that the origin of the derogatory phrase "Indian giver" was the Western bafflement by the practice in traditional cultures of keeping the gift moving, whereas Westerners instinctively try to remove property from circulation. For Hyde, one gift begets another in an almost magical way. This, he argues, is the point of many folk tales, which show that something horrible will happen if the flow of gifts is redirected into the exchange of commodities. When the gift is protected as property, it perishes; when it is passed along, the giver receives even more. Gifts are durable, then, only in transition. Their value, or wealth, resides not in ownership but in dispossession.

The potlatch, for Hyde, does not exemplify the connection of generosity to destruction. Instead, Hyde suggests that all giving involves destruction only in the sense that the gift moves from one hand to another. The real destruction occurs when an object is consumed by an individual rather than by the momentum it receives from being given. Something, however, must keep this movement going, and to explain this, Hyde turns not to the potlatch but to Malinowski's analysis of the *kula*. For Hyde, true giving always forms a circle. The circularity of giving means that nobody ever receives a gift from the person to whom she or he gives a gift. Thus, "each donation is an act of social faith" (p. 16). What is given returns, but only circuitously, through the countless detours that the gift creates, and so giving blurs the boundary between self and group by widening the individual's sense of belonging. The gift is the erotic expansion of the self from the self-gratification of the ego of one and the closed relationship between two to the dynamic ego of three or more. Hyde explicitly connects the circle of giving to the cyclical and holistic patterns of nature. In both cases, the system is self-regulating, and only immobility is dangerous. "With the gift, as in love, our satisfaction sets us at ease because we know that somehow its use at once assures plenty" (p. 22). Giving assures affluence and abundance; ownership legislates scarcity.

Hyde's basic insight is that the momentum of the gift, its locomotion, carries it from one place to another, thereby converting the restless energy of excess into the stable structure of reciprocity. Nevertheless, he comes dangerously close to praising the gift on the basis of its return, thus portraying it as a good investment. "Our generosity may leave us empty, but our emptiness then pulls gently at the whole until the thing in motion returns to replenish us" (p. 23). His connection of giving to the social circle helps explain how generosity leads to social solidarity, but it also limits the power of giving to a fairly specific, even elite group. The artists give of their talents, for example, to a community of aesthetes who appreciate artistic value above and beyond the limitations of the market, but it is unclear how the giving that unites this social group can expand to include other groups or to affect society as a whole. Hyde does address this issue by suggesting, in an interesting phrase, "the gift moves toward the empty place" (p. 23). Giving, he thinks, moves toward inclusivity, not exclusivity, but if giving is prompted and sustained by the circle of the tightly constructed social group, then it is difficult to understand how circles expand and grow. "The gift grows because living things grow," he writes (p. 27), borrowing from the natural fecundity of nature. The increase of the gift, however, is made possible by the continual shuffling of goods within the circle; once giving slips out of that circle, its motivation and maintenance become extremely problematic.

Blake Leland raises similar criticisms. "Hyde's essay insistently employs a system of metaphors which portrays the psycho-social institution of the gift in terms of circularity, of a bounded zone of coherence and vitality within which a lively erotic fluid flows: the social group is a body and the gift is its blood."[44] As a result, "An ego of one becomes an ego of many" (p. 40). Hyde captures the potential for gift giving to expand the self and to alter social relations, but only by translating the isolated, individual self into a larger, social version of itself. Hyde claims to recover the eros of giving, as opposed to its logos, but Leland thinks Hyde is indebted to the logos of theology: "Ideally this circle has no definite circumference: it approaches the theological" (p. 40). On the contrary, I would suggest that Hyde is not theological enough. His work is still bound by the logos of exchange and calculation. If, for Marx, logic is the money of the mind, for Hyde eros is the logic of social solidarity, the capital that creates the social group. Eros is within logos, compelling it forward, from the individual to the social, but the logos is not transformed. Eros works only within boundaries, only by the operation of exclusion, which is always strategic, calculative, logical. Hyde tries to hold eros and logos apart, but the result is that he mystifies their relation. As Leland explains: "In effect, Hyde's *eros* protects itself from itself by treating what must be an essential element of its own internal logic as if it were externally derived" (p. 43). By striving to purify the eros of giving from the logic of exchange, Hyde ironically portrays giving in a very unerotic manner.

Hyde leaves us with this crucial question: Can the gift create a circle that does not end where it began? In other words, can the gift create a community of both excess and exchange? In chapters 3 and 4, I, too, connect giving to the circle, but the circle is the one encompassed by an initial surplus of giving and is directed toward an ultimate harmony of mutuality, a circle identical to the unbounded generosity of God, who unites eros and logos by permitting our giving to be both excessive and reciprocal. The theological circle of giving—the church, inasmuch as it continues and galvanizes God's giving—is, in principle, unlimited and open. To enter into this circle is to acknowledge a debt that takes the form of a prior giving that carries one forward into more giving. As Hyde suggests, the true gift does not impose an impossible debt or demand simple repayment; instead, the gift asks our participation in its continuing journey. For many today, however, the idea of an initial obligation is disagreeable and burdensome. We want to receive, but we are afraid of being bought. The gift limits rather than bestows our freedom. In chapter 2, I argue that precisely the refusal to enter into the circle of the gift—which demands some form of gratitude—is at the root of the theory of squandering. Squandering is a kind of giving that denies exchange, and since theology often portrays God as a purely excessive giver, it is important to examine squandering more closely before moving on to the doctrine of God.

2

Squandering

I always exaggerate, that's my weakness.

Dostoevsky, *Notes from Underground*

Only the exaggerations are true.

Norman O. Brown, *Love's Body*

Gratuitous means, according to the *Oxford English Dictionary*, "free, spontaneous, voluntary"—something freely granted or given without claim or merit, without, that is, the possibility of exact compensation or direct repayment. It derives from the Latin *gratia*, meaning favor, and *gratus*, meaning pleasing. *Gratuitous* is also related to *gratitude*, the act of being thankful (as well as to other words like *gratify*, *gratulate*, and even *agree*).[1] The gratuitous begets or summons gratitude: we are grateful for something that is given uncaused, for no reason—or at least for reasons internal to our benefit and external to the interests of the giver. The gratuitous act occupies a difficult temporality: it is not motivated by the expectation of a return (the future), by the requirements of the situation (the present), or by a prior obligation (the past). The gratuitous is occasional, both in the sense of happening now and then and in the sense of causing a special occasion (the reception of a gift calls for a party, just as most parties involve gift giving), and this lack of regularity or predictability makes it appear almost without motivation.

Rarely, during the course of daily affairs, are we given something in an absolutely spontaneous manner, without discernible cause or sufficient reason, so it is arguable that all of these definitions of words that are still commonly used presuppose a theological horizon (and perhaps even demand a theological warrant). In fact, the language of giving immediately raises religious images and issues. One of the *Oxford English Dictionary's* earliest entries on *gratuitous* is a 1690 exposition of the Lord's Prayer: "Our pardon is free and gratuitous; for whatsoever God doth he doth it freely." Arguably, the model for that which is freely given is the grace of God, and even today we use the word *graceful* to refer not to *what* is given but to *how* a gift is properly given—an act that is effortless, that is prompted not out of need, desire, or struggle but, instead, emerges from a centered overflow of energy that has no external obstacle or constraint. Interestingly, an act that is graceful is a gift in itself, regardless of intention, purpose, or outcome, because we are grateful to witness such beauty and ease.

At one extreme the gratuitous can imply something that is reckless, wild, and abandoned. This case is what I called in chapter 1 squandering, a kind of hypergiving in which the graceful act is completely incommensurate to the situation and oblivious to the consequences. In a more moderate sense, when the intention of the act is more closely correlated to the benefit of the givee, the gratuitous simply means that which is freely given, but even in this case the giving, to be gratuitous, must transgress the expected and the required. Reflection on this broad range of significations is important. Minimally, the gratuitous is more than we could reasonably expect or even understand, but if the gratuitous is an act for which it is difficult to state the reason, how is it to be differentiated from the random, the irrational, and the superfluous?

Etymologically, the superfluous is that which overflows. It signifies a relationship that is disproportionate—a river swells and floods over its banks—and thereby extravagant. The superfluous can denote the dangerous and destructive, that which upsets necessary boundaries, or the abundant and the luxurious, that which is fecund and profuse. A synonymous word, *extravagant,* originally meant that which wanders out of bounds, straying, roaming, erring. It is prodigal, indeterminate, and rootless because (like the son in the famous parable) it is not bound by the transactional structure of giving, receiving, and returning. Although *extravagance* has a more positive resonance than *superfluous* (wandering can be the beginning of an adventure, whereas that which overflows can be disorienting as well as renewing), both words point to the problem of the antieconomical gift that is gratuitous. To receive such a gift is to be lucky, and to give it is to waste or squander. Once cut off from a reason, an interest, or a claim, the gift can become indistinguishable from the accidental, arbitrary, and irrelevant.

Gratuitous acts, then, like the giving of a gift, can be met with gratitude, but they can also be puzzling. That which is gratuitous is excessive in the sense that it is underserved, unwarranted; it goes beyond regular and ordinary interaction. Perhaps this is why the word *gratuitous* today is almost always used in the pejorative ("gratuitous violence," for example). Gratuitous acts are not located within the normal economy of bartering, exchanging, and trading, all of the activities that comprise the basic bonds of sociability as well as the economy proper: *do ut des*. I do something for you because you do something for me.[2] Gift giving resides uneasily at the border of economics. If exchange presupposes a relationship between independent, rational, self-interested agents, then the problem remains of articulating what relationship gift giving either requires or creates. Indeed, the extravagant logic of gratuity seemingly renders any constructive or positive response difficult, if not impossible. Excessive acts almost by definition defy the usual customs of reciprocity and obligation.

Taken to an extreme, that which is sheerly given, that which is there for absolutely no apparent justification, would be not only extravagant but also superfluous. That which is given without cause or reason could be given to anybody and for any purpose. The appropriate response to such spurious thereness is not gratitude but bewilderment and perhaps even terror. How does the gratuitous lead to gratitude and not simply to surprise and perplexity? Can giving be gratuitous on one end and equally gracious on the other? In other words, can the gift be both squandered and returned? I argue in this chapter that the theory of squandering is closely connected to the rejection of gratitude as an appropriate response to the gift. Although I agree with much of this critique of gratitude, I argue that the gift without a return makes for no gift at all, and so in the next two chapters I develop a theological theory of giving that simultaneously preserves the excess of generosity and promotes the return of the gift.

Against Gratitude

What is gratitude?[3] Frederick J. Streng has argued that gratitude is a universal and basic human response to life. Taking both verbal and nonverbal forms, gratitude is the way we offer thanks not only to God but also to "hidden resources of blessing in existence, to human providers, and to the provisions themselves (e.g., plants and animals that are eaten)."[4] Gratitude is diffuse: it is the opportunity to recognize any external priority, from the debt of our birth to the aid of all of those institutions that make us what we are. To be at all is to be thankful, beholden. Gratitude thus signifies various kinds of dependence and obligation, from bondage to praise and even worship. It can be an aspect of a vague attitude or intense emotion, or it can be organized in value systems, elaborate rituals, and daily, habitual activities. In all of its forms, it is an attempt to correspond appropriately to something that is simultaneously excessive and beneficial.

Gratitude, then, is the responsive side to a beneficial relationship, and such expressions comprise our moral core. Conversely, to be ungrateful is to be both immoral and antisocial. Philosophers have traditionally regarded the indefensibility of ingratitude as self-evident.[5] Yet, they have been uneasy about generalizing moral rules and arguments from the experience of gratitude. Gift-gratitude relationships involve special treatment and particular attachments, so they are not easily reconciled with the standard moral requirements of impartiality, objectivity, and universality. Gratitude toward a benefactor couples moral obligation with personal preference and interests, like friendship and family. Gratitude seems to be as much an aspect of etiquette as morality.

As etiquette, gratitude is an index of social solidarity and support. All cultures have rituals and discourses that place the gratuitous in a reciprocal context, enabling the givee to name the excessive and address the giver, but the expressions of gratitude can vary widely. In an essay on giving in southern India, for example, Arjun Appadurai argues that "in a highly hierarchical society, the nonverbal expression of gratitude is very closely tied with the nonverbal etiquette of rank in general."[6] Bodily posture, lowered or averted eyes, the use of honorific titles, and tones of deference are both expressions of gratitude and acknowledgments of the interplay between social superiority and subordination. Direct expressions of gratitude are rare in traditionally structured societies because giving is taken to be a duty correlated with rank and office. Giving is rooted in a system of relations that comprises the politics of the social group. As Appadurai explains: "The reluctance of benefactors to be directly thanked for their generosity is, in part, rooted in the pervasive feeling that every act of generosity is built on some other one and that the direct expression of thanks, in suggesting a terminal source of generosity, is dangerously misleading and must therefore be carefully hedged" (p. 17). Rather than expressing gratitude, the proper response to a gift is simply to (eventually) return it. Giving, then, maintains the relations of reciprocity that provide the moral foundations for traditional, hierarchical societies. Giving and exchange are not in conflict; instead, giving is the primary form that exchange takes.

In Western, market-dominated societies, giving and exchange have become increasingly differentiated, which makes gratitude especially important. Gratitude can still be an aspect of contractual relationships, as when businesses give presents in order to sell goods.[7] We are grateful for some things even when we have bought them, as when a medical procedure saves a life, and we are thankful in spite of the fact that the doctor's action was required and compensated. Most often, though, token gestures of gratitude ("have a nice day") mechanically accompany acts of exchange as a way of softening and personalizing the calculation involved in buying and selling. Gratitude as a nearly meaningless way of adding warmth to exchange must be expressed automatically and inauthentically, without much effort or sincerity. To be profuse in an economic transaction is to raise suspicions.

Contrary to exchange, gift giving is a relationship of more private than social significance, most frequently practiced among close friends or relatives. The simple expression in English, "Thank you," by contrast to the rituals that Appadurai discusses, is an abbreviated verbalization of gratitude that emphasizes equality, not hierarchy. In acts of giving, gratitude indicates a bond of loyalty, appreciation, and goodwill, pledging not an exact return of the gift but a continuation of the mutual rendering of assistance and comfort. We misunderstand a gift when we try to repay it too quickly or too equally; such promptness looks too much like exchange.[8] If the gift is not to be returned, quite literally, or if the gift does not function to establish and perpetuate a social hierarchy, then the gift does not merely do nothing: it gives rise to gratitude, which is a way of returning the gift without really returning it. Gratitude is a substitute for the countergift, the promise of a return that would not be a return, that is, the promise of further, commensurate gifts, when the time is right. It is a settled disposition that involves continuous respect and honor, and it vows future action based on imagination and reflection, not automatic equivalence.

Though gratitude serves to separate giving from exchange, the distinction is not an easy accomplishment. Gratitude must be given appropriately, acknowledging the gift but not the debt the gift might seem to create. Otherwise, it can cancel or negate the act of giving. For example, even the expression of a "thank you," which can seem to be a kind of repayment, can make the giver anxious; it is often met with a "forget it," "don't mention it," or "it was nothing," phrases that are not meant to be taken literally but heighten the gratuity of the original act while emphasizing the inappropriateness of a precisely corresponding act. The proper expression of gratitude is an art; it functions as a way of restoring balance in a gift-giving relationship without explicitly reducing that relationship to exchange.

Almost in spite of itself, however, this formulation seems to treat the relationship between the gratuitous act and the response of gratitude as an exchange based on equivalency. The philosopher and sociologist Georg Simmel articulates this approach by beginning with the assumption that "all contacts among men rest on the schema of giving and returning."[9] A relationship based on gratitude, then, is not different in kind from exchange and reciprocity. Indeed, for Simmel, gratitude is an aspect or implication of exchange, not a different kind of exchange altogether. It is what remains of an exchange, the trace of something owed that the exchange does not exhaust. Simmel calls gratitude "the moral memory of mankind" (p. 388), a kind of socially constructed but nonetheless universal feeling of guilt. "Once we have received something good from another person, once he has preceded us with his action, we no longer can make up for it completely, no matter how much our own return gift or service may objectively or legally surpass his own" (p. 392). Gratitude, then, is a necessary consequence of reacting to a prior action; it is the feeling that accompanies dependence and passivity. This fact of obligation — an inner relationship that persists even when the outer relationship has ceased — functions as a key element in social stability and collectivity. Gratitude is owed; to fail to express it is to violate the logic of compensation and thus to risk banishment from the moral community. Morality occurs in the return, but Simmel continues to value a giving that is not bound by gratitude. "Only when we give first are we free" (p. 392). To give is better than to receive, yet if every exchange creates a response of obligation and debt, it is unclear how a first gift ever can be freely given. In fact, in Simmel's view, the gratuitous is not purely free and graceful; gratuitous acts intend the gratitude they receive. Gratitude is an extra but not accidental return that the gratuitous produces, a form of labor that the initial investment purchases. For Simmel, then, gift giving is just another name for economics; exchange is the form that excessive giving always takes.

If gratitude is owed — and we do frequently use the awkward phrase, "a debt of gratitude" — then it is easy to understand how its expression can become problematic. Gratitude is a kind of expected gift, something that earns credit when adequately supplied, which raises all sorts of puzzles. The question immediately arises whether gratitude should be expressed at all. At one extreme, the person who gives gratitude can seem to be docile and submissive; at the other extreme, withholding gratitude can appear arrogant and egotistical. Gratitude is equally perplexing for the giver. If gratitude upon the reception of a gift is morally required, then the giver who does not receive gratitude is justified in judging the ungrateful recipient. Yet, condemning ingratitude makes the original gift suspect; such begrudging complaints suggest that the giving was not free and gratuitous. On a general level, then, gratitude seems obligatory, but on a specific level that requirement cannot be spoken or otherwise indicated.

In addition to this psychological level, there is a sociological dimension: gratitude frequently carries a symbolic meaning that has broad cultural consequences. Because gratitude means the accreditation of debt and dependence, it is readily subjected to the forces of politicization.[10] Arguably, one of the basic conflicts in modern society is between those who counsel in favor of the expression of gratitude and those who insist that gratitude should be suppressed or perhaps postponed until future gifts make it unnecessary. In the first case, gratitude is a vote of confidence in the institutions that produce the benefits for the givee, thus promoting loyalty to the status quo. Its expression is a basic affirmation of the necessity of order and of one's place in the natural hierarchy of things. Its rejection, from this perspective, is based on envy, the inability of sullen and resentful recipients to recognize the superior heights from which the gift comes.[11] In the second case, gratitude is a dreary obligation imposed on those who are forced to receive because they do not have anything to give. Gratitude is given begrudgingly, not from envy but from an obstinate longing for justice and equality. Gratitude from this perspective is a form of submission, and its opposite is either active contempt or passive indifference. Hence, the politics of gratitude divides into two opposing parties: those who can give and thus want others to appreciate what they receive, and those who cannot give and thus do not want to be compelled into gratitude. Gratitude comes to represent either inclusion in or exclusion from the structure of rewards and benefits of a given society.

The assumption in both groups—one representing gratitude as a way of conserving the present distribution of goods and the other connecting the denial of gratitude to defiance and discontent—is that to give is to have power and to receive is to be powerless. A theological horizon informs this assumption. The traditional doctrine of God, after all, portrays God as a giver but not a receiver. Giving is better than receiving because it is a sign of grace as well as strength. By implication, the activity of the gift marks the givee as passive and weak. Gratitude gives speech to a *dis*graceful impotence. Given the correlation of gratitude with a burdensome imposition, it is not clear how gratitude can ever be expressed without resentment or reservation. If gratitude merely completes the process of exchange, then it is redundant and irrelevant; if it is a response demanded by the gratuitous gift, then it signals a subservience that inevitably results in bitterness and frustration. To conceptualize receiving as an act of freedom equal to the freedom exercised in giving, reception cannot be limited to gratitude. A free assertion of gratitude should take the form of further giving, not the acknowledgment of an unpayable debt. In the first chapter I argued that the act of giving—oscillating between the extremes of excess and exchange—was a difficult accomplishment; now it should be clear that the act of receiving is equally challenging.

One way to respond to the difficulties of reception is to articulate a theory of giving that denies or disregards any constructive account of the destination of the gift. This type of theory, what I called in chapter 1 squandering, celebrates the freedom and spontaneity of the gift by disconnecting the rhetoric of giving from any positive deliberation on the intended audience of this rhetoric. By telling only part of the story of gift giving, squandering thereby risks removing the gift from the concerns of justice and mutuality. In fact, squandering, which intensifies the action of the gift, is an attempt to go beyond the gift, to give beyond gift giving, but the questions remain of what such giving is for and to whom it is given. In the next two chapters, I try to protect the excess of squandering from its most self-defeating expressions by putting it in a larger context, that is, by completing the account of this rhetoric with a reflection on the multiple and possible destinations and audiences of excessive giving. In this chapter, I analyze the configuration of hypergiving in terms of two of the most significant writers on giving, Ralph Waldo Emerson and Friedrich Nietzsche, thinkers who so closely ally giving with freedom that they leave little room for an affirmative evaluation of the gift's obligation and return. Whereas Emerson and Nietzsche emphasize squandering, the recent work of Jacques Derrida—with which I end this chapter—shows how giving, unsteadily fluctuating between excess and exchange, is nearly inconceivable and thus impossible. Derrida shows that an inability to elucidate the destination of the gift, the possibility of a community created by the gift, leads to a reflection on the end of giving, which tends to give giving over to exchange. The undue stress put on squandering thus serves to reinforce the dominance of economics and exchange.

Throughout my discussion, I argue that the defense of hypergiving is not, in the end, an adequate account of generosity, but I also argue, in the next chapter, that this result cannot be corrected simply by emphasizing the reciprocal aspects of giving. Indeed, reciprocity without excess gives generosity over to cynicism. What is needed is a way of thinking about reciprocity that preserves excess in all of its freedom and spontaneity.

Emerson and the Denial of Debt

The greatest achievement of Ralph Waldo Emerson, whose vision of self-reliance significantly influenced Nietzsche,[12] was, according to Harold Bloom, "to invent the American religion."[13] In common with other North American romantics, Emerson wanted to pattern both his life and his writings according to the dynamic of a ceaseless surging forth of fecund energy. He extols power in the service of creativity and encourages revolution through innovation. His prose is meant to embed the particular individual in the universal rhythms of history's progress and nature's profligacy. He begins the essay "Experience" with "Where do we find ourselves? In a series of which we do not know the extremes, and believe that it has none."[14] The disproportionate features of humanity's environment make "extremes of generosity" (p. 150) incumbent on those sufficiently farsighted and courageous. Yet, he does not praise excess for its own sake, disregarding the economy in which the self can profitably participate. Although he often writes of the power of genius to reveal hidden horizons of possibility, he also knows that the part must humbly take its place in the connectedness of the whole. "A certain compensation balances every gift and every defect," he observes. "A surplusage given to one part is paid out of a reduction from another part of the same creature" (p. 57). Giving follows the trope of synecdoche (the substitution of a part for the whole) more than hyperbole; giving is a partial expression of a larger network, and thus giving should reflect and participate in the balance that governs the whole.

The law of balance makes giving risky and strategic; deficiency is the other side of excess. Emerson strives to show the individual how best to synchronize the miniature drama of the self with the ebb and flow of magnificent but impersonal nature. The task of a life is to ride the Edenic rhythm of bountiful nature so that giving outweighs taking, and thus what one receives is what one makes. "Benefit is the end of nature. But for every benefit which you receive, a tax is levied. He is great who confers the most benefits" (p. 65). To give is better than to receive because it demonstrates an active and proportionate participation in the thrust of history and nature. "Be a gift and a benediction. Shine with real light, and not with the borrowed reflection of gifts" (p. 90). Giving is the prudent expression of an economy that operates to harmonize and maximize the complex rhythms of power and progress. "He only is fit for this society who is magnanimous; who is sure that greatness and goodness are always economy; who is not swift to intermeddle with his fortunes" (p. 120). The best excesses are the product of a thrifty economizing. To give is to find that balance wherein the self, in harmony with fecund nature, grows without limit and expands without regret.

The benefit of giving is best presented in the essay entitled, "Gifts." Emerson rejects the idea of an original dependence or debt, the feeling that, as he puts it, "the world is in a state of bankruptcy" (p. 305). To envision that owing is more original than giving would be to disallow giving altogether. Emerson wants to free giving from guilt (from response, or responsibility). He characterizes giving as the pleasurable and playful parody of paying; one act is as free as the other is compelled. Giving corresponds to the flowers of nature or the fruits of the garden, both of which are extravagant in their charm and delicacy. Beyond flowers and fruits, though, Emerson thinks giving is a difficult challenge. Most gifts are token apologies for gifts because "The only gift is a portion of thyself" (p. 306). Echoing Mauss's interpretation of *hau*, Emerson suggests that we can bring to the other only who we are. Giving, then, is the fruition of self-creation.

To give is to *be* abundantly. Reception, by contrast, is a reminder of our need for supplementation and thus our lack of abundance. "We wish to be self-sustained. We do not quite forgive a giver" (p. 306). Receiving a gift from love is relatively easy because "that is a way of receiving it from ourselves" (p. 306). Otherwise, receiving raises the unpleasant feeling of debt and dependence. Indeed, to receive is to fall, to mar the originality, individuality, and innocence of one's own giving. Receiving upsets the logic of priority and derivation, calling into question the very concept of a "first." The only way that the distressing nature of receiving can be ameliorated is to turn giving into exchange. "The gift, to be true, must be the flowing of the giver unto me, correspondent to my flowing unto him. When the waters are at level, then my goods pass to him, and his to me" (p. 307). Without the possibility of equivalent repayment, the receiver is obliged to express gratitude as a vague substitution, which can never seem enough to compensate for the gift. Gratitude is a form of punishment; it is the admission of an unredeemable debt. To escape gratitude, one must be a great giver; that is, one must subvert the exchangist logic implied in reception by the spontaneity and strength of generosity. To give to a great giver is really to receive; to be such a giver is to take without obligation or debt. "You cannot give anything to a magnanimous person. After you have served him, he at once puts you in debt by his magnanimity" (p. 307). The best that we can do, short of practicing such magnanimity, is to leave giving to fate. "We can rarely strike a direct stroke, but must be content with an oblique one; we seldom have the satisfaction of yielding a direct benefit, which is directly received. But rectitude scatters favors on every side without knowing it, and receives with wonder the thanks of all people" (p. 308). Being the person who does not need to receive is the best way of becoming the person who knows how to give.

Emerson's model of giving is carefully calculated to maximize the benefits of strength, independence, and power. The relationship between Emerson's thought and the emerging dominance of the market economy in the United States (as well as the expanding western frontier) is complex,[15] but his portrait of giving does not provide an alternative to the competitive entanglements of capitalism. With an inestimable influence, Emerson was the first to articulate the North American fantasy of acting the spendthrift without incurring any debt. Indeed, the Emersonian giver is slyly capable of reaping a profit without appearing greedy or anxious. Magnanimity hides prosperity and acquisition. As Cornel West argues, "The Emersonian self—much like the protean, mobile, performative self promoted by market forces—literally feeds off other people. It survives by means of ensuring and securing its own excitement and titillation."[16] Such giving is cunning, not excessive, and ironic, not hyperbolic. The flowing current of exuberant American optimism is circular but not in any simple, repetitive way. "The one thing which we seek with insatiable desire," Emerson writes, "is to forget ourselves, to be surprised out of our propriety, to lose our sempiternal memory, and to do something without knowing how or why; in short, to draw a new circle."[17] Surprise is the satisfaction the self receives (or gives itself) when it (conveniently) remembers that it has forgotten the gift. Emersonian giving extends and enfolds the spiral of the self, guarding the rotation from tedium and imposition by forgetting that all giving is also returning.

When applied to things divine, this attitude leaves no room for a response of gratitude toward a first giver. In a dramatic reversal of the usual ordering of the God-human relationship, Emerson writes, "The magnanimous know very well that they who give time, or money, or shelter, to the stranger—so it be done for love, and not for ostentation—so, as it were, put God under obligation to them, so perfect are the compensations of the universe" (p. 146). The Emersonian giver is self-made, not God-given. This giving is so expansively circular—the part becoming indistinguishable from the whole—that it even has the power to draw God into its orbit, obliterating (erasing, canceling, overpaying) the debt implicit in any reception. Emerson denies divine benevolence by transferring the synthesis of giving and creating from God to humankind, a move repeated by Nietzsche. Giving is a form of creation, but instead of creating something other (as in the Genesis account), for Emerson, giving creates only the self. The part the self plays in giving is the whole of giving. Only through such giving can God be forgiven for an otherwise asymmetrical priority and initiative.

Nietzsche and Self-Giving

In the foreword to *Ecce Homo*, Nietzsche says that he has "given mankind the greatest gift [*das grosste Geschenk*] that has ever been given it."[18] This present is *Thus Spoke Zarathustra*, a book for all that Nietzsche thought none could really understand. Indeed, the gift of *Zarathustra*, a book that spends a great deal of time discussing the practice of giving, is not meant to be readily or easily received. One has to have the right ear, he says, to comprehend the tone (style, rhetoric, package) in which the gift is given. I suggest that, for Nietzsche, this kind of gift is the only kind that can be given because he denies the possibility of the ordinary exchange of gifts as that is usually understood. Nietzsche pushes the excessive aspect of giving to its furthest extreme, so that the logic of excess can be examined in its purest form. For Nietzsche, authentic giving must be a kind of squandering (he uses the terms *Verschwendung* and *Vergeudung*), a ruthless release of energy that recklessly transgresses limits for no apparent reason or purpose. Such gratuitous giving is motivated by the graceful exercise of autonomy and power, an attempt to rise above the social struggle for recognition and reciprocity. The purpose of giving, the end of the gift, is internal to the giver. Indeed, Nietzsche asks in *Ecce Homo*, "How should I not be grateful to my whole life?" (p. 37). For the squanderer, the only kind of appropriate gratitude is what the giver gives the self because his gifts have been given to himself. Notice, for example, the repeated refrain, "O my soul, I gave you," in the section in *Zarathustra* entitled, "On the Great Longing." Giving constitutes not a social circle of obligations but a constricted circle of one, in which the other and the self become one and the same.

As many commentators have argued, none of Nietzsche's ideas can be separated from the form of their presentation, which is definitely true of his theory of generosity. I cannot exhaustively analyze the structure of squandering here, but I do want to give an outline of it, and any commentary must begin with Nietzsche's rhetoric. How he presents his gift on gift giving is, to a significant extent, what that gift is. Both activities, the gift and the presentation, can be analyzed according to the shape of excess, or hyperbole.[19] Much of Nietzsche's writing is concerned with excess (*Übermass*), from the affirmation of mystical, Dionysian unity in *The Birth of Tragedy* to skepticism about ecstasy in *Human, All Too Human*, and from the compact intensity of the aphorisms in his middle style to the ranting of the prophet in *Zarathustra* and the final feelings of exuberance and self-aggrandizement in *Ecce Homo*. Nietzsche pushes language to extremes, just as he thinks all giving must be excessive. Giving, like speaking or writing, should break rules and transgress the expectations of moderation and sociability.

Indeed, the hyperbolic tone of Nietzsche's texts, which assemble a variety of (sometimes contradictory) perspectives, is provocative, shifting, and unsettling. This proliferation of voices is not, though, a manifestation of a fault, a lack of cohesion or consistency, but a further expression of power and of generosity. The authority of the implied author controlling these voices stems from the vastness of his ambition and the intimidation of his self-assurance. As Henry Staten explains, "Where there is no appeal to additional authority, only the discourse *of* power can be a discourse *on* power."[20] Nietzsche's theory of energy expenditure is directly related to his own experiments with style: he is trying to articulate and practice (put into play) a smooth, exuberant, autonomous, and joyful release of word and deed from all anxiety, fear, and resentment. His voice must range so broadly because it is trying to mimic the economy of a soul indebted to no external source, dependent on no others, reacting to no lack or insufficiency. His style is hyperbolic in both its comedic and polemical extremes because he speaks from the standpoint of an overflowing that willingly squanders the truth he has struggled to obtain. He oscillates between mistrusting his present readers to idealizing future ones, and the result is that he frequently writes to and for himself, just as his theory of giving suggests that giving is only for oneself, born from an immense solitude (tinged with anger? revenge? resentment?), in which he has given himself a place above the giving of all others.

Zarathustra begins with the endless giving of the sun and ends with a potlatch, or party, that the prophet throws for the "higher men." In between, Zarathustra is almost constantly talking about giving. Although he is a teacher, implicated in a relationship of self-donation to his disciples and followers, he resists the connection of pedagogy and other-regard. He sojourns among the rabble because he is "weary of my wisdom, like a bee that has gathered too much honey."[21] The notion of giving as an overflowing, as with many aspects of Nietzsche's theory of generosity, has theological roots, which I further explore in the next two chapters. Nietzsche is drawn to the imagery of overflowing because it connotes a generosity that is natural, graceful, and unforced. Overflowing begins with a surplus of power, not the insufficiency of need. Nietzsche thinks that the Christian view of giving, or charity, originates in weakness, envy, and resentment. "I give no alms," says Zarathustra. "For that I am not poor enough" (p. 11). The problem is in understanding what it is exactly that Zarathustra does give. Zarathustra himself is unsure; he uses the language of giving but must also subvert it, because giving implies a mutuality that Zarathustra does not desire. At times, Zarathustra praises giving as a form of excessive loss and dissolution: "I love him whose soul squanders itself, who wants no thanks and returns none: for he always gives away and does not want to preserve himself" (p. 15). More frequently, Zarathustra argues that authentic giving does not involve self-denial or suffering: "Why sacrifice? I squander (*verschwende*) what is given me, I—a squanderer with a thousand hands; how could I call that sacrificing?" (p. 238). The brinkmanship of squandering displaces sacrifice as strength confronts weakness and health opposes illness.

Jacques Derrida and others have made much of the fact that the German *Gift* once had the sense of both present and poison, and *Gabe* can mean either gift or dose (as in a dose of medicine);[22] much of Nietzsche's work seems to conflate the two. Against (and perhaps parodying) Aristotle's celebration of giving as the bond of friendship, Nietzsche wants to remove giving from any positive consideration of the other. "Compassion for the friend should conceal itself under a hard shell, and you should break a tooth on it."[23] The best way to honor a friend is to wage war against him. Nietzsche suspects that we give to our friends because we do not sufficiently love ourselves, and thus we try to make our friends give us what we do not know how to give ourselves. True friendship is possible only when nothing is needed, and thus what is given need not be returned.[24] "I teach you the friend in whom the world stands completed, a bowl of goodness—the creating friend who always has a completed world to give away."[25] Nietzsche also rejects the connection of giving to broader social circles of justice and the distribution of wealth: "How can I give each his own? Let this be sufficient for me: I give each my own" (p. 69). Indeed, Zarathustra gives to his followers in order not to alleviate their pain and ignorance but to distance them from his giving and thus force them to receive what they give for themselves. He does this by giving nothing, which demands a mixture of creativity and destruction: "Verily, such a gift-giving love must approach all values as a robber; but whole and holy I call this selfishness" (p. 75). The overman, like God in the traditional theology of the doctrine of creation, does not so much give as create; what he gives is a new and original act that is not responsive to a prior giving and not intended to engender bonds of mutuality and support. Such giving must be ex nihilo, a free, spontaneous, gratuitous event. Consequently, the squanderer begins to look suspiciously similar to the God whom Nietzsche has pronounced dead. What Nietzsche rejects returns as what only he can give.

In the section entitled "The Gift-Giving Virtue" ("Die schenkende Tugend"), Zarathustra wants to be alone. His disciples, however, persist, and he reluctantly agrees to talk about giving.[26] To prompt him, the disciples give him a gift, "a staff with a golden handle on which a serpent coiled around the sun."[27] For Zarathustra, the gold represents giving at its best because it is both rare and useless. The gift should be an expression of power, like the sun, but it also must be cunning, like the serpent, in order to extricate itself from a relationship rooted in dependency. Zarathustra's speech is tinged with melancholy, because what he speaks about is not what it appears. The circle of the gift, he insists, begins and ends with strategies of taking. "You force all things to and into yourself that they may flow back out of your well as the gifts of your love." (p. 75). Degenerate forms of giving are an attempt to manipulate the givee by pretense and illusion, ignoring the fact that what is given is really taken in a power relationship built on need and obligation. The feeble gift, no matter how generous, inevitably deteriorates into the relationship of host and parasite. The strong giver does not break these hypocritical bonds with altruism but instead gives in full recognition that what is given is first stolen (not received). Strong giving is beyond the binary logic of the good and bad of morality. It does not seek grounding in some transcendental value or otherworldly orientation. Instead, it matches the proliferating rhythms of the earth and the body, matter not spirit. "Let your gift-giving love and your knowledge serve the meaning of the earth" (p. 76). When Zarathustra finishes this speech, he broods in silence and then confesses that he might have deceived his followers. In a strategy that anticipates the basic gesture of Derrida's work on the gift, he has to take back what he has said about giving, what he has given, because otherwise it would not be a true gift. "Now I bid you lose me and find yourselves; and only when you have all denied me will I return to you" (p. 78). Like Christ,

Zarathustra must be absent in order to be fully present; unlike Christ, however, Zarathustra does not promise a return of what was rejected but now denies what was given in the first place.

The gift, for Nietzsche, is not a simple activity; readers of Nietzsche should not be tempted to idealize it as a solution to personal and social quandaries. Indeed, Nietzsche recognizes that it is fraught with complexity, danger, and ambiguity; that is why he is drawn to it. Although at times he reduces all giving to the motivation of selfishness, he also distinguishes between two diverse economies, which are inextricably intermingled. Typically, he articulates an unlimited economy connected both to the fecundity of nature and to the mechanism of the powerful will. He opposes to this an economy of reserve based on timidity, fear, and prudence. His celebration of strong giving is not an attempt to purify giving from the machinations of calculation and exchange. Giving is not a private sphere of warmth and intimacy, as opposed to the rigors of the economy. On the contrary, giving is agonistic, and the individual must be hard in order to be generous. Staten argues that Nietzsche defends generosity as a metaphysical idea but couples it with a realistic psychology of self-interest; Staten further suggests that there is "a curious sort of conceptual contamination or synecdochic slide" between the two.[28] The noblest squandering is initiated and protected by appropriation, even exploitation; the two movements augment each other. Accumulation is the necessary prerequisite for expenditure, and calculation is its milieu. Giving is not a pure form of what is mixed in exchange. It is a way of turning exchange inward in order to circumvent some of the restrictive implications of mutuality and reciprocity. As with Emerson, synecdoche displaces hyperbole; giving is a partial expression of self-affirmation. The gift does not metaphorically fuse together two otherwise unrelated persons, nor does the gift hyperbolically transgress and transform the expected relations of exchange; instead, the gift is the species term for the genus of the self, an extension of the self that does not go further than the self is able or wants to go.

The conclusion Nietzsche draws from this argument is that all activity is essentially nonmoral. To describe an act as moral is to attribute to it an imaginary framework that can serve only to conceal the actual dynamic of exchange from both the actor and the recipient of the act. If all acts are basically self-interested, then the problem becomes one of deciding how best to manage one's own interests. Nietzsche's direction of thought is not to deny the possibility of other-regarding activity but to reconceptualize it along lines that are not dictated by the false opposition of altruism and selfishness. Self-denial is accepted only as a means of furthering self-advancement. Other-regard becomes possible as an expression of power, strength, and pleasure; otherwise, the attempt to act for the other can be only a mask for weakness, envy, and resentment.

If squandering occurs within an economy of abundance, in which energy is overproduced, compelling a sovereign and even impersonal expenditure of goods regardless of their effect on other systems of circulation, then the opposite of squandering can be discerned in the word *sacrifice*, predicated upon an economy of scarcity in which the shortage of moral value clashes with the overproduction of desire, and only through the deprivation of the latter can the former be stimulated and produced; that is, only through rigorous and abstemious self-control can something, anything at all, be given to the other. In one case, the ample gift is a Neoplatonic emanation, a serene overflow of an internally self-perpetuating machine, a hydrological system in which supply, disconnected from demand, entropically proliferates, disperses, and disseminates, not to restore some original equivalence or achieve a future harmony but to fulfill a unique function: the disposal of the by-products of a blessed state of strength, the sheer exercise of power. In the other case, exiguous giving is made possible only by constriction and concentration, by a prior loss, a humbling that controls and redirects the circulation of energy, an intervention into the system that breaks a closed economy in order to spend not surplus but minimal and necessary goods before the system has the opportunity to balance its accounts according to the self's own needs for equilibrium. Needless to say, Nietzsche is against sacrifice; religion misrepresents the economy of the noble soul. There is no outflowing of energy that is unrelated to the pleasure and interests of the agent. Other-related activity is always governed by a self-centered economy, although some economies are more self-affirming than others.

No matter how much Nietzsche wants squandering to be amoral and atheological, self-denial persists in his work, and this vestige of theology demands interrogation. Indeed, Nietzsche valorizes squandering as an ethic superior to both philosophical and theological versions of generosity. Whereas squandering is a dynamic and transgressive expression of energy, Nietzsche suspects that giving is ordinarily governed by a resentment against the flux of nature and an envious desire for a state of power that would protect oneself from the vicissitudes of time. Such giving originates in weakness or sickness; instead of exercising power, this giving tries to imitate what it lacks, and thus it speaks from bitterness, not strength. More specifically, giving is traditionally connected to a petty version of self-denial, a paltry attempt to transcend the natural limitations of the body by the spiritual act of negating this world in favor of a world to come. Nietzsche calls this variant of giving *asceticism,* which is the product of an introspective turn, an attempt to arrive at the truth by paring away all that is excessive or inessential. In both its Platonic and Christian forms, asceticism is the drive away from complexity and toward the ideal. Nietzsche, by contrast, wants to embrace a strong version of self-denial, a negation that does not rely on the affirmation of another world but rather affirms that which is messy, convoluted, and scattered. Zarathustra, for example, learns to say yes to time, which is another way of saying that Zarathustra learns how to give, because the gift is returned only eventually and unpredictably, over time, and thus the gift is given in a horizon of temporal openness that cannot be measured, calculated, and kept.

Squandering requires self-affirmation, but it also repeats the structure of self-denial at a great cost. Even though Nietzsche criticizes the tradition of asceticism and sacrifice from the ancient priests through Platonic philosophy and Christian morality, he advocates a generosity that is bounded by discipline rather than given over to desire. Squandering for Nietzsche is not governed by eros, the sensual desire for the other, the lure of beauty and merit. Such desire is foolish in that it is not regulated by mastery and control. The economics of squandering must be planned, arranged, and managed so that power is maximized. In any economy, the weaker parts must be sacrificed for the profit of the whole. What the squanderer finally denies is that part of the self that is strengthened by receiving what cannot be self-given. Squandering is thus a kind of selfish sacrifice that spends excessively by borrowing from exchange.

Consequently, the Nietzschean giver is playing a game in which the ball thrown turns out to be a boomerang. What begins as an incipient erotic spilling outward reveals itself, in the absence of concern for the other, as a masturbatory conceit. As Staten writes: "An economy that pours itself out endlessly into itself, therefore preserves itself even as it squanders itself because there is only itself from alpha to omega. But the price of this self-preservation is eternal, absolute solitude" (p. 184). Strong giving is thus unrelated to sympathy, the shared suffering (*Mitleid*) that is the basis of both Christian morality and liberal humanism. This is not to say that Nietzschean giving is a way of avoiding pain or suffering; indeed, squandering at times seems based on a kind of pantheistic affirmation of the negation of suffering, a consequence of the triumph of the strong, who are able to turn their suffering into occasions of quiet celebration and sober reflection. What squandering is not connected to is considerations of mutuality, in which what is given is given over to others in order to encourage more giving for the good of the group as a whole. Nietzsche's excess is not an ecstatic bursting outward toward the other;[29] it is not an irrecoverable and thus eccentric expenditure of loss that gives birth to a new relationship to the other. Squandering is the exchange in which the self is guaranteed a profit. As Zarathustra says, "What returns, what finally comes home to me, is my own self."[30] Through self-surpassing, not self-sacrifice, the self can grow in wisdom and power. The expansion of the sovereign self, its manifest destiny, is the closest Nietzsche comes to a metaphysical unity toward which all things merge and dissolve.

In the end, the truth of squandering, its cost, is that others must pay the terrible price for such powerful profligacy.[31] Exchange for Nietzsche is a zero-sum game in which one person's profit must entail another person's loss. All surrender turns out to be appropriation; giving is always a form of taking. The strong version of self-denial thus harbors a seed of resentment that seems impossible to dispel. If squandering is not for the other, then it must always be open to the possibility of hurting the other as a way of compensating for the cost of the struggle for sovereignty. As Staten argues, "The creditor who enjoys inflicting suffering performs an act with a structure identical (even if one act is real and the other imaginary) to that of the Christian slave who takes vengeance on the powerful by imagining their sufferings in hell."[32] The violence of squandering is true on both an individual level and a social level. Nietzsche wants to avoid the horizontal flow of love, which would disperse the power of giving into the uncontrollable channels of social obligation and custom. His metaphors are vertical, not horizontal. He wants giving to serve an upward function, a pyramidal purpose. The point of this ascending movement is the great man, who is both the paradigmatic giver and the ultimate receiver. The squanderer is, whether predictably or paradoxically, the pinnacle in this spiraling of energy. Nietzsche's ideal economy is organized in order to squander the masses so that certain sovereign individuals may accumulate sufficient energy for their own acts of squandering.[33] The great man is the product, the purpose of the profligate economy of both society and nature, the various drives of exuberance that only the genius can organize and control.[34] Everything else is, quite literally, waste. Dionysian generosity is blind to the consideration of the social whole, which inevitably entangles sovereignty in the rules and customs of sociability. Squandering is the action of ascendancy that spends others in order to save the self.

Nietzsche's theory of giving has influenced many aspects of postmodern philosophy.[35] Georges Bataille and N. O. Brown are two modern-day Nietzscheans, trying to recover a sense of excess that could rejuvenate social relations while at the same time continuing the Enlightenment project of defending and supporting the sovereignty of the autonomous individual. Bataille returns squandering to its religious roots by connecting it to primordial acts of sacrifice, as well as modern experiences of violent loss like gambling, luck, inebriation, accidents, sex, and mystical longing. For Bataille, excess, what he calls *expenditure* (*dépense*), is a religious act of dispossession and sacrifice in which loss is made the source of an ecstatic despair.[36] For Brown, Dionysus and Christ are interchangeable in a synthesis of the outlandish and the moral. Giving is a way of celebrating the life instinct by fusing sexual desire and social needs in a playful, earthy exuberance.[37] Both thinkers risk running into an aporia because they try to recover a purposeful dimension to excess. Moreover, they locate excessive giving as an activity of the isolated individual, even as the way in which the individual can be most free and independent, and so they minimize the communal aspects of giving.

Although Nietzsche is at once more radical and more conservative, he faces similar problems. His discourse on squandering is meant to upset any and every moral notion, but it is also contextualized in a moral framework that utilizes excess for specific purposes. For Nietzsche, excess taken to an extreme is disconnected from any considerations of reciprocity. Indeed, it is possible to argue that Nietzsche's affirmation of ascendancy and health itself masks a fear of decay and suffering. Nietzsche is afraid of the bonds and obligations that would draw him into the midst of the rabble. He risks siding with the victors, the dominant, the strong at the expense of those who are most in need not only of gifts but also of the empowerment of giving. His desire to return to a pre-Christian view of giving, in which excess can overpower and control exchange, is itself an affirmation of unreality every bit as hopeful and fantastic as Christianity. As Staten suggests, "Nietzsche claims to affirm this world, yet he finesses the issue by affirming a version of this world that is really *another* world, long ago and far away, and perhaps a world that never was."[38] Squandering is wishful thinking, but it is also not very far from Walzer's definition of giving as the exercise of ownership over private property. It is an index of the self's willingness to reject the possibility that excess can create new forms of exchange. Instead, excess is for itself, the sign of the strength to will away reciprocity in the oblivion of an internally generated extravagance. Excess is both the origin and the end of the gift, as if giving prompted by gratitude is not giving at all. Here giving has gone beyond the gift; in fact, it has gone so far that it belongs (returns) to the giver alone.[39]

Derrida and the End(lessness) of Giving

In a way, deconstructionism has always been a critique of the event of the gift.[40] Indeed, the resemblance between the structure of philosophy and the event of the gift provides Derrida with a distinctive account of both. For Derrida, there is no ideal reality or first principle (consciousness, presence, being) that is represented by a detour through history, language, and the world and restored to its purity by an act of understanding. Derrida suspects that metaphysical systems repeat theological stories by narrating the plight of meaning as an innocent essence subjected to an unfortunate fall; language becomes the impure mediation of meaning, and the task of philosophy is to redeem the really real from the messy contingencies of space and time. For Derrida, the given cannot be so easily returned because what is external to the really real is actually internal. Mediation is not an accident, separable from the essence of meaning. Language is present, for example, from the very beginning of meaning. Consequently, there is no original given that is not already altered by its reception and return. Likewise, the route of understanding is always marked by passages that do not lead back to an ultimate origin or starting point. To interpret is not to return to a given but to give something other than what was given in the first place. In sum, the beginning of meaning is marked by its end, and interpretation is as much giving as it is return.

With Derrida I can bring my analysis of giving to an end because he endlessly announces its closure. He capitalizes on the circularity or reciprocity of giving in order to interrogate the very possibility of the inauguration of giving. If giving always comes around, he seems to be saying, then how does it get started in the first place? Without a first giver, giving can never begin, and yet we do give all the time, so perhaps the problem is with the apparatus of our conceptualization. Indeed, Derrida's work on giving is also an examination of the limits of philosophy. For Derrida, the extravagance of the gift (*don*) makes it a particularly suitable symbol for the "other" and all the problems of understanding otherness in general. If understanding can only know that which is regular, balanced, and proportional, then the excess of the gift is a threat to the measured categories of understanding. Nevertheless, the fact that giving initiates an exchange is the very precondition of all understanding because only that which is given can be responded to in reflection and comprehension. In these Derridean aporias, the polarities of excess and exchange fall apart. Derrida is drawn to Nietzschean squandering, but he realizes that it leads literally nowhere. He is also drawn to the work of Mauss, but he knows that "giving" the name of gift giving to certain practices in archaic societies is not a nonviolent and disinterested investment. Indeed, for Derrida, the gift is other, and thus unnameable, yet the discourse on giving persists; we must try (and fail) to understand the gift, but such uncertainty means that we cannot know what we have been given or if we ever give anything in return.

Analyzing Derrida's *Given Time*, his most comprehensive work on giving to date, is a challenge because Derrida's prose goes in circles by circling around his topic without ever quite entering into it.[41] The figure of a circle is, of course, a mythic symbol of great power, and it threatens to surround and beleaguer any discussion of giving. The problem is this: If giving constitutes a circle, the trope of reciprocity, then is it giving at all? "It will besiege us all the while that we will be regularly attempting to exit [*la sortie*]" (p. 8). The circle is the most apt figure for the economy and for the circulation of goods in exchange. Economy is ruled by the law of the circle, what Derrida calls the "*odyssean* structure" (p. 7) of exile and appropriation. What is given *must* return. Derrida is asking whether there is a rule other than this law, a kind of grace that circulates outside the economy of exchange. This would be the geometrical structure of the gift—a circling that would be circuitous, imitating the circle but never ending where it begins, a nonidentical repetition or disjoined loop.

Is this shape a stable configuration? Does it continue or interrupt the repeating pattern of the economy? Provisionally, Derrida suggests, the gift can be defined as that which must *not* be returned. This is Derrida's own law of giving: "If the other *gives* me *back* or *owes* me or has to give me back what I give him or her, there will not have been a gift, whether this restitution is immediate or whether it is programmed by a complex circulation of a long-term deferral or difference" (p. 12). The gift must not be exhausted (or consumed) by the process of exchange. Yet the gift, by obligating a countergift, is also a form of exchange. Indeed, the very fact that we can think about what is given implies that giving is an aspect of exchange; our thinking is a way of receiving and returning the gift. By simply asking about the gift, though, we risk reducing giving to exchange and thus begin an impossible task: "It is perhaps in this sense that the gift is the impossible. Not impossible but *the* impossible" (p. 7). By both transgressing and perpetuating exchange, the gift represents the attempt to escape the inescapable. The excess of giving is a tangent that never quite touches the circle of exchange, and since we live within the closed geometry of the circle, we can never know whether the rupture of excess has occurred. Given this characterization, gift giving is a challenge to exchange in just the same way that Derrida's deconstructionism is a challenge to the predominance of metaphysical thinking; in both cases, the challenge is necessary but impossible, and so it can be carried out only in the most cunning manner.

Derrida's very definition of giving intentionally moves contradiction into the center of this act: "For there to be a gift, *it is necessary* [*il faut*] that the donee not give back, amortize, reimburse, acquit himself, enter into a contract, and that he never have contracted a debt" (p. 13). In other words, the gift cannot be received as a gift. Simple recognition, let alone praise, commendation, or acknowledgment, is enough to annul it. "Why? Because it gives back, in the place, let us say, of the thing itself, a symbolic equivalent" (p. 13). Even (perhaps especially) gratitude destroys the gift:

> The link between morality and the arithmetic, economy, or calculation of pleasures imprints an equivocation on any praise of good intentions. In giving the reasons for giving, in saying the reason of the gift, it signs the end of the gift. The equivocal praise precipitates the gift toward its end and reveals it in its very apocalypse. The truth of the gift unveils only the non-truth of its end, the end of the gift. (p. 148)

The end (meaning, purpose) of the gift can only be its closure, in the literal sense of its abolition. The gift, therefore, cannot be a gift (or appear as a gift) in order for it to be (to really be) a gift, either to the donor or the donee.[42] "But its very appearance, the simple phenomenon of the gift, annuls it as gift, transforming the apparition into a phantom and the operation into a simulacrum."[43] The authentic gift, then, once given, must be completely gone; it must disappear. It must be not. (Here Derrida seems influenced by the connection of giving and destruction in the potlatch.) It must be given in an absolute secrecy, unsigned and unnamed. However, if the gift is no longer a gift when it is given, how can we subsequently talk about it, let alone receive it? "The simple identification of the gift seems to destroy it" (p. 14). To talk about it is to try to take it back, to try to get something out of it, to find out where it goes, to track it down, to circle around it. Such a pursuit violates the logic of giving. Therefore, once the question of the gift is asked, answering it is no longer possible—even though the gift does encourage some kind of response.

Nevertheless, Derrida continues to encircle his elusive quarry. Time, he notes, is often portrayed as a circle, so the question arises: What is the time of the gift? Derrida oscillates between two options: all gifts are untimely, in the (perhaps Nietzschean) sense of being surprising and spontaneous, but they also give time, in the sense of plotting the course of an origin, reception, and return. At first, Derrida resists the circular imagery of the gift's return. Gift giving cannot be caught in a hermeneutical circle that only knows (gives) what it already presupposes (receives). Derrida knows that giving is possible only at the instant of an effraction of the circle. Only on this condition can the gift take place; otherwise, the gift's excess is merely the energy that keeps the closed circle rolling. But how can we ever know if this instant has occurred? Like Kierkegaard's attempt to locate and isolate the instant that constitutes the madness of faith, Derrida wants to locate an instant that is not a part of time. "In this sense one would never have the time of a gift" (p. 9). The gift, then, is never present, like the moment right now that Augustine claims can never be known. If we experience time only through memory and anticipation, time as present is time without being, that is, nothing. The gift, what is given in the present moment without thought of past or future, cannot give time. "If there is something that can in no case be given, it is time, since it is nothing and since in any case it does not properly belong to anyone; if certain persons or certain social classes have more time than others—and this is finally the most serious stake of political economy—it is certainly not *time itself* that they possess" (p. 28). Derrida does not want to imply thereby that the gift is timeless; instead, it is momentary, always passing and never present, and therefore impossible.

Yet, there is more productive relationship between giving and time. Derrida can also say that what the gift gives is, in a sense, time. It gives what he calls waiting time, given time: "The gift is not a gift, the gift only gives to the extent that it *gives time*" (p. 41). Or "*there where there is gift, there is time*" (p. 41). The custom of giving is to delay restitution. The gift is thus not only event (event language heightens the excessive features of giving, its suddenness and disconnectedness) but also process because the gift structures a certain rhythm of expectation and decision. "The thing is not *in* time; it is or it has time, or rather it demands to have, to give, or to take time—and time as rhythm that does not befall a homogeneous time but that structures it originally" (p. 41). Every gift has its own time. The givee must decide what to do with the gift, how and when and in what form to return it. The gift is a beginning that continues through the middle of the reception and seeks an end, which is in turn another beginning. The gift thus lends itself to a certain poetics of narrative, but what does narrative give to the gift? Derrida holds open the possibility that where conceptuality fails in understanding the gift, narrative can succeed.[44] In telling the story of the gift, a narrative can account for its delayed return while resisting the reduction of giving to exchange. In the next two chapters, I point to the Christian narrative of giving as a framework that tensely preserves both the event (the unrefundability) and the process (the circularity) character of giving.

What story does Derrida think giving creates? Derrida knows that the form of his presentation, the lecture (now a text) in which he seeks the meaning of giving, is itself—like Nietzsche's *Zarathustra*—a kind of gift. Derrida knows that any discourse on the gift is performative, an example of what it is describing. Thus, the gift-discourse must itself be a gift, if it presumes to explain or narrate what giving is:

> This is an unsigned but effective contract between us, indispensable to what is happening here, namely, that you accord, lend, or give some attention and some meaning to what I myself am doing by giving, for example, a lecture. This whole presupposition will remain indispensable at least for the *credit* that we accord each other, the faith or good faith that we loan each other, even if in a little while we were to argue and disagree about everything." (p. 11)

So this exchange has the form of a gift, and thus the nature of giving can be read from the dynamic of the reader's interaction with the text as well as the text's actual content. A close reading of this book should leave any reader with the impression that Derrida's work gives his readers the gift of making the gift seem almost impossible but also strangely necessary. If giving is impossible, or nearly so, then his discourse must embrace and intensify that impossibility while still retaining something of the form of the gift. This strategy distances the reader from the gift and seems to teach that the best way to receive the gift is not to return something equivalent but to deny it, to put it away without it being recognized as a gift, to give back, in other words, nothing.

The only way Derrida could give us the gift of a discourse on the gift is to negate the possibility of gift giving altogether; otherwise, what he gives us is something we could appropriate and return. Derrida's essay is radically unreadable, because he does not give us anything to which we can respond. His topic is impossible, and he refuses to let us take it any other way. He also cannot characterize his own work as a response, a dialogue with the traditional questions on this topic. Derrida places himself in this bind when he argues that restitution annuls the gift. By implication, Derrida's own discourse cannot be a response to a prior discussion. He is forced to claim that he is not just intensifying (or exaggerating) traditional discourses on gift giving, but leaving them behind:

> Even though all the anthropologies, indeed the metaphysics of the gift have, *quite rightly and justifiably,* treated *together,* as a system, the gift and the debt, the gift and the cycle of restitution, the gift and the loan, the gift and the credit, the gift and the countergift, we are here *departing,* in a preemptory and distinct fashion, from this tradition. That is to say, from tradition itself. (p. 13)

Given his theory of giving, Derrida has no other choice than to reject all other theories; otherwise, he is giving back to the tradition what he has received, which would result in the reduction of tradition to exchange and in the obliteration of the gift.

Perhaps, one might wonder, giving is something we grasp intuitively but have trouble explaining. If this is the case, then the gap between what we feel and what we can know could be closed by reference to a transcendental solution. Philosophy could demonstrate how our experience is trustworthy by appealing to the ultimate conditions of all human knowing and doing. Derrida suspects that this Kantian move merely reiterates the original problem; how can that which is given in our experience be illuminated by the provision of universal standards? How can reason respond to the gift without reducing it to exchange? "This gap between, on the one hand, thought, language, and desire and, on the other hand, knowledge, philosophy, science, and the order of the presence is also a gap between gift and economy. This gap is not present anywhere; it resembles an empty word or a transcendental illusion" (p. 29). Theories are powerless here. For reason to give explanation to the gift is to deny the gift altogether. Thinking can only measure actions that are repeatable and regular; thought thus risks its own destruction at this limit. Any attempt to think through the gift relies on the very distinction that thought must try to cross. The theoretical coordination of the orders of giving and knowing, whether it follows the logic of identity or contradiction or even some form of Hegelian sublation, would only bring the tangential nature of giving into the orbit of circulating reason. "What must be interrogated, it seems, is precisely this being-together, the at-the-same-time, the synthesis, the symmetry, the syntax, or the system, the *syn* that joins together two processes that are by rights as incompatible as that of the gift and that of exchange" (p. 38). Giving and exchanging are so close that they are merely different. So what is the difference?

> The difference is precisely that of the *excessive*. An essential exaggeration marks this process. Exaggeration cannot be here a feature among others, still less a secondary feature. The problem of the gift has to do with its nature that is *excessive in advance, a priori exaggerated*. A donating experience would not be delivered over, *a priori*, to some immoderation, in other words, a moderate, measured gift would not be a gift. To give and thus do something other than calculate its return in exchange, the most modest gift must pass beyond measure. (p. 38)

I continue to explore the relationship between hyperbole and giving in the next two chapters. At this point, it is important to note that hyperbole, for Derrida, cannot be related to the give-and-take of conversation, and thus it is impossible to attend to excess in a constructive manner. For Derrida, hyperbole is not one form of language among others but that which defies language altogether. Hyperbole is the silence within which the gift must be both given and received. Hyperbole, that which is always more, is the secret of the gift, but once spoken (shared, revealed, given) it is no more.[45]

As much as Derrida complicates the Nietzschean accent on the excess of giving, he can also define giving in terms of excess alone. He is tempted by and, in turn, drawn to accelerate the logic of extremity. If giving is possible at all, it is only as an act that defies daily conventions and ordinary expectations. The gift must be a surprise. "No gift without the advent of an event, no event without the surprise of a gift."[46] Even more, violence may be considered one of the preconditions of the gift: "If it remains pure and without possible reappropriation, the surprise names that instant of madness that tears time apart and interrupts every calculation" (p. 147). The gift and the event are both unique acts that do not fit any preconceived pattern. The gift is thus related to chance and luck: "The gift and the event obey nothing, except perhaps principles of disorder, that is, principles without principles" (p. 123). Indeed, Derrida wonders what a gift would be if it were not really given: "What would a gift be in which I gave without wanting to give and without knowing that I am giving, without the explicit intention of giving, or even in spite of myself? This is the paradox in which we have been engaged from the beginning" (p. 123). In the end, though, he recognizes that giving must be intentional, and he looks for some way in which giving can be both careful (reciprocal) and carefree (excessive). "There must be chance, encounter, the involuntary, even unconsciousness or disorder, and there must be intentional freedom, and these two conditions must—miraculously, graciously—agree with each other" (p. 123). Derrida seems to be playing with a problem analogous to the traditional theological puzzle of how human giving can be both free and guided by God. The possibility of grace is the limit of his investigation.

Derrida admits that this all sounds a bit mad: "The truth of the gift is equivalent to the non-gift or to the non-truth of the gift. This proposition obviously defies common sense" (p. 27). How do you render an account of that which does not balance? The gift is both *alogos*, that is, without reason, and *atopos*, without place, "and thus it means the extraordinary, the unusual, the strange, the extravagant, the absurd, the mad" (p. 35). Even in Mauss's text, his attraction to the potlatch shows the insinuation of madness into any discussion of the gift. In fact, madness could be defined as that which does not return, that is, as the gift. This madness "manages to eat away at language itself. It ruins the semantic reference that would allow one reasonably to say, or state, to describe this madness, in short, it ruins everything that claims to know what gift and non-gift *mean to say*" (p. 47). The fact that Mauss tries to capitalize on the return of the gift shows how he misunderstands giving.[47] According to Derrida, Mauss denies excess by trying "to define the right rule, the right economy: *between* economy and noneconomy."[48] He embraces gift giving in moderation. The result is he "announces perhaps a sort of paradoxical *hubris*, the *hubris* of the right measure" (p. 64). It is a good compromise. Good gifts are always returned; their profit must be reinvested. This is Mauss's own way of paying back the gift, by writing about it so generously. Derrida senses a Rousseauist scheme operative in this move; Mauss wants to portray giving as natural, not excessive.

> The anthropologist proposes to *give back* and to *come back* in a circular manner to the good example, to return to the good inheritance that archaic societies have given or rather bequeathed us. The inheritance that is thus passed down is nothing other, finally, than nature. It is nature that gives, and one must show oneself worthy of this gift." (p. 66)

The naturalization of giving fits in well with Mauss's political goals. Generosity and order are not in conflict; instead, they presuppose and complement each other. The problem is, Derrida knows, that equivalence is never given; it must be achieved: "To say that *one must* reach equivalence and that equivalence is good is to recall that it is not simply given and that giving is not taking. There is at the outset neither real equivalence nor semantic equivalence: To give does not mean to take— on the contrary!" (p. 67). The philosopher or anthropologist can never presume to do away with exchange by hypothesizing giving into existence. Nor can giving be reduced to pure exchange: "We are not through with this 'logic,' and what is more one is never through with it" (p. 67). Exchange and giving reside together, in the same logical space, yet their relationship cannot be fully categorized or distinguished.

If the gift must be denied in order to be received, is it enough to unconsciously repress the memory of the gift? Indeed, could gratitude be the form of this repression, an unconscious ruse, a calculated noncalculation that feigns forgetting? Does gratitude say both "thanks" and "no thanks," thus dismissing the debt that the gift intends to create? Derrida also rejects this solution: "For there to be gift, not only must the donor or donee not perceive or receive the gift as such, have no consciousness of it, no memory, no recognition; he or she must also forget it right away and moreover this forgetting must be so radical that it exceeds even the psychoanalytic categoriality of forgetting" (p. 16). Repression puts into reserve that which is forgotten, so that it can still be given over to the consciousness. Derrida is after an absolute forgetting and the correlative giving that would make such forgetting possible.

There are echoes of Heidegger here. For Heidegger, Being is a gift, the *es gibt*, there is or it gives, that which manifests itself when understanding receives the truth.[49] This original giving of beings is difficult to receive; indeed, the story of philosophy is about forgetting, an ingratitude that constitutes the history of philosophy's attempt to reduce the presence of Being to the particularities of beings. Giving thus becomes exchange: the manifestation (the givenness) of Being is turned into an exchange (calculation, mastery, ownership) between the understanding and beings. For Heidegger, the gift of Being cannot be restricted to the exchange between two subjects, who are at once in a relationship of manipulation and power. As Derrida notes, "One would even be tempted to say that a subject as such never gives or receives a gift."[50] The original giving of Being must precede subjectivity and thus all humanisms. "There where there is subject and object, the gift would be excluded" (p. 24). The structure of the gift, then, for Heidegger, is also the structure of Being, that which can be thought only when it gives itself, but not as some *thing* (or commodity) to be appropriated, analyzed, and returned. Being can be thought only in its difference from beings, which is giving. In Heidegger's hands, this interpretation of Being calls for a meditative and poetic encounter, a form of intellectual gratitude for the presentations of truth that language gives and the philosopher receives.[51] In Derrida's interpretation, Heidegger's gift of Being is a futile attempt to remove the givenness of truth from the reality of exchange; if Being is the gift, and thinking involves measurement, then Being must be nothing. All we are left with is beings, which can be exchanged but not given, unless their difference from Being can be thought. In chapter 4, I discuss the possibility of thinking of the gift as higher than Being, a "more than" which calls into question our attempts to establish "what is."

Can giving precede Being? That is, can the question of giving be asked prior to the question of what is and what is not? The French philosopher Emmanuel Levinas, whose sense of responsibility for the other is informed by a profoundly Jewish understanding of the priority of the neighbor and the stranger,[52] has argued in *Totality and Infinity* that ethics is prior to metaphysics, which might provide a way of thinking about giving that circumvents the ambiguities of theoretical explanation. Derrida seems to appeal at one point to Levinas's argument that the intrusion of the other is the beginning of morality.[53] For Levinas (whose distance from Emerson cannot be exaggerated), if the ordinary exchange of objects cannot break out of the circle of self-concern, a first giver, an external force that serves to initiate this break, can open the self to something radically other. Levinas conceptualizes otherness in terms of an asymmetry that resembles and radicalizes the relationship of giving. He portrays the other in terms of vertical metaphors of height; the very exteriority of the other breaks the bonds of desire that encompass the self. Ordinarily, he agrees, we try to grasp the other in terms of use, service, function. "Labor remains economic; it comes from the home and returns to it, a movement of Odyssey where the adventure pursued in the world is but the accident of a return" (pp. 176–77). Authentic otherness surpasses this appropriation, and thus the other becomes a (unpaid) teacher: "The calling in question of the I, coextensive with the manifestation of the Other in the face, we call language. The height from which language comes we designate with the term teaching" (p. 171). The face of the other is infinite, resisting containment in any conceptual totality. This infinity is both extravagant and binding, placing me in a debt that can be paid only by substituting myself for the other. What the infinity of the face finally teaches is the demand that we not kill: "The being that presents himself in the face comes from a dimension of height, a dimension of transcendence whereby he can present himself as a stranger without opposing me as obstacle or enemy" (p. 215).[54] The other is the gift that allows us to be in a relationship that is not determined by power and desire. Ethics thus precedes metaphysics just as giving precedes exchange.

Derrida doubts, though, that such otherness is so purely unrelated to exchange. As he suggests: "Finally, the overrunning of the circle by the gift, if there is any, does not lead to a simple, ineffable exteriority that would be transcendent and without relation. It is this exteriority that sets the circle going, it is this exteriority that puts the economy in motion."[55] With Levinas, the other intrudes as a forceful given—demanding, deliberate, always already there. For Derrida, however, the very language of otherness makes it ambiguous. Otherness is not only ethical; it is also constructed, construed, and spoken. It is not only what we submit to but also what and how we reply. If the gift is always asymmetrical—that is, excessive—then how can it be received without saying something in return and thus upsetting its asymmetry? The rhetoric of the reply thus problematizes otherness.

In an essay on Levinas, Derrida questions the possibility of thinking about or receiving such otherness; even to express gratitude would be to negate or compensate the gift: "Before any possible restitution, there would be need for my gesture to operate without debt, in absolute gratitude."[56] To return the gift is to violate the height of the transcendent face, yet not to show gratitude is to reject the gift altogether. This dilemma makes responding to Levinas exceedingly difficult, and it forces Derrida to write in a double bind, showing both gratitude and ingratitude. Every gift has its wage, yet to return the gift is to wager against giving itself. Indeed, all commentary results in betrayal; all gifts must be denied if they are to be returned. As Simon Critchley explains: "Ingratitude does not arise like an accidental evil; it is a necessity or fatality within ethical Saying."[57] By writing about Levinas, Derrida is forced to interrupt the primacy and priority of the other; the best that he can do is to write in such a way that he invites other interruptions, since he is unable or unwilling to pass along that which was given to him.

In the end, the gift is a question of language; everything returns (and thus must be returned) to language. "In short, one must not only ask oneself, in something close to rapturous wonder, how it is possible that to give and/or take are said this way or that way *in* a language, but one must also remember first of all that language is as well a phenomenon of gift-countergift, of giving-taking—and of exchange."[58] Derrida means, in part, that the gift, using terminology from his earliest works, is the trace of meaning that language promises but never gives us in the present. The gift is analogous to the surplus of meaning implicit in every communicative act. Another analogy is possible: the text is the given, and commentary is the return. "The most apparently direct writing, the most directly concrete, personal writing which is supposedly in direct contact with the 'thing itself,' this writing is 'on credit': subjected to the authority of a commentary or a re-editing that it is not even capable of reading" (p. 100). Derrida does not mean to imply that "writing is *generous* or that the writing subject is a *giving subject*" (p.101). The writer, like all subjects, is defined by the operation of capital:

> As an identifiable, bordered, posed subject, the one who writes and his or her writing never give anything without calculating, consciously or unconsciously, its reappropriation, its exchange, or its circular return—and by definition this means reappropriation with surplus-value, a certain capitalization. We will even venture to say that this is the very definition of the *subject as such*. (p. 101)

The writer is not generous; language is. The power of language is not only the gift of thought but also the production of babel: meaning is proliferated in ways that cannot be controlled. "This hypothesis of a dissemination without return would prevent the locution from circling back to its meaning" (p. 48). Language is the gift that makes the discourse on giving both possible and impossible. The best commentary on giving would continue that discourse in unexpected and unusual ways. To give is to complicate, obfuscate, mislead, and confuse.

Derrida is trying to formalize the rules of a language game that has lost its horizon of meaning, depleted of any practice that could give it shape or substance. He realizes that the further he pushes excess, the less the gift looks and acts like a gift: "To overtake the other with surprise, be it by one's generosity and by giving too much, is to have a hold on him, as soon as he accepts the gift. The other is taken, caught in the trap" (p. 147). Certainly giving can be both good and bad, as captured in the French, *donner un coup*—"to give a gift" or "to give a blow." Giving does involve considerable skill, what could be called a kind of deception, in which the gift does not draw attention to the giver. Yet in Derrida's futilitarian hands, problems multiply in almost comedic ways. Indeed, he sustains the impossibility of his subject matter only with the interminable persistence of his attempt at understanding. His style is both comfortless and heroic, a retreat from or evacuation of meaning that looks at the same time like an advance or a marching forward. His discourse is underwritten by a strategic (and yet essential) hesitation or indecision that enables him to prolong what he does not want to say. To account for the gift, to theorize its destination, is to reject the gift altogether, yet the gift demands some sort of response. Within this dilemma, Derrida is tempted by the possibility (which Borudieu affirms so simply) that there is no giving: this is the given that Derrida reticently receives and questioningly returns. The object he pursues has no logic, and thus it cannot really be analyzed. To talk about it is to talk about something else. Likewise, to give it is to give something else. The problem is of his own sly crafting in that he has rejected gift giving as the very precondition of his discourse. He seeks an excess without reciprocity, and then finds reciprocity wherever excess pretends to be. He simultaneously drives both poles of giving to opposite extremes while insisting that they must meet at some unimaginable point.

At times, Derrida seems to desire an absolute giving, an ultimate squandering that would be totally unreserved. "The gift, if there is any, will always be *without* border" (p. 91). Such a gift would be a giving without an object, a giving accomplished in total secrecy.[59] Derrida has hyperbolized the Christian discourse on giving because the gift that must not be (as it is) given is, after all, a Christian theme: Jesus, God's gift, is sacrificed (God disappears in or withdraws from the cross of Jesus), and Jesus teaches that giving must take place in private, that is, nowhere (Matt. 6:1–4).[60] Sacrifice becomes inward, subjective, spiritualized in Christianity, seen only by God and not by others. Yet in Christianity, the gift that is "not given" is not thereby nullified; it is reborn in the Christian's freedom to give again and in the power of the giving community that is the church. At the instant that the gift is given up, it returns, not as reward but as the condition of further giving. For Derrida, by contrast, once a gift takes a definite form, once it is understood or received, the "more" is not more. "As soon as it delimits itself, a gift is prey to calculation and measure."[61] Mauss's desire for appropriation and reform is clearly rejected. All attempts to organize giving, whether governmental or religious, transform giving into exchange: "As soon as almsgiving is regulated by institutional rituals, it is no longer a pure gift—gratuitous or gracious, purely generous. It becomes prescribed, programmed, obligated, in other words bound" (p. 137). Indeed, giving can be organized, defended, and explained only because it is already economical, already imitating what it seeks to deny.

Although Derrida occasionally strains after the theological, at the same time he sees it as clearly impossible. The gift is infinitely repeatable and never the same.[62] There is no first gift, because to give is always at the same time to receive. Giving never begins, but as a possibility within the logic of exchange, it also never ends. Religions play on excessive giving only to profit from exchange. "Sacrifice will always be distinguished from the pure gift (if there is any). The sacrifice proposes an offering but only in the form of a destruction against which it exchanges, hopes for, or counts on a benefit, namely a surplus-value or at least an amortization a protection, and a security."[63] An ultimate excess that enters into relationships of mutuality without surrendering to exchange would seem to be modeled by God's grace, but to the extent that religion always replaces grace with exchange, Derrida cannot accept it. The appeal to grace ("a sort of adoring and faithful abdication, a simple movement of faith in the face of that which exceeds the limits of experience, knowledge, science, economy—and even philosophy"[64]) merely mystifies the ways in which excess always becomes exchange and subjects excess to the manipulation of those who need magic. So Derrida is left with a cunning but frustrating subversion of his own topic, a doubleness or duplicity within which the most he can do is erect new obstacles by intensifying old quandaries.

For Derrida, we cannot finally think the difference between giving and exchange, just as the ontological difference between Being and beings also always eludes our grasp. Giving and exchange neither contradict nor repeat each other. They can be subjected to neither dialectics not analogy. Their difference, at once both excessive and calculated, is the condition of both their possibility and impossibility. Difference itself remains unthinkable, even as it provides the condition for all of our thinking. There is no difference that can be represented as an origin, a source, a given that does not itself partake of the ambiguities of that which it gives. There is no giving, *unless* it can be shown that excess does not negate exchange, while exchange does not nullify excess. Ironically, Derrida emphasizes the heterogeneity of excess and exchange so completely that they become indistinguishable, each hiding in the other, using each other, giving (or taking) from the other— exchange trying to improve itself by taking on the appearance of giving, and giving justifying or explaining itself as exchange. Such dissembling creates debts that cannot be paid. Giving desires a reward; exchange pretends to give. In the next two chapters, I want to show how Christian giving affirms both an ultimate excess and a comprehensive reciprocity without contradiction or separation. In other words the Christian God answers to Derrida's demand that excess be driven to extremes, but God also pushes that extremity toward reciprocity without reducing excess to exchange. In the grand sweep of God's giving, excess and mutuality meet without one becoming or overcoming the other. This argument involves a rejection of the traditional notion of divine giving by revising the relationship between excess and reciprocity on which it usually rests.

3

The Theo-Economics of God

In the deeps are the violence and terror of which psychology has warned us. But if you ride these monsters deeper down, if you drop with them farther over the world's rim, you find what our sciences cannot locate or name, the substrate, the ocean or matrix or ether which buoys the rest, which gives goodness its power for the good, and evil its power for evil, the unified field: our complex and inexplicable caring for each other, and for our life together here. This is given. It is not learned.

Annie Dillard, "Total Eclipse," from *Teaching a Stone to Talk*

Profusion, not economy, may after all be reality's key-note.

William James, *Pragmatism*

The first and second chapter argue that the excessive either obliterates the possibility of an appropriate return or is immediately entangled in the predictable and mundane circularity of reciprocity. In the first case, the excessive is irrelevant, only negatively connected to social relations; in the second case, it is undialectically submerged in its opposite. Either way, excess comes to nothing. The gift is exchange hyperbolized, and yet gift giving seems to be merely a way of embellishing or enhancing the unbreakable logic of barter and trade. The ambiguity of the trope of hyperbole points to the central difficulty in gift giving. Does the gift exaggerate, in a pejorative sense, the encompassing calculations of exchange, or is there the possibility of interruption, disruption, and transformation? Does hyperbole merely heighten the customary trans-actions of this for that, or does its height beckon a mode of agency that radically threatens the dominance of "more of the same"? Moreover, is the disruption of the gift only a temporary reprieve from the persistence of exchange, or is it a genuine alternative, an antieconomy sustainable on its own terms? How can we relate or join together the two thematics of excess and exchange? Can the gift be *both* excessive, as a sign of strength and abundance, *and* sensible, that is, reciprocal in both intention and effect? Can the gratuitous be *both* playful, pleasurable, and free *and* productive in the sense of entering into and changing social relations and cultural formations? What does the gratuitous do? In sum, does excess have an ethics?

Giving the Given Gift

Can the pair gratuity and gratitude be distinguished from exchange without running the dangers of the rhetoric of squandering? Can the gratuitous lead to a gratitude that is empowering, not humiliating? It is possible to portray gratitude as a unique response to a unique offering, a relationship that includes elements of both excess and reciprocity. This approach to giving is rooted in theological presuppositions, and it is the Christian grammar of gratuity and gratitude that I want to explicate, critique, and transform through my own proposal about gift giving. Theologians traditionally have wanted to maintain the gratuitous nature of God's acts without sliding into the languages of either superfluity or exchange. This is not a simple task.[1] The trick of theology is to show that the gifts of God—primarily creation and salvation—are simultaneously free and undeserved, yet binding and obliging. Heresies characteristically err in one direction or the other, emphasizing either the freedom of God's grace without any need for response on our part or the demand that we earn and deserve God's giving through our own efforts. Theology traditionally keeps together, without separating or conflating, both sides of this issue. God's gift as both promise and demand thus creates a covenant, a set of obligations both ritual and moral, that emerges as a sign of and response to grace. In Christian theology, the covenant is the particular economy of God's giving and our return, but the use of the term *economy* raises serious questions about God's involvement in the world.[2] We can hardly apply the modern and narrow use of that term to divine agency, but the persistence of its application to God makes us wonder how divine benevolence actually works. The central question is how we can return that which is excessively given. How is the gift both free and demanding, both gratuitous and obliging? How does grace create the covenant? What kind of economy operates within the covenant?

Theologians from every Christian tradition emphasize gratitude as the principle of participation in the covenant. The central resource for this focus is the Christian practice of worship, which, according to Geoffrey Wainwright, is essentially nothing else than the free response to God's free gift: "The gratuity of worship expresses the character of salvation as gift: a gift to be actively enjoyed."[3] In the eucharist especially, thanksgiving serves as the paradigmatic response to God. Wainwright is aware that his account of doxology as gratitude raises the problem of reciprocity: What is it, exactly, that we are giving back to God in return for God's gift, and how can we repay that which is given for no reason? Thanks itself, Wainwright argues, is the return of the gift, an acceptable, even if not precisely equivalent, substitute for that which is given: "In worship we take in the outpouring of God's creative and redemptive love, and we offer in return our thanks and supplications. In this personal exchange we are coming into the moral and spiritual likeness of our Lover" (p. 462). Our freely given gratitude is a mimetic representation of God's grace, and thus we are led to give as God gives. This logic of worship as thanksgiving presupposes the possibility of responding to a gratuitous gift in a gratuitous fashion, but such logic seems, prima facie, illogical. If we can respond in a proportionate and adequate way to God's gifts of creation and salvation, then how can we maintain that those gifts are freely given, for no reason? That is, how is God's giving both asymmetrical and reciprocal, both unreturnable and returnable, both free and exchanged, or, in other words, gratuitous but not superfluous?

Attempts to clarify the donative language in theology usually focus on the doctrine of creation. God creates not out of any need or for any reason; God creates freely, graciously, out of nothing (ex nihilo). Behind the basic doxological response of thanksgiving, then, lies an even more fundamental theological presupposition. God gives freely, as Langdon Gilkey has shown, because God is transcendent.[4] That God is the creator of all things means that there is only one source of all that is and that source precedes, sustains, and governs all that is. Our existence is "a gift from beyond" (p. 87), but God's existence is completely self-sufficient. God does not need anything external to God's self, and thus the creation is the one actual instance of a purely gratuitous gift. We cannot ask why God creates. If there were a reason, then God would be motivated by something external to God's nature, a situation that would threaten God's infinity and sovereignty. God practices agape, disinterested love, not eros, love that is driven by desire and need. Gilkey explains the traditional position: "If God needs the world in order to complete or enrich His being, then His creation of the world is not 'free.' It is a necessitated and therefore impersonal act, to which God 'is compelled by His own unfulfilled nature" (p. 109). Nothing moves God in the sense of coercing God's will; God moves because

God wills. To be sure, what God creates is good, but God does not create because of the good. God must necessarily will God's self, but all other divine willing is born of a radical voluntarism, which deepens the mystery of grace and creation.[5]

Some theologians have tried to argue that God creates not from an act of the will but from the overflow of goodness itself. Pseudo-Dionysius talks about the *bonum diffusivum sui*, the good naturally spreading outward, in a process of ecstatic dissemination, and Bonaventure reflects this theme of centrifugal surplus in his image of God as the *fontalis plenitudo*, the fountain of fullness and plenty.[6] Although this cluster of images is recurrent in Christian theology, most theologians have tried to avoid language that echoes the emanationism of Neoplatonism: if creation is modeled on the organic metaphor of an external overflowing of God's internal activity, then God's creativity would seem to be natural, automatic, and inevitable—not deliberate, decisive, and free. Thus, theologians traditionally maintain that the act of creation is not exactly like the spilling over of a fountain. It is more intentional than that, and yet it is also not like human gift giving, in which someone gives something to somebody, because in this case that which is given exists before it is given and could be obtained in ways other than the act of giving. In fact, traditional theologians are forced to acknowledge that we have no analogies from human experience whatsoever for a creation that begins with nothing. God must be, then, wholly other, and creation is a mystery that can be only symbolically construed.

According to the traditional perspective, God's benevolence is not like human giving or nature's fecundity because God is utterly transcendent, free from the encumbrance of reciprocity that even the most extravagant human generosity presupposes and promotes. As the Thomist E. L. Mascall argues, "It is possible to assign motives for the acts which our human wills perform, precisely because their freedom is limited; in the case of God there is no reason whatever."[7] Absolute freedom defines excessive generosity. If God gives because God wants or needs something in return, then God would be dependent, limited, and vulnerable. God would become implicated in a process that could alter or even damage God's very being. This is unthinkable in classical theism because it assumes that God's being is infinite, perfect, and simple and thus incapable of change. In Thomas Aquinas's definition of God as pure act (*actus purus*), God has no potentiality that God does not actualize. If God changed from a lesser to a greater state, God would be imperfect at the prior state, as well as subjected to the difficulties of growth and advancement. These arguments led Aquinas to conclude that God is complete, and, therefore, nothing can add to God's existence. By implication, we cannot give anything of real value to God. Mascall defends this position with an analogy:

> Now most fathers receive presents from their small children on their birthdays, and receive them gladly, in spite of the fact that the presents are usually quite useless and in any case have to be paid for by the parent in the last resort. They are none the less readily accepted because of that, and the normal human parent has a joy in receiving such a gift which far exceeds the satisfaction obtained from a much more expensive and useful present given by a business client or even by a grown-up friend.[8]

For Mascall, the most we can give to God are the "useless" gifts of praise and gratitude, because God's paternal nature is self-satisfied and self-contained. Mascall's analogy, however, works against him; he thinks that God, like all good fathers, does not really need useless gifts, but his own description of such gifts shows that they can be called useless only in a paradoxical fashion. All gifts are useless in the sense that they are more than we reasonably expect or minimally need, yet the useless is something that we cannot live without. We are who we are only through what we are given, which is always more than what we think we need. Indeed, I argue that God wants us to give excessively, beyond the requirements of utility, because that is the nature of giving, and this giving is what God needs and desires in order to be all that God can be. The desire to give is always connected to the need to receive; to give is to want to enter into the life of another in a risky way, giving oneself over to possibilities of frustration and incompletion. What God wants is not a token display of our gratitude but our further giving because God is involved in both how and what we give, staking his identity on the future of God's gifts.

Gilkey is a careful observer of how the traditional view of God's transcendence has become the target of increasing criticism from many revisionist theologians. These contemporary theologians accuse this position of portraying God as essentially unrelated to the world, incapable of change or sympathy. One of the classical terms for God's transcendence is *aseity,* the idea that God is self-sufficient because self-derived (*a se*) rather than derived from some external source (*ab alio*). A passage from Anselm shows the difficulty of connecting God's aseity to the Christian idea of God's suffering compassion and generosity:

> But again, how art thou at once compassionate and impassible? For if thou art impassible, thou canst not suffer with others, and if thou canst not suffer with others, thy heart is not wretched out of sympathy for the

wretched — but this is what compassionate means. . . . Yes, thou art compassionate according to our sense, but not according to thine. For when
thou lookest upon us, wretched as we are, we feel the effect of thy
compassion, but thou dost not feel emotion. So, then, thou art compassionate, because thou savest the wretched and sparest those who sin
against thee, and yet thou art not compassionate, because thou art not
affected by any share in our wretchedness.[9]

Such a God, many theologians now maintain, is closer to the spec-
ulations of Greek metaphysics than the story of the crucifixion of Jesus.
The predicates of impassibility and immutability were attributed to
God as a way of emphasizing God's uniqueness, but they also honor
autonomy and independence as the highest values. God is the unmov-
ing first cause who orders our thinking and gives our restless souls
eventual rest. God does not need to give to an other because God's love
is fulfilled in God's desire for God's self; nevertheless, God does give as
a way of inviting humanity to participate in this eternal bliss. At best,
God's giving (as with Thomas Aquinas) is connected to the divine will;
it is a decision that originates in the mystery of God's freedom. It does
not involve any movement and does not implicate God in real relations
with the benefactors of this decision.[10] At worst, God gives only to
God's self, a closed economy that makes our own giving redundant. In
the classical model of theism, God gives, but God does not share, in the
sense that God does not share in the destiny of the gift, its messy
movement through the perils of the world, and the difficult labor of
its return.[11]

Gift giving provides an important perspective to challenge the classical model of theism because it both continues and undermines many
aspects of the traditional pairing of the divine gratuity and our gratitude. Although gift giving presupposes an excessive initiative, it also
involves relationships of real mutuality and sharing. Most radically,
this perspective inserts need and desire into the heart of God's being. It
is interesting that Islamic teaching suggests that God, too, is thankful,
indeed, that God exemplifies the virtue of gratitude in being thankful to
us for acknowledging God's gifts.[12] By contrast, Christian theology has
not wanted to connect the idea of God's generosity to the human
activity of reciprocal gift giving. Traditional Christian teaching suggests
that how God creates (rather than gives) is utterly different from how
we give (rather than create). We must start with something already
given, shape it, create something out of it, and then pass it along. We
also give with some expectation of return or reimbursement. God's
giving follows the pattern of neither impersonal economic calculation

nor mutuality practiced within the confines of the closed group. By starting from nothing, God's act of creation is the ultimate gift, giving being to that which was not before, but, like Nietzschean squandering, it is not an act that graciously participates in the to-and-fro expectation of a return. Indeed, the rule that seems to govern this logic is the following: *God receives only what God gives.* Although this seems like a model for a self-giving that denies otherness, it actually is an act we cannot understand based on our own experience because God really neither receives nor gives. It is hard, then, to know what it would mean to embrace a doxology that portrays thanksgiving as the imitation of God's free giving; surely, imitation requires understanding. How can we give something back to God if our giving is not analogous to God's giving? Moreover, what can we give to God, if God does not need our gifts? Can you give something to someone who does not need anything? Finally, how can God's giving be free and yet demand gratitude as a kind of repayment? How does God's gratuity work, and what is the gratitude that excess engenders?

Here I examine several theological positions with reference to the problem of how God gives and how we are to return those gifts. I begin with a discussion of Calvin because it is in the Protestant Reformation that both the transcendence and the gratuity of God receive special emphasis. Contrary to stereotypes about Calvin's portrait of an austere and frugal divinity, Calvin's God is boundlessly generous and gracious. Nevertheless, the structure of this generosity needs careful attention. I use Calvin as the primary example of the traditional Protestant notion of a giving God, but I also discuss one of Calvin's modern heirs, Karl Barth, who likewise defends the traditional notion of God's transcendence as a giver who does not need gifts. For Barth, God does not give, in the sense of giving something to somebody; instead, God only creates, in the sense of calling into being that which did not previously exist. Both Calvin and Barth situate God's giving in the mode of excess, to the point where mutuality is threatened, if not intentionally obliterated. The question is whether the logic of excess alone is appropriate to Christian worship and practice. In this regard, I examine several challenges to this traditional depiction of God in terms of what they have to say about the dynamic of giving: I look at Charles Hartshorne, Sallie McFague, Mark Taylor, and Peter Hodgson. Hartshorne, McFague, and Hodgson try to modify the traditional concept of God's transcendence by emphasizing mutuality and partnership. Generally speaking, they portray God's relationship to us as one of exchange, not excess. Taylor represents a special case because he radicalizes God's immanence in order to emphasize not exchange but gratuity, to the point where excess becomes ubiquitous and thus meaningless. In contrast to these alternative constructions of God's gift-giving activity, which also raise insurmountable problems about the nature of God's involvement in the world, I offer my own conception of the gratuity of God by setting it in a trinitarian framework. In the next chapter, I develop this framework in more detail.

My reflections are guided by the idea that if we are to be able to conceive of gift giving as both an activity of God and as a human virtue rooted in that activity of God, then we must avoid two opposing extremes. Giving can be neither completely gratuitous nor totally reciprocal. The traditional view emphasizes the gratuitous nature of God's creativity, but at the risk of abandoning any coherent notion of reciprocity. The critiques of this position, I argue, approach the opposite mistake of substituting reciprocity for gratuity. I want to argue that divine gift giving is both excessive and reciprocal, or rather, it is reciprocal precisely because it is excessive. The doctrine of God's transcendence does not mean that God has only external relations to the world and thus does not need the world. It should be taken to mean that God's giving is an abundance, an excessive giving that initiates, sustains, and solicits a response from the one to whom God gives. God's immanence is this reciprocity, the idea that God "needs" our gifts and desires our giving. One of the most terrible things in the world is to take away from somebody their capacity to give, which can be done *both* by not giving the other anything to give in turn *and* through an extravagant giving strategy that does not allow for reciprocity. True gifts create return gifts, but it does not follow that giving therefore is always controlled by a logic of equivalence, of measuring this for that. For the return response to be solicited, the gift itself must be excessive, wonderful, unexpected. My governing insight, then, is the following: *divine excess begets reciprocity.* Without excess, reciprocity becomes calculation, bartering, exchange; without reciprocity, excess becomes irrelevant, anarchic, and wasteful.

The Christian model of giving follows a triadic pattern or logic that holds together both excess and mutuality throughout the whole process. This can be seen from the simple claim that God's giving initiates, solicits, and sustains all of our own giving. Following the trinitarian nature of this scheme, it should be noted that God is the Giver, the Given, and the Giving. That is, God gives, and God can even be said to give recklessly, but God does not give randomly, for no purpose or reason. What God gives is both God's self and the givenness of things that allows us to recognize, multiply, and return God's gifts. But God is more than just the giver and the given. God is also persistently involved in our giving, sustaining our participation in the unfolding of God's great generosity. To participate in giving is not only to give but also to receive — that is, to have something at stake in the process as a whole. God gives excessively, to the point of the given, as a way of empowering relationships of mutuality and reciprocity. In the end, what God gives is the power of giving itself, the possibility that we can all participate in the movement of giving with the hope that such generosity will be enhanced, organized, and consummated in God's very own becoming. God is, then, the Giver, the Given, and the Giving, in such a way that God's giving is a form of receiving that creates even more giving in turn.[13]

These three moments in God's giving can be analyzed separately because they constitute distinct phases in a coherent process. Moreover, these moments correspond both to the three elements of giving with which I began chapter 1 and to a trinitarian framework. To borrow George Lindbeck's strategy, which, in turn, is dependent on Ludwig Wittgenstein, I treat these moments as "rules" that mark the boundaries to, and provide the conditions for, any proper discourse on divine benevolence.[14] I do not mean to suggest that my three rules of divine giving describe the basic grammar or structure of all Christian discourse on this topic. These rules are as much imaginative hypothesis as comprehensive description. They emerge from my readings of scripture and theology, but they also respond to the philosophical conundrum on giving that I developed in chapter 1. They both illuminate and challenge Christian thinking about giving, just as they both resolve and critique philosophical thinking about giving. These rules, then, are the basis for my criticisms of the various theologians I analyze in the next sections, and in the next chapter I return to these rules for further exploration and elaboration.

First, God gives. There is a first giver (the initiative quality of this giving is what theologians call God's prevenience), and this giver models all appropriate giving. Giving does not originate with us; it is not something for which we are completely responsible. Instead, it is something to which we are responsive. Giving begins as a lavish intrusion into our lives that calls forth something from us that could not otherwise come to be. The way that we are called and what we are called to do are equally excessive. The source of giving is also the norm. God the Giver is what I am calling the first person of the Trinity, who is traditionally understood as the Father. (I should make it clear that such abundant giving can be characteristic of either gender, so there is no theological warrant for maintaining the exclusively male pronoun.)

Second, what God gives is given, in the sense that it is given for us but also in the sense that it is there for us to choose what we will do with it. The "given" usually means something that is just there, not given by a giver. Thus, the given can be possessed because it is there for the taking. God's gifts can be owned because they are really given, but they can also be received and returned in the spirit in which they were given. Gifts are always already there, before we give them to others; we must decide what to do with them. Giving involves both response and initiative, and thus the gift simultaneously promotes obligation and freedom. Moreover, what God has given is always more than we can utilize, which means that the economy of God's giving is based on abundance and not scarcity. What the given tells us is that God does not merely give; instead, God splurges, abundantly. We can give, in turn, because the given exceeds and thus sustains, enhances, and empowers our capacity to turn taking into giving.

The two traditional forms of God's gifts, creation and salvation, represent the two complementary sides of the given. The doctrine of creation encapsulates the idea that the gift is really given—that is, it is distinct from the giver—and thus it gives us the freedom to receive or reject it, to deny it, or to pass it along. The incarnation emphasizes the connection of the gift to the giver: at stake in every given is the being of the giver. The gift is not just there; it is also an extension of the giver, resonating with the shape and force of the initial giving. I agree, therefore, with those theologians who subordinate the doctrine of creation to Christology, but not because creation can be received as a gift only in the form of the particular gift of Jesus Christ. In my terms, the particular gift of Jesus Christ shows that the given is the giver. In other words, creation can be acknowledged as benefit (received as a gift) because it is shaped by the giving of God as that is revealed in Jesus Christ. God as Given, then, is how I am referring to the second person of the Trinity, the Sonship of Jesus Christ. Jesus is the moment in which God lets go of God's self to become completely other, and so what God gives is not only the given, but also God's own self. The gift is given, squandered, recklessly abandoned, to be given again or not, according to how it is received.

Third, God's giving is a form of receiving. Gratitude is a static notion, an uneasy response to a giving that should not or cannot be returned or passed along. God, I argue here, gives to us in order to create a community of givers, enabling us to move the gift along in acknowledgment and action alike. The best form of gratitude is to be empowered to give without resentment (due to extrinsic obligation) or expectation (based on calculation). We do not give in order to receive for ourselves but in order to give something back to the God who gives. Our giving is not governed by the logic of compensation and return but by the desire to follow the essential dynamic of all gifts, which is to return them to their origin, in God, by giving them to others. By receiving our gifts, God solicits our giving even when that giving does not seem to make a difference, or when it seems too difficult to give. God preserves, directs, and continues our giving, no matter how limited our own imaginations or strengths. When we give to others, then, there is a very real sense in which we are giving to God. We do not have to choose between giving to God and giving to others; by giving to others, we are participating in the momentum of God's giving, which multiplies and disperses gifts even as they are directed to the one Giver. The glory of the receiving God, however, cannot be an end point that puts a stop to the process of giving. Instead, God receives in order to give again even more abundantly; God blesses and sustains this strange economy of giving by returning what is given in ways that defy our desires and expectations. God the Giving, who is also God as a receiver, corresponds to what traditionally is called the Holy Spirit.

In sum, according to the Christian theory of giving, when we give, we give the given gift, what has already been given, adding to it what we can, and directing it to the glory of God. God makes possible our giving by an activity that precedes, surpasses, and sustains all of our gifts. God's special economy provides a contour that shapes and empowers our own antieconomic acts. I have chosen to call this process, both God's giving and our own, *gifting,* in an attempt to synthesize both the activity of giving, its verbal form, and the idea that giving begins with a prior giving and with something already given, its nominative form. The neologism *gifting* should remind us that the gift precedes and empowers giving, and that giving is always in response to a prior gift. This verbal noun is intended to conjure both the act and being of giving, because it is an act that has its form in the being (or, better, becoming) of God, which is in turn a kind of activity. The gifting God gives not as a supplement or addition to who God really is but as the act that constitutes God's own self. The gifting God puts God's self at stake in God's gifts, so that the giver, the given, and the giving are no longer easily distinguished. We, in turn, can give this gift, thus becoming the people who are created by this activity. Our own gifting involves the gift that we always already are, as well as the openness to others that giving hopes to become. Gifting, then, is not a marginal activity that complements other forms of interaction. The gift is not one object among many. In opposition to the reckless amorality of squandering and the vigilant conservation of exchange, gifting is the unreserved act in which we are most truly ourselves, supported and sustained in the dynamic becoming of God, finding ourselves by losing ourselves in the other, fusing action and being in a tensile process that is held together by God's own power to become God's self in the expenditure of the gift.

Calvin and the Labor of Gratitude

One of the most interesting readings of the traditional understanding of God's generosity can be found in Brian Gerrish's recent *Grace and Gratitude*.[15] Gerrish takes as his focus one of the primary themes of Calvin's theology: the idea that God is the fountain of all good, the *fons omnium bonorum*. Gerrish is obviously trying to correct the popular image of Calvin's God as a capricious tyrant. Calvin's God is the epitome of liberality, offering humanity a great and lavish abundance of goodness. To illustrate this theme, Gerrish notes that Calvin uses the images of fountain and father interchangeably in describing God. The familial images, not the natural one, dominates the *Institutes*, but both metaphors acknowledge the benefits God bestows through creation, providence, and redemption. Gerrish points out that Luther also liked the fountain image; in his *Large Catechism*, Luther called God "an eternal fountain overflowing with sheer goodness; from him pours forth all that is good and is called good."[16] Calvin also knew Seneca's *De beneficiis*, where Seneca writes: "God bestows upon us very many and very great benefits, with no thought of any return, since he has no need of having anything bestowed, nor are we capable of bestowing anything on him" (p. 38). Calvin's use of the filial image, however, is meant to personalize Seneca's notion of an arbitrary God who is nearly indistinguishable from the good that comes from nature itself. For Calvin, God's love is more like a parent, both father and mother, than an overflowing fountain, because God acts intentionally and specifically for our benefit. Yet, such love does not implicate God in a parental relationship of mutuality and reciprocity, and here Calvin is more influenced not only by Stoic and Neoplatonic imagery but also by the voluntarism of nominalism. God does not give out of a sense of obligation or need; God gives because God freely chooses to do that. God gives according to God's nature, because, like a fountain, giving is what God does.

Given the basic fact of God's awesome generosity, it is difficult to understand why people find it so hard to acknowledge and respect

God's giving. Humans are in the privileged position of being spectators to the theater of God's giving, but people are frequently blinded or bored by this glory. Indeed, Gerrish argues that Calvin understands sin to be thanklessness. The image of God that constitutes humanity is not some inner essence but the graceful activity of thankfulness. Gerrish quotes Thomas Torrance: "Calvin practically equates the *imago* with the *actio* of gratitude." (p. 44) The sin of Adam was irreverence for God's giving, an apathetic pride that Calvin often zealously denounces. This sullen ingratitude is something of a mystery. If God's gifts are so abundant, why are they so difficult to appreciate? True, Calvin thinks that not everyone receives the equivalent benefits, but all have more than enough to motivate thankfulness. Nevertheless, ingratitude stubbornly prevails.

Perhaps it is the very indiscriminate abundance of God's giving that makes indifference so seductive. What is everywhere is easy to overlook. Moreover, people are not content merely to receive this perpetual giving; they want to claim some form of giving as their own. Whatever the status of the mystery of ingratitude, it makes necessary the particular reconciliation of Christ as the basis of all authentic thanksgiving. Christ is the access to God's fountain of goodness. God's giving is thus not wanton; instead, God distributes God's goods along genealogical lines: only the Son gives us the Father. Two theological mistakes are possible at this point. First, Christ does not initiate God's love. It is wrong to say that God is not loving until the coming of Christ. Second, it is also wrong to say that the atonement is "a mere change in our own subjective consciousness by which we come to realize that God is not, after all, a judge but a father" (p. 60). Christ neither begins nor confirms God's giving; rather, Christ intensifies and thus guarantees God's love in order to ensure the radically generous distribution of God's goods. Christ actually shares the honor of sonship with us, enabling our adoption and thus our reception of the family inheritance. We receive these benefits through faith, which is not primarily a cognitive assent but an existential confidence in the inclusivity of God's goodness.[17] Faith changes us from passive spectators to active participants in the drama of God's goodness.

God's goodness in the arena of creation, then, is subordinated to the action of redemption. Salvation from ingratitude is the one true gift. As Gerrish quotes Calvin: "The reason why God bestows everything on us in Christ is so that we shall claim nothing for ourselves, but ascribe everything to him" (p. 86). This theological move conveniently provides Calvin with a vantage point from which to criticize the medieval penitential system. In Gerrish's own words: "Forgiveness is a gift of sheer liberality: the creditor who gives a receipt for money paid does not forgive, but only the one who, without payment, cancels the debt out of kindness" (p. 92). The old self is not weak but perversely strong; revolution is demanded, not reformation through education. Grace is not pedagogical; it "is not assistance but a new act of creation" (p. 94). In God's gift giving, then, God controls not only the act of giving but also the act of receiving. Calvin agrees with Augustine that God rewards his own works, so that even our merits, what we are able to give to God, are gifts of grace. God does this not out of an exercise of power but from an extravagant indulgence. The most we can do is to offer a sacrifice of praise because to try to repay such excessive generosity in order to balance the account with God would be an insult, not an appropriate response.[18] Nevertheless, Gerrish cannot avoid the language of exchange to illuminate the gift of grace: "The sacrifice of thanksgiving is presented to God only by those who, loaded with his boundless favors, repay him with their whole self and everything they do."[19] Is gratitude connected to the burden of an impossible debt, or does it spring forth from the same gratuity as grace? Is a gratitude based on insolvency and irreciprocity possible? In order to reconcile excess and exchange, Gerrish is forced to argue that gratitude is the response that allows us to do nothing as a way of doing something; it thus keeps the focus on what God has done and is still doing.

Calvin is fond of saying that Christ is the food of our souls and that insight provides the basis for the centrality of the eucharist in Calvin's theology. The eucharist is the liturgical enactment of the themes of grace and gratitude: "The Lord's Supper is a genuine feast (*convivium*), a holy banquet (*sacrosanctum epulum*), which recalls to our memories that Christ was made the bread on which we continually feed" (p. 13). People, prone to thoughtlessness, need this special occasion of God's giving. Calvin's paradigmatic person is a "eucharistic man," a phrase Gerrish borrows from Gregory Dix:

> Over against the dissatisfied "Acquisitive Man" and his no less avid successor the dehumanized "Mass-Man" of our economically focused societies insecurely organized for a time, Christianity sets the type of "Eucharistic Man"—man giving thanks with the product of his labors upon the gifts of God, and daily rejoicing with his fellows in the worshipping society which is grounded in eternity.[20]

Mediating between Luther and Zwingli, Calvin argues that Christ is really given in the sacrament. Christians do not simply partake of the benefits of Christ; they partake of Christ's very presence. The sacrament is an act primarily by God, not humans. Nevertheless, what is given is not a localized gift that can be found only in this ritualized form. What is given is a continuation and exemplification of what God is and does at all times, the giving that is a constant with God but only periodically and inadequately perceived by those to whom God gives. The very irregularity of our capacity to receive this gift makes its concentration in the eucharist necessary.

Gerrish has succeeded in drawing attention to a truly majestic theme in Calvin's work, the twofold movement of grace and gratitude. Yet, the way in which both Gerrish and Calvin persistently discuss gratitude in the economic terms of repayment, exchange, debt, and labor is troubling. Gerrish quotes a significant passage from Calvin: "The same thought keeps coming back to me: that there is a risk of my doing an injustice to the mercy of God by laboring so painstakingly to assert it—as if it were doubtful or obscure! But because we are so grudging that we never concede to God what belongs to him unless very strongly constrained, I shall have to insist on it at a little greater length."[21] What Calvin thinks keeps returning, and so his thoughts can reach out to God only when coerced. This quotation encapsulates Calvin's dilemma: to labor at gratitude is contrary to that very attitude, and yet gratitude is a kind of labor. Only God's love, for Calvin, is laborless. If gratitude correlates to grace, it should be simple, easy, and free, yet it must be, on Calvin's own admission, enforced, compelled, and constrained. Indeed, this is arguably the essence of religion: it takes time, effort, preparation to express gratitude to God; rituals of gratitude must follow meticulous rules, which, in turn, require a division of labor, a diversity of roles that, when sufficiently organized, efficiently accomplishes the given task. Gratitude is what a gift buys, or what a gift produces, and the whole process is expensive and difficult. In fact, it seems an aspect of the excessive logic of gratitude to always go "a little greater length" because it must be unsure of itself: it is both appropriate and impossible, both demanded and unsolicited, both spontaneous and compelled, both proportionate and token. Gratitude is bound by the rule of "etc.": if true gifts are excessive, then so must be gratitude. It is essentially hyperbolic, not because it must feign an embellishment but because what it says can never fully and truly be said at all. Gratitude, then, cannot know when to stop, and perhaps that is why it must be so carefully organized and ritualized—otherwise, it would not know how to begin.

Calvin is right to voice some misgivings here: to match the traditional transcendent creativity of God, responsive gratitude would have to go on and on and on. Where could it possibly end? How could it possibly be enough? A gift that is unique and perfect is more demanding than giving, and it correlates with a gratitude born of guilt, not joy.[22] The singular and unrepeatable gift is not deserved, and therefore it cannot be enjoyed. In sum, for Calvin, God's gift in Jesus Christ reveals the depths of our ingratitude toward God's giving in and through creation. A gift that compensates for something rejected is more reprimanding than rewarding. It demands respect for the order that ingratitude disrupts, requiring a belabored and not ecstatic response. In terms of my three rules, God's giving controls the given so that what God receives is the same as what God gives. Consequently, our gratitude is an expression of our inability to give. We give gratitude because we cannot give anything else. Such thanks can never compensate for our more basic thanklessness. The resulting gratitude would have to try to prove itself by an infinitely anxious and strenuous labor, but how could such futile labor possibly be called – gratitude?

Karl Barth and God's Freedom

Karl Barth's theology in the *Church Dogmatics* portrays a dynamic God who is best understood as an action, not a principle, idea, or substance: "God is who He is in His works."[23] Barth can make this claim because in Jesus Christ the being of God is revealed as a specific kind of activity. For Barth, there is no knowledge of God beyond or beside the sheer fact of this revelation, and what is revealed in Jesus Christ is God's freedom to be for us, which is, first of all, God's ability to become other than God's self. God's freedom, then, is the foundation for God's revelation and graciousness. Put another way, the gift of revelation testifies that God is both sovereign and gracious. Indeed, for Barth, true sovereignty entails the capacity for gratuitous action. God's freedom means that God is self-complete and self-satisfied, yet God nonetheless chooses to lovingly act for an other: "He ordains that He should not be entirely self-sufficient as He might be. He determines for Himself that overflowing, that movement, that condescension. He constitutes Himself as benefit or favor. And in so doing he elects another as the object of His love."[24] For Barth, love is not possible without freedom. Actions motivated by necessity or by bonds of reciprocity cannot be gracious, free, and loving. Freedom, however, does not mean caprice. God's decision to be for us is not an incidental aspect of God's being. God is for us from eternity. God's freedom and God's graciousness are inextricably interrelated, and the logic of that free grace already says everything that can be said about gratitude: "To thank means to acknowledge that it is a question of accepting a pure gift, whose reality has no basis elsewhere than in the goodness of the Giver, in view of which, therefore, we can only glorify this kindness of the Giver."[25] The only answer to *charis* (grace) is the eucharist.[26]

Barth's Christocentrism would force him to be very suspicious, of course, of the theological program I am developing here. He would not want to subject the discourse about God's activity through Jesus Christ to the terms of the model of gift giving. Through revelation, God masters and controls our knowledge of God's self. Jesus Christ reveals an eternal decision that neither conforms nor corresponds to any merely human hypothesis or analogy. Nonetheless, it is central to Barth's theology to portray God's love as "overflowing, free, unconstrained, unconditioned,"[27] so that asking after the nature of that generosity is appropriate. Moreover, in the lecture fragments that belong to *Church Dogmatics* IV/4, the volume on the ethical implications of God the Reconciler on which Barth was working at the time of his death, Barth does rely on the language of gift giving to illuminate divine agency:

> To give thanks is to acknowledge as such a gift that someone else has freely given. The children of God know that they live only by the freely given gift of their Father, which consists of the fullness of his being and work for them and in them. The first motive of their movement to him, which as a basic note decides and determines all that follows, is that they owe him the boundless acknowledgment of his free gift, and knowing both him and themselves they have at least the will and desire to discharge something of this debt of thanks.[28]

Thanksgiving is the basic gesture of Christian life; it is the form of every response to God, from worship and praise to acknowledgment, reflection, obedience, and action. Gratitude is the only response that the gift of grace earns. It is, essentially, a recognition of need and debt: "Their thanksgiving and praise can be only that of those who have total need of him and his further free gifts (p. 88). Gratitude is the only possible correlation to an initiative that is free and undeserved.[29]

Barth does not praise gratitude as a worthy virtue in itself; it is not a practice that we can cultivate and develop. Barth suspects that gratitude "is often enough interrupted by their self-satisfaction, defiance, and forgetfulness."[30] Fortunately, God does not need our gratitude in order to be gracious: "It is by no means self-evident that he [God] should be pleased by their praise, that he who does not need it should seriously let himself be honored by their far too slender and often also far too bulky praise" (pp. 106–7). God hears our gratitude only because our "weak and dissonant voices are sustained by the one strong voice of the one by whose eucharist the inadequacy of theirs is covered and glorified in advance" (p. 106). The one to whom God responds in receiving our gratitude is, of course, Jesus Christ. Jesus Christ is the action of God, making our reaction always secondary and dependent. Jesus is the gift that God both gives and receives. Our gratitude, therefore, does not really give or do anything. It just happens: "Gratitude can only take place."[31] It is an event, not a process. If gratitude does anything at all, Barth argues, by definition it cannot be real gratitude: "Where man repays like with like, there is no question of thanksgiving but only of transaction: we are at the market which is ruled by the mutual adjustment of supply and demand, value and price" (p. 217). The grace of gratitude is a gift of God.

The content of the divine action in Jesus Christ displays a God who is loving, who is willing to humble God's self before the world, manifesting God's power in powerlessness. The divine condescension, however, does not display a contradiction or even a tension in the midst of God's being. God's giving is first and foremost trinitarian: "He does not exist in solitude but in fellowship. Therefore what He seeks and creates between Himself and us is in fact nothing else but what He wills and completes and therefore is in Himself" (p. 275).[32] The incarnation is not a new event in the life of God but the revelation of who God eternally already is. The man Jesus brings (gives, adds) nothing to God that makes him worthy of this divine election. "That this is indeed the case may be proved conclusively by the absoluteness of the gratitude and obedience with which this man stands before God and submits Himself to Him."[33] The fullness of the Trinity, however, makes God not only self-sufficient but also inclusive. In willing to exist in the mode of the Son as well as the Father, while at the same time willing that the Son should become one with the person Jesus Christ, God chooses to include humanity in God's being. God thus participates in our suffering; only at the point of utter weakness and impotence is God's true power made manifest.

Sheila Greeve Davaney argues that we should be careful not to infer that Barth is defending a general definition of divine power as powerlessness. Weakness is not being praised here as really strength, in some paradoxical, Pauline fashion. God is consistent: God can determine God's self as powerless precisely because God is omnipotent. God can be for an other because God is sufficient for God's self. The crucifixion is an indication of God's ultimate freedom to determine God's self as God chooses. Davaney voices an important dissatisfaction with this idea of divine power: "Despite Barth's claim to the contrary, there remains the suspicion that although lowliness is not improper to God, the real power is behind the cross and Jesus is merely an occasion for the illustration of power."[34] The problem lies with Barth's emphasis on divine freedom; God can be other than God's self, but this is a choice God makes (and thus, though Barth never quite says this, did not have to make). God is constrained only by the impossibility of self-contradiction. God is free to be other than God's self, and this freedom for otherness is who God is, but who God is does not necessarily include God's being with and for us. It is important to note, however, that Barth is careful to emphasize God's freedom not in order to suggest that God could have chosen not to be for us but to magnify the sense of the gratuity of grace. God's giving is never compelled; this seems to be the chief mystery of faith for Barth. "God loves because He loves," Barth writes.[35] God is the one who loves in freedom.

For Barth, the doctrine of creation highlights God's freedom to love by emphasizing creation's goodness for humanity. "Creation is benefit because it takes place according to God's beneficence, and therefore according to the supreme law of all benevolence and *bene esse*. Creation is blessing because it has unchangeably the character of an action in which the divine joy, honour and affirmation are turned towards another."[36] Barth argues, however, that we do not know the benefit of creation from direct observation alone; we can know it as such only because it is grounded in the event of Jesus Christ. Only from this more specific gift of love can we make sense of ourselves in the givenness of the world around us: "Man finds what a person is when he finds it in the person of God and his own being as a person in the gift of fellowship afforded him by God in person."[37] Creation is the environment (presupposition or precondition) for God's self-determination to become other in Jesus Christ. Creation is that which makes God's self-giving in Jesus Christ possible and productive. It has no independent status of its own.[38] The gift of Jesus Christ requires a vehicle or a "packaging" for its delivery; in Barth's words, creation is the external basis of the covenant of grace, and redemption is the internal basis of creation. Barth pushes the priority of Christology over creation to the point where the latter seems to be an afterthought to the former, not a gift in itself. As a result, gratitude is the specific response to a particular gift, not a pervasive and perhaps vague feeling or a constitutive dimension of human existence: "To believe in Jesus Christ means to become

thankful."[39] For Barth, there can be no general human response to the
basic givenness of God's works. Gratitude takes only one shape.

The unyielding verdict (centered in Christ) on the goodness of creation is a high point in Barth's theology, but it does raise problems
about sin and evil. He is forced, for example, to view evil as purely
privative (*das Nichtige*) and to conceive of the limitations that the created
environment imposes on humanity (the shadowside, *die Schattenseite*,
of loss, decay, and death) as the dialectical counterpart to creation and
thus also a basically good aspect of creation. More problematical for my
purposes, since creation is considered a gift only in relationship to the
gift of Jesus Christ, who is none other than God, creation is not really
given over to the givees—who tend toward sin, for unfathomable
reasons—for their own deliberations. The gift does not have a destiny
apart from God's self-determination. For Barth, God only gives God's
self, and since what God gives is eternally who God is, the gift of
salvation is determined from the very beginning, regardless of how we
receive or return it.[40] "The love of God does not await my response to
love to be eternal and omnipotently saving love."[41] God's giving is
objectively complete and efficacious, independent of any subjective
response. In other words, God's providence is total and final. Although
God's plan for the world does not conflict with human autonomy (he
argues that, through the Holy Spirit, God's intentions are harmonized
with human agency and, furthermore, true human autonomy is obedience to God anyway[42]), God's preservation and governance of the
world, as with the incarnation, is a by-product of God's own self-
determination. Divine providence is not, then, affected by the ways of
the world; humans cannot alter or add to God's thoroughly pre-
established intentions, but they can become most fully themselves by
conforming to and following God's providential rule. Indeed, Barth
sometimes defines *gratitude* precisely as the acknowledgment of divine
foreordination. "To be thankful of our own free will it is necessary that
we should have unconditionally acknowledged the divine foreordination of our free will. It is in this acknowledgment that gratitude to God
consists."[43] God gives us freedom by determining our justification from
the very beginning, so that we do not have anything to prove, to God or
to anybody else, but we also do not have anything we can give, because
nothing is our own.

More than any other modern theologian, Barth has preserved and
intensified the traditional notion of the purely boundless, unrestrained,
and excessive generosity of God. We simply cannot ask why God gives;
that is the sheerly given datum of revelation. That God is not dimin-

ished by generosity implies that God does not give as we do, so we must look to God to learn what giving really is. Such giving is discontinuous from all human activity; God is not what we would be if we were God. The divine excess does not dissipate God's fullness. This excess is so singular, however, that it threatens to create a massive dependence that must be acknowledged but can never be rectified or even redressed. God's excess does not beget reciprocity: "Grace would not be grace if it were not free, but were conditioned by a reciprocal achievement on the part of the one to whom it is addressed."[44] Although Barth frequently discusses human freedom, it is difficult to understand how God's giving can be connected to anything but a passive reverence toward God's control. Barth's God monopolizes generosity. God's giving is determined by an eternal choice that is rooted in the power of God's self-determination, and thus it risks being unrelated to the actual process of gift giving as we experience it in time. God's giving is not a response to or desire for an other, nor is it the beginning of a risky project that culminates in receiving transformed that which was given away. God gives because that is who God chooses (and has always chosen) to be. For all of Barth's emphasis on God as activity, then, Barth does not allow God to be part of the activity of giving, which is so much a part of human religious experience.

In sum, for Barth, God's transcendence means that the giver gives all; there is nothing left to be given by anybody else.[45] Moreover, nothing can be given back to God. That is, our countergifts do not shape or affect how God gives: "Even out of its [the creature's] gratitude there cannot arise, then, any expectation of divine election."[46] God's giving is controlled by God's freedom to determine God's self, regardless of external factors or causation. Such giving cannot create giving in others because this gift does not have a life outside the giver. The gift need not even be received: "Grace cannot be called forth or constrained by any claim or merit, by any existing or future condition, on the part of the creature. Nor can it be held up or rendered nugatory and ineffective by any contradiction or opposition on the part of the creature. Both in its being and in its operation its necessity is within itself" (p. 19). In the end, giving is an oddly static notion when applied to Barth's God; the divine gift is not a given, in the sense of something that is there, given up to an other. Instead, the gift remains an attribute, perhaps the definition, of God's life, not something in which we can participate as partners in a perpetual process. Barth uses the language of giving, the language of being for an other, but it is a language that refers only to God. Even when giving appears in human affairs, it is really a capacity of God alone. Graced acts of giving always signify divine authorship. In fact, giving can be described solely with the proper name of Jesus Christ. Every gift is signed with that particular signature. Barth's portrait of divine giving begins and ends with the first of my three rules: God gives. Although this makes for a majestically focused, theocentric celebration of God's central and abiding excess, it cannot provide the foundation for a Christian theory of mutual generosity, a language that encompasses God's involvement in acts of giving that are also our own.

Charles Hartshorne and God's Reciprocity

In many ways, Charles Hartshorne's theology is the complete opposite of Karl Barth's. Whereas Barth focuses on the revelation of Jesus Christ, Hartshorne begins with a metaphysical understanding of all reality, including the reality of God. Hartshorne's metaphysics follows the work of Alfred North Whitehead by presupposing that reality is basically continuous, interconnected. There are no gaps in reality, no regions of essential mystery, impenetrable ambiguity, or wholly otherness. The universe is a closed totality that is in principle analyzable into a set of fundamental, descriptive statements. For Whitehead, as well as Hartshorne, these descriptive statements must try to do justice to the idea that all of actuality can be defined by internal relations to past actualities and conceptual relations to future possibilities. Each moment of experience is involved in a tug-of-war that both pushes and pulls the entity into being. The consummation of this battle for existence is a moment of aesthetic satisfaction or harmony in which each entity becomes what it is. This language is obviously metaphorical, and both Whitehead and Hartshorne sharpen it by using technical terms that both appeal to these metaphors and claim a more precise explanatory power. Indeed, Hartshorne's metaphysics encapsulates a deeply rhetorical view of the world, in which all relations are based on the gentle art of persuasion. What is important to note is the radical force of these suggestive ponderings: reality is in flux, ever changing; interrelated entities arise out of each other, attain self-satisfaction, and then perish, to leave themselves as building blocks for future creations.

Much of Whitehead's philosophy is an attempt to show that this fundamental insight—that reality consists of a flux of interrelated events and not unrelated substances—is not trivial or fleeting. He grounds his intuition and thus gives it lasting theoretical power in an elaborate model of what he calls actual entities or occasions. These entities are "the final real things of which the world is made up. There is no going behind actual entities to find anything more real."[47] From God to "the most trivial puff of existence in far-off empty space" (p. 18), all of reality can be characterized in terms that derive from an analysis of actual entities. This ambitious claim is formalized in what Whitehead calls the ontological principle: "Actual entities are the only *reasons,* so that to search for a *reason* is to search for one or more actual entities" (p. 24; italics his). All explanations and abstractions must be immanent to the given facts of reality, and this gives Whitehead's program an empirical, almost scientific feel. Yet Whitehead's ambition is also grandly theoretical. The categories of metaphysics are operative in all experience, whether we are aware of them or not. In his characteristically modest fashion, Whitehead writes that the world never takes a holiday from these universal categories (p. 4). As Hartshorne notes, the principle of continuity is the "supreme law of rationality."[48]

Hartshorne adopts this thoroughly social view of reality, which emphasizes the relatedness of all objects to each other. Relation, synthesis, dependence are not additions to any given entity but part of the entity from the very beginning. The idea of independent, concrete substances is an abstraction that does not do justice to the complexity of reality. *Novelty, relationship, and becoming* are the key terms that replace the traditionally static metaphysical vocabulary of *sameness, substance,* and *being.* These metaphysical arguments apply equally to God. Indeed, for Hartshorne, God strictly and uniquely exemplifies all metaphysical categories. In applying this scheme to God, the point at which Hartshorne breaks from Barth and traditional theology becomes clear. God and the world are correlated; their relationship is necessary. There is no first act of creation in which God initiates a relationship with something other by calling it into being out of nothingness.[49] Nevertheless, God is not merely one part of the world. God has a dipolar nature, what Whitehead calls primordial and consequent and what Hartshorne calls abstract and concrete. In God's abstract nature, God transcends the world in the sense that God is related to it in a way superior to any other relationship, but in God's concrete nature God is essentially (internally, not externally) related to others. Although God's constancy provides the abstract goals (what Whitehead calls eternal objects) for the coming-to-be of every occasion, God also changes as the world changes. The world adds to God's concrete experience. God is the self-surpassing world's partner, guiding and receiving the world's moments of experience and returning them as renewed and reinvigorated possibilities for further development.[50] God's power, then, involves both activity and receptivity. God is uniquely aware, sympathetic to, and involved in the ongoing unfolding of actual events in the world. God includes (by integrating and remembering) all experiences in God's own life, thus preserving the world in a quite literal way.

God's interaction with the world is guided by perfect knowledge and full involvement. It is a giving that is ruled as much by reciprocity as the giving of Calvin's and Barth's God is governed by excess. Indeed, it is a basic proposition in Hartshorne's theology that God's interests coincide with the interests of the world. God's persuasion of the world, therefore, can be understated, not exaggerated; God need not appeal to interests that are not God's own. In other words, God's activity in the world is not self-sacrificial. This follows logically from the description of God as essentially related. There is no gulf that God must traverse in order to be heard or understood. God and world are intimately joined, each literally feeling the other. God is not self-determined first and then secondarily related to the world, and so what takes place in the world essentially comprises who God is. God, then, needs the world. The growth of the divine life demands the harmonization and integration of ever-new experiences. Like an artist, God continually creates an aesthetic whole from the fragments of worldly becoming. This does not mean that God uses the world for God's own purposes, regardless of the best interests of the world. Instead, Hartshorne argues, "in God there is indeed perfect agreement of altruism and egoism. For whatever good God may do to any being anywhere, he himself, through his omniscient sympathy, will inevitably enjoy."[51] The interests of God coincide with the interests of the world, so there is no conflict in God between acting for God's self and acting for an other. This is one of the ways in which God is superior to us. Our limitations force us to choose between our own good and the good of others. God does not need to make this decision at all. The good toward which God tries to persuade us is God's very own good.

It is difficult not to conclude from this line of argumentation that what God gives to the world is really given to God's self. To the extent that God enables actual entities to achieve rich and harmonious syntheses in the present, these climaxes of experience, in turn, become the stuff that God receives, remembers, and cherishes in the future. Anything that God does now (investment) increases God's enjoyment later (profit). Love here does not mean the overflowing counterbalance to the inner independence of a free individual. Instead, love, or giving, is regulated according to an ever-expanding circle, or spiral, in which what is given always returns. God's giving is not gratuitous, extravagant, or excessive, but prudent, measured, balanced, and symmetrical.[52] As a result, the three moments of the gift-giving dynamic become confused and indistinguishable. Without real separation in these moments, giving is reduced to receiving. That is, the dynamic of giving, which includes risk and excess as well as release and abandonment, is reduced to reception and return. The problem here is that Hartshorne develops a dipolar, not a trinitarian portrait of God. In my terms, God's giving and receiving are not mediated by a gift that is really given and thus subjected to its own relatively independent destiny. Without this middle term—the something that is sheerly given—giving and receiving collapse into each other, and, in fact, Hartshorne emphasizes the third moment of the gift-giving dynamic at the expense of the first, an initial excess.

Hartshorne thus can make the startling claim—an exact reversal of the traditional understanding—that God is in debt to us because he is the primary receiver:

> To God each of us is dearer than wife to husband, for no human being knows the inner experiences of another human being so intimately as they are known to God. And to know experiences is to appreciate them; for the value of experience is just the experience itself. As we are indebted to a few persons for the privilege of feeling something of the quality of their experiences, so God is indebted to *all* persons for the much fuller enjoyment of the same privilege. God is not conceited or envious; therefore he has no motive for wishing to escape or deny this indebtedness.[53]

It is hard not to come to the same conclusion about Hartshorne that I reached concerning Barth. God monopolizes giving, except here God does so not by giving abundantly but by receiving abundantly. God abstractly sets the aims that God concretely and excessively receives into God's own experience. Hartshorne's God is not the giving but the receiving God, who gives in order to receive and who receives whether or not we even intend to give. This God is the Emersonian self writ large, a cunning agent who manages to turn every loss into a gain. It is difficult to understand how what we give to God can be called a gift at all. God takes everything from us, so that who we essentially are is what God receives. Moreover, if God wants our experiences, not our gifts, it is implausible to believe that God's gifts to us necessarily would be in our best interests. God's giving is directed not toward the particular goods of individual entities but toward the greater good of God's own ever enlarging self.[54] All of our giving ends in God's metaphorical harmonies. God takes it all, and such self-insured and all-encompassing receipt threatens to render incoherent the mutuality and reciprocity that Hartshorne initially set out to develop and defend.

Sallie McFague and God's Embodiment

Sallie McFague's use of metaphor to reform the traditional notion of God's transcendence is more direct than in Hartshorne's metaphysics, but the consequences of her position are very close to Hartshorne's.[55] McFague is critical of traditional notions of transcendence on both eco-logical and feminist grounds. The idea of a distant, omnipotent God not only reflects and reinforces images of patriarchy but also devalues God's relationship with the world and discourages human stewardship for it. If God is totally in control of history and capable of massive intervention at any moment, then the fate of the world is in God's hands, not human-ity's. McFague wants to shift the vocabulary of theology to mutual, shared responsibility by reconceiving the idea of God's power and in-volvement in the world. Moreover, she wants to overcome the dualisms implicit in the emphasis on God's transcendence: spirit/flesh, mind/ body, subject/object, male/female. Her methodological solution to these problems is to recover the rhetorical substructure of theological language as a way of subverting the conceptual framework of transcendence. For McFague, all language about God is metaphorical, an attempt to say what something is by drawing a rich, complex, but basically incomplete comparison. The "as if" of a good metaphor provides a kind of model from which concepts can be drawn, but the primacy of metaphor—and metaphor's very flexibility—means that concepts can be challenged by reimagining religious language at the level of rhetoric. McFague's own project of remembering the metaphorical origin of conceptuality enables her to dismember the rigid conceptual scheme of traditional theism. Her goal is to replace the literalized tropes of God as father, king, and judge with the innovative images of mother, lover, and friend.

Central to this shift in language is a key insight that serves as a ruling metaphor for McFague's new theological vision: the idea of the world as God's body. McFague does not mean the world *is* God's body; instead, she suggests, as the word *as* implies, this idea can function as a new metaphor by which God's relationship to the world can be reconceived. McFague worries that the traditional, monarchical model portrays God's power as essentially arbitrary: God can do whatever God wants, and thus God oscillates between domination and benevolence. Indeed, traditional accounts of God's benevolence often develop that trait as a counterbalance to God's freedom and God's right to judge and con-demn. If God can dominate the world, the argument goes, then how much more wonderful is God's decision to love. God can forgive because God first can demand. The problem here, according to McFague, is a model of God that makes any divine act (and by implication divine agency in general) disconnected from the world in the first instance: "The king's power extends over the entire universe, of course, but his being does not: he relates to it externally, he is not part of it but essentially different from it and apart from it" (p. 65). If God's power is defined apart from God's compassion, then God's benevolence seems strangely secondary to who God is and what the world is. The gap between God and the world can be bridged only by a decisive and difficult venture, by an act that is sacrificial and altruistic. McFague wants to begin with continuity, rather than discontinuity. If the world is like God's body, then God knows the world immediately, empathetically, and directly. Moreover, God is vulnerable to what is done to the world, which imbues our relationship to the world with added significance.

The metaphor of the world as God's body is figurative, McFague insists, not descriptive. It is meant to change the way we think about God. McFague realizes that the risk that resides at the literal level of the metaphor is pantheism, but she thinks this danger can be avoided by realizing the full range of the analogy: just as we are not our own bodies, neither is God to be reduced to the world. Furthermore, she elaborates this basic metaphor by developing three other images of God, all of which emphasize the agency and personality of the divine: mother, lover (*eros*), and friend (*philia*). All three images emphasize the physical intimacy of God with us, an intimacy that is based in God's own need for companionship and love. The mother and lover images are rooted in biological processes that tend to portray God's love as natural and intuitive. The image of friendship heightens the sense of God's free choice to enter into relationship with the world and with us. McFague knows the Aristotelian argument that friendship is possible only between equals. She quotes Aristotle's remark: "If one party stands at a vast remove, as God does, there can be no question of friendship."[56] What she finds fascinating about friendship is the way in which it forms when two or more people are working on a common project with a single goal. *Philia* is the invitation to partnership, our companionship with God rooted in our shared relationship with the world. The world, she says, is where we meet and befriend God; the dramatic rhetoric of sacrifice is replaced by the simple gesture of being (in the sense of holding, touching) with each other.

McFague's visionary theology is refreshing and moving; she does not hesitate to connect God's relationship with us to our very concrete relationships with each other and with nature. A difficulty, however, stems from her eagerness to overturn the theological tradition. She tends, I want to argue, to give an undialectical response to some of theology's excessive depictions of God's transcendence; to criticize one extreme by emphasizing its opposite only compounds the original problem. She uses the (quite appropriate) image of God as Mother, for example, to expound the idea that God gives in a familiar and instinctive way to that which is really still a part of God. McFague is imagining with this metaphor the intimacy that obtains between a mother and a young child, but parental giving is not always so reciprocal. The image of God as a parent should capture some of the pain of giving that is surely an aspect of all generosity. Giving to children means, in part, letting go of the gift of children as they grow up and leave the household. Indeed, the whole process of raising children suggests that what is given is never completely returned to its source. Children go out into the world, giving in turn to their own children and to others, but they do not give back all of what they have received. At some point, parental giving moves from an initial excess to a letting go or stepping back, in which giving enters into the life of the other only by the disappearance or withdrawal of the self, with the hope that thereby something new will be born again.

The same set of problems apply to McFague's idea of the world as God's body. McFague imagines the organic unity of the world as the precondition for God's agency; the processes unfolding in the world are the sites of divine agency. However, if the world is God's body, it is actually more difficult either to think of God as giving to the world or to think of the world as the gift that empowers human freedom and responsibility. Indeed, the world as God's body is not given by God; rather, the world is God's given in the sense that it establishes the limitations to and the means for God's agency. God may add intentionality and creativity to worldly processes, but it is confusing to think of God (or anybody, for that matter) as giving something to one's own body.[57] It is true that we are frequently told that we owe it to ourselves to give to ourselves, but such giving borders on narcissism. Does God merely give to God's self when God gives to us?

For McFague, as with Hartshorne, giving is already given; mutuality is so inclusive that the dynamic of giving is threatened. McFague tries to avoid these problems by stressing the idea that the world as a whole is God's body. Thus, God is not immediately connected to each individual in the world but to the world in its totality. This provides some distance between God and individuals, allowing God to give not what people want but what they need, since the needs of the world as a whole doubtless conflict with the wants of individuals. It is not clear, however, if this transcendence is sufficient for the conception of God as a gift giver, especially given McFague's use of the imagery of lover and friend. McFague ends her book talking about a worldly transcendence; "The transcendence of God in our picture, whatever it does mean, cannot be understood apart from the world, or to phrase it more precisely, what we can know of God's transcendence is neither above nor beneath but in and through the world."[58] She suggests that we need to learn how to think small, not big, with regard to God. God's transcendence is found in the complexity of the world, in its everyday details, its rhythmic patterns, and its internal infinity. Yet, I am left with the suspicion that this God is too close to us to be able to give to us. In fact, her theological method reverses the priority of God's giving relative to our own: God's giving seems to imitate the giving that we see all around us. Ordinarily, we give only to those we already know and from whom we have already been given. Giving is circumscribed by an intimate circle that provides a protective boundary of belonging.

True, for McFague the circularity of giving is not defined by tribal or familial loyalties; it includes the whole world. Her ample vision succeeds in articulating the ultimate horizon or telos for all giving, the absolute mutuality embodied in the gift's return. Nevertheless, this closed system of giving cannot do justice to the excessive nature of giving, the idea that giving involves an initial squandering that only subsequently results in a return. Her metaphors point to a giving that is very physical, an act that is more like touching than like gift giving. To give here is to give in, to literally encompass or enter into the other, so that giving to the other borders on giving to the self. She downplays the beginning of the gift, which is, to a significant extent, to give away. The metaphors of mother, lover, and friend do not adequately emphasize the hyperbolic dimension of generosity. Giving is a metaphorical act for McFague; it draws together, fusing and synthesizing rather than spreading and multiplying. Consequently, McFague's giving does not endow the other with the capacity to give in turn; instead, such giving extends the domain of the self by enlarging the self's sphere of affectivity, to the point where inclusivity threatens to abolish giving altogether.

Mark C. Taylor and God's Radical Immanence

Mark C. Taylor's attempt to reconstruct theology by deconstructing it stands at the crossroad of two powerful paths of thought:

deconstructionism and post-Hegelian "God is dead" theology. His influential *Erring*,[59] which eagerly abides in the ambiguity of a/theology, relies on the two most significant representatives of these postmodern projects—Jacques Derrida and Thomas J. J. Altizer. I want to show that in *Erring* Taylor resurrects the death of God theology by burying it deeply in deconstructionism. Substantiating this claim is not an easy task because Taylor's arguments lead the reader to be suspicious of any attempts to analyze something that is so allegedly radical. In fact, analysis, which takes things apart and puts the parts into a systematic order, is itself being called into question by Taylor. The extremist rhetoric of *Erring* leads the reader to question any questions that are brought to the text. Indeed, it is not clear whether Taylor is deconstructing theology from a position outside theology or following the historical breakdown of theology from within.[60] Nevertheless, I argue that Taylor's vision is guided by the idea of a purely immanent God who is mired in an absolute relationality, but this idea self-destructs in Taylor's work, leaving no possibilities for the giving and receiving that constitute the real otherness that Taylor so earnestly seeks.

Taylor's early work on Hegel is a crucial preliminary to understand his appropriation of and differences from both Altizer and Derrida. Taylor agrees with Hegel that there is no self-relation that is not mediated by opposition to otherness. Identity always turns out to be difference, and, Taylor adds, "relation to other turns out to be self-relation."[61] Contradiction is inescapable, but for Taylor it is also unmanageable. In Taylor's hands, the dialectical unfolding of thought has no telos or goal. Taylor thus embraces a Hegelian ontology of relatedness that omits progress or ultimate reconciliation: "Relations are ontologically definitive—to be is to be related" (p. 274). Here Taylor is already following Altizer's amendment of Hegel. For Hegel, God comes to full self-consciousness through a journey into God's opposite, the finitude of the world. For Altizer, by contrast, God gives God's self completely to the world in order to free the world from empty consolation and false idolatry. God actually dies on the cross, an ultimate expenditure that intends human autonomy and freedom. Consequently, the absolute interrelativity of God and world is apocalyptically present in the collapse of the divine into the human. Absolute relatedness means absolute presence; meaning is not "out there somewhere" but radically here and now. Hell and heaven, death and resurrection, sin and grace—indeed, all binary oppositions—become indistinguishable.[62]

In *Erring*, Taylor gives a deconstructive twist to Altizer's position: instead of the realization of an absolute relationality based on the total presence of meaning, the death of God read through Derrida suggests the actuality of an absolute absence, and this totally present absence is the liberating message of a/theology. For Derrida, the term *presence* is a master trope that indicates any attempt to provide an extralinguistic foundation for meaning and interpretation. Against this metaphysical and theological search for stability and certainty, Derrida argues that the living present is constituted by a pure difference that cannot be identified, that is, subsumed under a categorical structure. In fact, we only know difference as a trace that remains after the failure of our attempts to establish identities: "What the thought of the trace has already taught us is that it could not be simply submitted to the on-tophenomenological question of essence. The trace is *nothing*, it is not an entity, it exceeds the question of *What is?* and contingently makes it possible."[63] This elaboration of difference (what Derrida calls *différance*) enables Derrida to undermine other philosophical projects from within without articulating a constructive position of his own. Difference—the absolute power of temporality that makes all language impermanent and nonmeaningful—can be written about only in a provisional way. "In marking out différance," Derrida explains, "everything is a matter of strategy and risk."[64] To write about difference is to play rhetorically (not to labor philosophically), in other words, to accept the simul-taneous promise and defeat of meaning in the otherness of words.

After his encounter with Derrida, then, Taylor abandons all on-tologies, both the ontology of relatedness he took from Hegel and the ontology of absolute presence he took from Altizer. Yet, he does not simply repeat the Derridean project. Introducing the death of God into the rhetoric of deconstructionism is the strategy and risk that Taylor undertakes. God's death is an absence that reverberates throughout all aspects of philosophy and culture. A key to Taylor's position is his basic agreement with Altizer's interpretation of the incarnation as radically kenotic. For Altizer, though, God's self-emptying makes all meaning absolutely immanent in the sense of purely present. Taylor does not reverse Altizer by making God's death merely absence, or nothing; instead, the incarnation denotes the total immanence of meaning in the play of differences that nullifies the opposition of presence and ab-sence. Only in the interplay of (the difference between) presence and absence is the radicality of God's self-negation realized. Consequently, all sense of coherent meaning is gone, including the notion of history, which is governed by a faith in absolute beginnings and endings, and the idea of the book, in which knowledge can be collected and orga-nized: "The impossibility to which the death of God points can be read in and as the eternal return of writing."[65] The Word of God is not bound in a single historical narrative; instead, it is continually rewritten in a radically open text that has no beginning and no end. What is left is what Taylor calls the Divine Milieu, the dispossession of the self and the dissemination of meaning scattered through the play of differences that constitutes our postmodern epoch.

The most important consequence of the divine immanence — understood as the interminable interplay of presence and absence — concerns the notion of the self. Taylor argues that the traditional idea of the transcendence and perfection of God was correlated to the notion of the stable identity of the self. Only by having a firm point of reference in a divine center can the self be construed as solitary, independent, and consistent. The decline in the belief in God should have revealed the fictive nature of the constant and fixed identity of the theological self; instead, however, humanists promoted the idea of the infinite self to take God's place. This transference of divine predicates to human agency only prolongs the problems inherent in theology. In fact, Taylor argues that the modern self is an anxious entity propelled by insatiable need and desire; only by assimilating otherness into its own emptiness can the infinite self find identity. Taylor criticizes the inhumanity of this economy of domination: "Eventually consumption becomes all consuming."[66] The modern self, then, is a consumer who seeks meaning (propriety) through establishing what is and is not its own — that is, by turning objects in the world into instances of property.

Giving up God by accepting God's ultimate giving deprives the self of a center, either in the God above or the soul within. The self is written, but without author or plot. The resulting destruction of both the theological and the humanistic self radically transforms traditional notions of generosity and gift giving. The death of God inaugurates a reign of excess. Only by recognizing the indeterminacy of all meaning, including the identity of the self, can the postmodern "self" be freed from the obligation to consume and dominate. Subjectivity is determined by the trace of differences that constitutes all meaning, a trace that itself can never be fully identified or conceptualized (that is, owned). The term *trace* signifies the relationality of meaning: "The emptiness of the trace is the full actualization of divine relativity rather than the realization of the nihil of the void. Relative subjects, enmeshed in a network that is both creative and destructive, possess neither solidity nor substantiality" (p. 141). Relations are primary and constitutive, but they are also arbitrary and random. The reign of difference means that one can embrace only a loss of identity — what Taylor refers to as the lack of a proper name—in which giving becomes purely rhetorical, without aim or context. Just as the search for meaning is ultimately profitless, authentic generosity should entail only loss and waste. Giving becomes gambling: "No longer possessive, the communicant seeks neither to secure his properties nor to preserve his propriety" (p. 142). Passion and compassion are indistinguishable; all activity is a giving to the other because otherness is the very precondition for agency in the first place.

Taylor's achievement is remarkable: whereas God's excess is usually argued from the concept of transcendence, Taylor succeeds in combining a novel articulation of the immanence of God with a reassertion of the classical notion of the gratuity of God's generosity. Indeed, Taylor's work substantially intensifies the tradition of divine gratuity, from Calvin to Barth, but disconnects that tradition from the framework of transcendence. God promotes excess by becoming radically empty and immanent, not by giving freely and graciously. Unfortunately, though, this fascinating combination of ideas is unstable and thus self-defeating. Although Taylor can argue that it is generosity that breaks the bonds of the proper, meaning-hungry self, he more often suggests that generosity is a by-product of a new vision of what the self truly is. Taylor risks reducing giving to an intellectual event: it is a matter of recognizing who we already are (or, better, who we are not) rather than doing something for an other. The action demanded is no action at all.[67] For Taylor, in fact, giving is not an excessive act that precedes and funds all subsequent giving; giving is only excessive to the extent that it is all-pervasive, universal in scope and reference.

The result is that Taylor collapses my first rule of giving into the second: excess is given; it is an ontological aspect of all activity, and thus it is hardly excessive at all. Giving is totally incarnate, but there is nothing given, in the sense of that which our giving passes along, and there is no prior empowerment of giving, in the sense of a first giver. The whole process of giving is present (and not present) all at once, so that none of its moments can be distinguished. Giving is all, but giving is given. Giving always already takes place within the given structure of difference.[68] If McFague diminishes God into the world following the model of the self and the body, Taylor turns God into a hyperintellectual experience of deferment and difference. His norm for generosity is the prodigal who does not return home. "For the responsible person who stays near home, there is something improper and disturbing about prodigality."[69] Drawing on the work of Georges Bataille and N. O. Brown, Taylor argues that true generosity must be reckless, accidental, and carefree. The hyperbole of giving in Taylor's rhetoric is intensified to the point of meaninglessness. Giving becomes another name for an absolutely ambiguous exaggeration: Every action is a gift to the extent that it plays between the differences that can never be fully reconciled or conceptualized, passing the self along from one permutation to another, in the frivolity of what Taylor calls mazing grace, the confusing anarchy of a/theology. When everything is already in the process of being given, it must be asked if anything is given at all, or if everything remains the same.

Peter C. Hodgson and God's Persuasive Dialectics

In a famous essay on Hegel, Barth wonders why he did not become for the Protestant world what Aquinas was for Roman Catholicism. Barth pays this compliment not only from due respect for the impressive completeness of Hegel's achievement but also from a recognition of Hegel as a worthy opponent. Both thinkers emphasize the activity of God, the becoming rather than being of God, and both were driven by an ambition to let that activity pervade and shape a comprehensive and total intellectual vision. Both think of God's self-differentiation as the basis for God's relationship to the world. Nevertheless, Barth was also compelled to admire Hegel because Hegel's characterization of God's action was also so opposed to his own. For Barth, the basis of God's activity is the election of the Son in the person of Jesus Christ, a free giving and restoring of all things unto God's self. For Hegel, God is active in a dialectical interaction with the world, developing in and through history, so that history as a whole, not the particular event of Christ, becomes the story of God's very own unfolding. For Barth, subjecting God to the dialectical logic of history takes away from the objective reality of revelation and turns God into an idol of humanity's own making. "Hegel, in making the dialectical method of logic the essential nature of God," Barth argues, "made impossible the knowledge of the actual dialectic of grace, which has its foundation in the freedom of God."[70] Barth's emphasis on the gratuity of God's generosity, then, serves as the pivotal principle by which he rejects all theologies that begin from a position other than the revelation of God in Jesus Christ.

Barth also thought that Hegel's time might still be yet to come. If many critiques of the traditional account of God's transcendence err in the opposite direction of God's immanence, then a more dialectical approach to these two modes of relationship might, in fact, be needed. Indeed, my own description of God's threefold giving might appear to be structurally very similar to Hegel's portrait of the self-evolution of God, and thus it is important to draw the differences. Peter Hodgson has served the theological community well by developing a contemporary appropriation of Hegel in his *God in History.*[71] Hodgson wants to salvage Hegel's central insight into the correlative interdependence of God and history, which are connected at the point of human praxis, without falling into the trap of Hegel's claim to absolute knowledge. Against Barth's warning not to transfer the actual relationship between God and the world into the being of God, Hodgson agrees with Hegel that without the world God would not be God. God is in history, and history is in God.

Traditionally, theologians have argued that God is simple in the sense that God has no parts, no aspects that might be in tension or contradiction with each other: God is an undifferentiated whole. Hodgson follows Hegel in arguing instead that God's existence is not completely self-sufficient or self-enclosed. Indeed, God's life is complex and evolving. God becomes God through the world: "The true infinite, the divine God, 'overreaches' and encompasses the finite, includes finitude, difference, otherness within Godself" (p. 62). God becomes God by passing over into another and returning to God's self in a process that closely resembles the dynamic of the gift. In fact, there must be all three elements of gift giving—a desire or need to give, a recipient to receive, and the eventual return of the gift—in order for God to be construed primarily as a free agent who nonetheless depends on the freedom of the other for self-understanding and self-development.

The world, then, is the difference, the given, that provides the possibility for God's development as a giver. Although Hodgson sometimes writes as if he wants to maintain the traditional idea that God is self-constituting, independent of the need for an other, he modifies that notion by arguing that part of that constituting process is God's constitution of the world as other than God, an otherness that God transforms through a supreme relationship. God gives the other in order to become a giver. This dialectical formulation allows Hodgson to avoid the extremes of current theories of God's immanence, and, in fact, he explicitly criticizes both Taylor and McFague.[72] Although God is embodied in the world, the world is best understood as the shape of what God is not, albeit in a moment within the divine economy. The given is born from the giver's self-negation. This is the basic outline of Hegel's dialectical logic: the universal becomes individual only by a sojourn through the particular, which is comprised of contradiction and negation.

The return of the gift raises the crucial and connected questions of God's purpose and our participation in the gifting process. The world is the necessary condition for God's self-differentiation, an aboriginal given that makes more giving possible, but the world, in turn, demands further mediation for divine development. The given must be returned to complete the initial giving. Otherwise, the gift remains a static aspect of nature and not the dynamic thrust of God's historical unfolding. Our giving enables God to be reconciled with the world, just as God's giving provides history with purpose and orientation, so that temporality is not arbitrarily open-ended. As it unfolds in history, the gift must have a direction or goal, a point at which God's giving and our return coincide. For Christians, Hodgson argues, Christology constitutes the horizon toward which the gift moves. The specific shape of God's giving, the particularity of divine universality, is the suffering, alienation, and death of Jesus Christ, and this provides the ultimate goal of historical development; God's concrete embodiment in Jesus Christ outlines the form through which God seeks to love the world toward freedom by reconciling the world with God's self. Only at that final extreme does God become the God who synthesizes freedom and love and thus shows us the way to our own paths of liberation. In that event, God is both loving (involved, related) and free (transcendent, gratuitous). In other words, Jesus Christ is neither pure grace, given whether we like it or not, nor an exchange or negotiation between the divine and the human; instead, Jesus Christ holds together excess and exchange in an event equally free and necessary. To encapsulate God's ability to bring together the two sides of the gift, Hodgson ironically borrows a phrase from Barth: God is the one who loves in freedom. For Hodgson, however, freedom is not identified with gratuity; instead, it is historically and socially construed: "Freedom is precisely presence-to-self in, through, and with otherness; it is intrinsically communal, social, synthetic" (p. 46). By giving God's self to the world and yet preserving God's freedom, God is, or furnishes, the shape of love-in-freedom, which is the final aim or return of history.

Hodgson is post-Hegelian in the sense that he no longer thinks that the comprehension of God coincides with the singular, progressive, and inevitable history of rationality that climaxes with Hegel's very own thought. He realizes that we live in a plurality of histories, in which progress is fragmentary and incomplete at best, and the struggle for freedom never fully prevails against the forces of domination and oppression. History is "a crazy patchwork, with holes and loose threads that threaten to unravel" (p. 161). Naming God does not procure a decisive and comprehensive interpretation of history. The telos provided by God is not totally unitary, because the shape of the freedom toward which we strive is plural and ambiguous. Providence is polymorphous. Hodgson wants a noninterventionist, nonmiraculous, and noncausal account of providence, "nonlinear in its teleology, and nonsuprahistorical in its eschatology" (pp. 42–43). God works toward an integration of freedom and love in history that is always undermined by the unexpected, the disorienting reversals of history that obliterate any easy notion of progress. God's power is limited, and the future is radically open. The plot of God's story and our history is neither comedy (in which everything works out in the end) nor tragedy (which gives irony the last word) but tragicomedy, the combination of historical contingency with preliminary achievements of Christlike love. Nevertheless, history does have a direction, to the extent that it conforms to the configuration of God's freedom in love. God shapes history in ways that we can acknowledge as responsible participants. God calls forth partnership, then, rather than obedience. By practicing the freedom to love in the midst of historical limitations, we take God's shape and make it our own.

Hodgson's retrieval of Hegel's dynamic conception of God without Hegel's pretensions to absolute knowledge (the equivalence of God's involvement in history with the philosopher's understanding of the structure and end point of that history) is a valuable framework for correcting traditional emphases on the transcendence of God. Nevertheless, from my perspective, several problems remain. Most important, it is not clear what God gives to the world. God provides shapes, "a shape rendered concrete by certain images associated with the ministry and death of Jesus" (p. 194), but shapes do not act in history. How, precisely, does God empower our struggle for freedom? True, Hodgson does insist on the efficacy of God's presence in history. God is actually present in the shapes of freedom that history partially realizes because God *is* that freedom. Hodgson's emphasis on the shape or gestalt of God is, however, curiously static.

The problem here is rhetorical. Indeed, one of Hodgson's most creative moves is to talk about God's influence on history in rhetorical terms. Borrowing from Whitehead, Hartshorne, and other process theologians, Hodgson argues that God is figuratively related to historical change: God refigures history by offering configurations of freedom in spite of history's various defigurations. Hodgson thus emphasizes

God's persuasive or rhetorical role in history: God "lures, empowers, and shapes human activity in the direction of transfigurative praxis" (p. 40). It is in liberating activity that we know God is at work with and for us. God is the shape of that liberation, which we embody by shaping history in ways that imitate God's configurative power. The specific rhetorical form of God's persuasive powers is, however, not the hyperbole of generosity but the metaphor of God's combination of freedom and love in Christ. Although he does at one point mention the need for "extravagance, paradox, hyperbole" (p. 210), more consistently Hodgson's God provides us with metaphorical images for imitation and actualization rather than empowers us with excessive giving, which we must receive and return. By drawing together freedom and finitude, hope and suffering, Jesus Christ is the metaphorical convergence toward which we should aim, not the hyperbolic splurge from which we are thrown and toward which we recoil.

God is a shaper, not a giver. Indeed, the shape that God gives is anticipated in the life and influence of Jesus Christ but finally discernible only in the whole of reality, the way in which all things hang together. God is driven by the difficult development of the structure of freedom and love, which has its own necessity and logic.[73] "This complex divine shape is not empirically observable or directly identifiable with any particular worldly structure since it is fully embodied only in the totality of the world."[74] This structure encompasses even God, so God alone cannot build it. The effect is that God's activity in the world is minimized. As with Hartshorne, Hodgson's God provides aesthetic, metaphorical standards toward which we can aim, but God does not actually give us the means for achieving those goals. The shape of God is hidden, and we find it only by creating it. Only through strenuous work, the hard labor (Hegel's *harte Arbeit*[75]) of rational effort, is freedom possible. The root problem is that there is no sufficient notion of grace here, in either God's agency or our own. The figure for human freedom is the act of figuration itself, the metaphorical (strategic, careful, deliberate) shaping of what is given in history and what is provided by God's own gestalt of freedom. The basic idea of God's gratuitous acts on our behalf—the traditional rhetoric of divine excess—is undermined by Hodgson's interpretation of the Hegelian dialectic, not because he prematurely synthesizes contradiction and negation with unity and affirmation but because he replaces the compelling momentum of hyperbole with the labored productivity of metaphor.

In a discussion of the doctrine of providence, early in his book, Hodgson focuses on a treatise by Thomas Aquinas, *De veritate*. For

Aquinas, the world is the product of a process of emanation from and return to God, *exitus et reditus.* God's relationship to the world as a whole contextualizes the more narrow economy of salvation. Hodgson argues that Aquinas sees providence as a kind of prudence, "which disposes in an orderly way means to an end by a kind of reasoning process, a practical reason."[76] God actively guides history by being the final cause toward which history moves. Humans can cooperate with this process by aiming at the common good in this life and the divine good in the next. All of these actions, God's and our own, must be measured by their given end, and thus prudence, the careful calculation about the relationship of means to ends, is the guiding virtue of both providence and salvation.

I cannot but suspect that Hodgson's doctrine of providence is, in a significant way, not too distant from Aquinas's doctrine. For Hodgson, God provides the metaphorical images that serve as the concrete goals that we can realize if we act in an appropriately mimetic fashion. Since we know that these shapes or forms are never completely present to us, we must act prudently, in full awareness of irony, without excessive hopes or ambitions. That prudence matches God's own cautious involvement in our existence, an involvement that offers us forms but does not give us too much for fear of displacing our own cooperation. God invests in our efforts, carefully measuring what is given by what is returned. Hodgson, in the end, situates the divine-human relationship in the sphere of labor, the logic of an economy of productivity and organization, not the excessive antieconomy of gratuity and grace. Although Hodgson, following Hegel, does the most of the theologians analyzed here to bring together God's excess (transcendence) and reciprocity (immanence), we still need a more systematic outline of how God is characterized by both of these features without reducing one to the other.

4

How Giving Works

The gift not only moves, it moves in a circle.

Lewis Hyde, The Gift

This Godhead is granted as a gift to all things. It flows over in shares of goodness to all. And it becomes differentiated in a unified way. It is multiplied and yet remains singular. It is dispensed to all without ceasing to be a unity.

Pseudo-Dionysius, The Divine Names

All of the theologians discussed in chapter 3 have wrestled with the problem of relating God's overwhelming generosity to human affairs and concerns. I have argued that a correlation needs to be drawn between God's practice of generosity and our own. The most difficult aspect of making this correlation is to relate the divine excess to human preoccupations with reciprocity. The goal is to portray the power of God's giving as sovereign but not dominating, free but involved. Pushing divine excess too far leaves little or no room for a human countergift, yet subjecting God to the logic of reciprocity diminishes the gratuity of God's grace. God either monopolizes giving or gives only in the form of exchange. None of these theologians satisfactorily accounts for a divine giving that both exceeds and maintains our own, initiating but also entering into acts that involve an extravagant outpouring and a cooperative return.

My criticisms of other theologians might inadvertently obscure the way my own methodology draws from several major theological options. First and foremost, I agree with Karl Barth that theology is a responsive discipline, that the abundance of God's grace is the given reality that theology must acknowledge as its very basis. Nevertheless, I insist that, no matter how mysterious, God's grace is not unrelated to the interconnected features of human existence. Because the world is full of grace, reflection on basic human practices, in the context of theological insight, can help illuminate spiritual truths. Indeed, an investigation of the very common and universal custom of gift giving can situate the otherwise ethereal topic of the mystery of God's love. Moreover, I find analogies between problems in the philosophy of generosity and the theology of grace, so that a dialogue between the two is fruitful and even necessary.

One of my main points is that giving involves unpredictable movement and change, while at the same time it creates a reliable architecture of belonging and community. God provides the structure of giving by participating in the activity of the gift; indeed, grace is that action. Against Barth, I draw from process philosophy the idea that God and the world are related in complementary ways, that God, in fact, changes along with the world. From process thought, I am especially in debt to the notion of mutuality, that God receives as well as gives. I cannot accept, however, the way process metaphysics tries to display God as an instance or example of rational rules that have no limit in their applicability. Process thought treats giving as an example of the necessity of internal relations, rather than as a historical and social process initiated by God and sustained through individual acts of grace. Metaphysics inevitably reduces the irregularity of excess to the measurement of exchange. Giving becomes a description (of the way things are) rather than an event (that could be otherwise).

Instead of relying on the abstract and universal schemes of metaphysics, I tend to see gift giving as a social structure that can be illuminated by what George Lindbeck has called "theological grammar" or linguistic rules. Gift giving is a social practice, so that it demands anthropological and sociological—more than metaphysical—description. Yet, Lindbeck's position tends to give religion over to social construction, so that human behavior is governed by reciprocal agreements and spiritual practice is bounded by communal norms, leaving little room for the surprise of grace. Lindbeck assumes that social systems are stable, so that their governing rules can be described with little ambiguity; under the influence of deconstructive thought, I see gift giving as both ordering and disordering reality in unexpected and unsettling ways. Moreover, the gift event never occurs in a pure form, so that its description is necessarily theological, constructive, and even speculative; to see the gift is to see something that in a way is not there, a dimension that resides uneasily but intimately with exchange. Returning to Barth's sense of the intrusive and determinative reality of God's excess, the idea that theology is not about social reality but divine, the rules that I am trying to articulate are not primarily descriptive of human enterprises. Instead, they are an attempt to describe a dimension that is at once human and divine, the ever present possibility of a giving that is supported and guided by an excess that supersedes all human generosity.

To clarify my response to these theological options, I want to examine more carefully what I have called the three rules of the Christian language game on gift giving. These are secondary rules, the formalization of the grammar and rhetoric of Christian generosity. The primary language of theology is given first in Scripture and subsequently in church history, and the primary response is doxological, both in the sense of the liturgy and in what broadly can be called Christian ethics or the Christian way of life. As I have already noted, the language of worship, which pervades every aspect of Christian living, is the language of thanks. By explicating gratitude in terms of the model of gift giving, I do not intend to make that language deeper but to safeguard it from various errors and confusions. Nonetheless, the rules I am defending have more than formal significance; they are more than a mere protocol marking pleasant speech and agreeable behavior. They entail substantive beliefs and promote certain kinds of action. These rules shape not only a language but also a community, the community that embodies God's gifting. These rules sketch a picture not of reality, of how Christians do, in fact, give, but of the permanent possibility of an ever-emerging while ever-receding counterreality, of how Christians can and should give, to others as well as to God. These rules, then, are presupposed by Christian giving, but they are also the object of theological reflection and liturgical response because they are the substance of the grace that faith receives and returns.

Tracing the outline of this framework is helpful because I suspect that theologians are too frequently tempted to idealize God's love. The result is that God's gratuity is removed from considerations of mutuality; excess is connected to ethics only in a belabored and haphazard manner. Reinhold Niebuhr's work epitomizes this interpretation of the covenant created by grace.[1] Throughout his career, he emphasized the absolute purity of God's love (agape) as opposed to the self-centered nature of human loving (eros). His portrait of agape gives it a vertical dimension that is frustratingly disproportionate to the horizontal range of human problems and concerns. God's love constitutes perfection, but human agency, as that is embedded in finitude and historicity, can experience and act on that love only in fragmentary and provisional ways. God enters vertically into human affairs while humans always divert God's love into the horizontal channels of give and take. God's excess is thus tangential to human exchange. The vertical is described without reference to the horizontal, and when the divine is translated into the human realm, the resulting tension forces it to undergo conversion, correction, and modification. The horizontal inevitably and tragically diminishes the vertical, and so to conceptualize agape as a force active in the realm of eros necessitates the handing of hyperbole over to litotes (understatement). Agape must be blunted to be present in human affairs. God's love is too much to sustain everyday practices.

Niebuhr is unable to articulate a way of understanding God's excessive generosity that preserves that excess and yet still does justice to the presence of grace within the bonds of reciprocity—the compromises and accommodations that comprise human sociability. By contrast, the language of gift giving can emphasize both excess and mutuality, but it must be carefully appropriated so that the dimension of verticality does not disappear altogether. Indeed, the emphasis on transcendence is a necessary way of formulating both the priority and the extravagance of God's benevolence, thus highlighting an essential feature of gift giving. It is even possible to connect an exclusive focus on God's transcendence with different understandings of human exchange and mutuality. Kathryn Tanner has argued, for example, that God's transcendence can be reconciled with a variety of political positions, so that one need not reject a strong version of transcendence in order to affirm both human freedom and community.[2] It is the very transcendence of God that gives space for human freedom and thus requires independent human action if solidarity and reform are to be achieved. Yet Tanner's own work, by showing the diversity of political and ethical positions that can be correlated to the notion of transcendence, demonstrates the need to think through more consistently the complementary notion of immanence. God's transcendence promotes human responsibility in giving, but God's immanence raises the more vexing issue of what God expects from our giving and, thus, what specific shape that responsibility should take.

God gives us room to give in a variety of ways, but how does God respond to and receive our giving? What kind of giving does God want? True, the majesty of God's transcendence protects theology from the encroachment of an exchangist mentality: What can I get out of God; what does God do for me? God is often sold as a commodity in the marketplace, and televangelists promise that God will literally reward their listener's donations, thus (falsely) advertising the church as a form of risk-free investment banking.[3] In an era of limits to economic growth and complexity in career advancement, the church is tempted to define

God as a magical giver, the one who guarantees outward prosperity on the basis of inward sincerity, trading material goods for spiritual obedience and regular tithes. God becomes a way of purchasing at a bargain what otherwise cannot be bought at any price—the American way of life. Nevertheless, emphasizing God's impervious otherness as a solution to such crass ideologies and idolatries runs the danger of compartmentalizing and thus minimizing the efficacy of God's grace. Moreover, against the idealism of the theologians, most Christians do tend to think of God's love as involved in a process that entails some form of reciprocity. Being a Christian means being implicated in a kind of economy, a structure of demands and benefits—a covenant. God asks us to give, and how giving is returned or rewarded must be articulated, however cautiously and carefully. In addition to transcendence, then, we need an equal emphasis on God's immanence to clarify God's receptivity to our own giving. Talking about gift giving is a way of crediting the practicality of God's love by examining it in a dialogue with the way many Christians really think it works anyway.

To talk about the architecture of Christian generosity should inevitably lead to that ultimate Christian edifice, the Trinity. The building metaphors, however, can be misleading. The Trinity is not so much the foundation as the propulsion of the gift process. If giving is an energetic venture, then it must be correlated to a dynamic design that gives it coherence, direction, and substance. Discussions of the Trinity traditionally have been more speculative than practical, but the recent revival of interest in this doctrine has developed it in more ethical than metaphysical ways. Catherine Mowry LaCugna tells the story of how the subordinationism of Arius, who portrayed Jesus Christ as a lesser God, moved theologians in both the Latin West and the Greek East to defend Christ as *homoousios* (of the same substance) with God.[4] The focus of theology shifted from God's involvement in the world to the equality of the three divine persons on an intratrinitarian level, concerned with sorting out the internal relations within the Godhead. Theology increasingly began from above, in a deductive manner; consequently, it was separated from the pressing matter of soteriology. In response to these trends, LaCugna wants to return theology to its practical roots in the economy of salvation. To do this, she announces her agreement with Karl Rahner's axiom that the economic Trinity (the action of God in the world) is identical to the immanent Trinity (as it is eternally in itself).[5] To know God is to know how God acts in history, because, as Barth insists, what God does is who God is. God's giving is who God is, and to know that giving is also to know ourselves. Thus, it is crucial to ask what kind of economy God both embodies and encourages. How does God's giving also organize our own?

LaCugna notes that *oikonomia* comes from *oikos* and *nomos*, the management or law of the household. The economy of God's activity is the way in which God organizes the household of God's creation. LaCugna argues that we can know the threeness of God's being because this is how God acts in history for our salvation. God is essentially other-related, ecstatic, and passionate. Such fecundity makes God's life our own; God *in se* is God *pro nobis*: "The incomprehensible God *is* God by sharing, bestowing, diffusing, expressing Godself. The gift of existence and grace that God imparts to the world is not produced by efficient causality, largely extrinsic to God; the gift is nothing other than God's own self."[6] The Trinity is the structure of an extravagant overflowing that breaks through the boundaries of self-interest and concern. Drawing on Pseudo-Dionysius and Bonaventure, LaCugna argues that "goodness is self-diffusive, not self-contained" (p. 353). Love naturally seeks affiliation. Selfhood is found in community; only the dispersion of love establishes identity. To explain how this excess is both expansive and inclusive, LaCugna adopts the classical theological term *perichoresis*, the notion that each divine person coinheres in the other in a vital and compelling fashion. This dynamic and reciprocal interpenetration allows God's involvement in the world to be both unified and plural. The Trinity, then, represents the possibility of a society of individuals who are both free and connected through acts of excessive and mutual giving.

LaCugna further pursues this idea of relationality by developing an ontology of personhood that synthesizes freedom and obligation. "Personhood requires the balance of self-love and self-gift" (p. 290). The essence of personhood is the capacity for freely chosen self-transcendence toward the other. Unfortunately, at this point in her work, LaCugna comes close to subjecting the dynamic of the Trinity to a metaphysics of personhood rather than the process of giving itself. I want to argue that authentic gifts are not an expression of personality or a capacity of personhood because they precede the individual and their momentum connects the individual to a larger whole. The gift is not controlled by the intention of the individual; the gift has its own amorphous and fluid energy, which moves it along in unpredictable and even faceless directions. What I have learned most from LaCugna is the emphasis on the idea that God's being is in giving; giving is who God is. From this starting point, it is important to think through God according to the hyperbolic logic of giving, not the metaphysical anthropology of subjectivity. Giving is a process that occurs along the boundaries between persons, calling into question the duality of internal and external, self and other; personhood is as much an effect of giving as giving is a product of personhood. Indeed, the gift problematizes the notion that I belong to myself, and thus giving raises the most basic question of what is really real; its structure is more suitable to an ontological rather than anthropological analysis. Nobody has done this in a more original way than Jean-Luc Marion, who does not subordinate the gift to the question of reality but rather interrogates the idea of "what is" from the perspective of the gift.

Giving and Being

Jean-Luc Marion has most consistently pursued the possibility of defining God in terms of giving (the Christian notion of charity or agape) rather than Being (the most general metaphysical idea and thus the foundation of philosophy).[7] For theology, Marion seems to be insisting, the foundational question is, What does it mean to give? not, What does it mean to be? With God, giving precedes Being: "If, to begin with, 'God is love,' then God loves before being, He only is as He embodies himself—in order to love more closely that which and those who, themselves, have first to be" (p. xx). Marion argues that philosophy has imposed on God metaphysical names, like the first cause and the ground of all beings, that distract from the revelation that God is as God gives. Marion accepts Nietzsche's critique of the moral God who orders the universe; this God can be nothing more than a projection of our own desires and wishes. A God who is something can always be thought otherwise; to think the true God is to risk thinking nothing, a God who gives rather than is.

The death of the idol of God, however, should not give way to a thinking about God, perhaps influenced by Heidegger's late meditations, that equates God with the foundational notion of Being rather than a being. Although Heidegger marvels at why there is something rather than nothing, the wonder that begets metaphysics, his agnosticism forces him to seek the ground of Being from within Being, thus shifting from the question of why Being is to what and how it is. The philosopher's Being is that which manifests itself whenever something is, but for the Christian, Being does not have to be; the Christian answer to what Being is thus depends on the intensification of the mystery of why. The Christian senses in the gratuity of all that is the mystery of a thrower as well as a thrown. Indeed, God precedes Being by an original and extravagant giving. God gives existence by being other than a mere existent, that is, by being love. Being is gift, and the real name of God is charity. God's giving does not explain or minimize the mystery of Being; on the contrary, the gratuity of God's giving is that mystery.

What disconnects giving from philosophical accounts of Being is the simple fact that the gift does not have to be: "For the gift does not have first to be, but to pour out in an abandon that, alone, causes it to be; God saves the gift in giving it before being."[8] The gift has no preconditions, and so it is an ideal analogy for the attempt to think God without reference to the conditions of possibility that philosophy expounds. Like LaCugna, Marion draws much inspiration from Bonaventure and Pseudo-Dionysius.[9] Whereas Aquinas follows the classical tradition of using *esse*, or existence, rather than *bonum*, or the good, as the first divine name, Marion agrees with Pseudo-Dionysius that God creates out of the diffusion of goodness, not a free act of the will. This means that God's nature cannot be understood according to the categories of Being; instead, God as *hyperousia* (beyond being)[10] is disclosed in "the gesture of a giving as much imprescriptible as indescribable, which receives the name, in praise, of goodness."[11] Love is that which is self-given, and God can be known because God gives God's self. Giving is the way in which God must be received as well as named. Marion agrees with Barth that theology has a *positum*, something external that begins and shapes theological discourse. Giving is the being of God, which is more than the Being that philosophy seeks to know and understand. God is not the essence of Being but the beginning of giving.

A crucial implication of this move is that our relationship with God is ethical before it is cognitive.[12] The ethics of reception is marked by humility. The very act of praise denotes a distance that is appropriate to the gift: the length the gift traverses cannot be simply reversed or annulled. We recognize the good as the self-propelled gift of love that knows no restrictions: "Thus love gives itself only in abandoning itself, ceaselessly transgressing the limits of its own gift, so as to be transplanted outside of itself."[13] Such giving cannot be subsumed under the categories of existence because it is pure excess: "Agape passes all knowledge, with a hyperbole that defines it and, indissolubly, prohibits access to it" (108). Marion emphasizes this point by writing the word *God* with a cross through it to signify the impossibility of thinking this event as an aspect of Being: "The cross does not indicate that G⊗d would have to disappear as a concept, or intervene only in the capacity of a hypothesis in the process of validation, but that the unthinkable enters into the field of our thought only by rendering itself unthinkable there by excess, that is, by criticizing our thought" (p. 46). The gift crosses Being with an excess that opens existence onto another dimension. The gift does not presuppose some mode of existence or *dasein*; instead, the gift gives what is and thus precedes and surpasses the understanding of Being. Even the ability to question Being is already given, so that "what is" is already preempted, pressured, and challenged by what seems to be not.

Marion presses his argument by distinguishing between two modes of reception, what he calls the idol and the icon. Only by recognizing God in the transgressive and intrusive movement of the gift can we turn away from the facile idol and to an authentic icon. The idol fascinates and captivates us because it is essentially of our own making; it seizes hold of our gaze in an invisible mirror that gives us only ourselves. It is fabricated by—while at the same time concealing—our own investments, but it cannot ultimately hold us because it gives only what we already are, so we desert our idols easily. For Marion, the categories of philosophy, when applied to God, are conceptual idols that try to fix God as a form of Being, subjected to our gaze. The icon, by contrast, envisages us, correcting the gaze by calling on it to surpass itself.[14] The icon is an excessive event, and Marion draws on the logic of hyperbole for explanation: "The icon recognizes no other measure than its own infinite excessiveness [*démesure*]" (p. 21). The idol, which gives to the gaze only that which the gaze brings to it, represents an economy of self-enclosed return; this economy must continually produce new idols for consumption in order to entertain and distract the gaze from seeing itself clearly (that is, from seeing that it sees only itself). The icon, by contrast, need not be subjected to the forces of novelty—what Kierkegaard called the aesthetic and spoke of in terms of the rotation method—because it follows the pattern of the excessive gift. Only as a gift can we release God from the quotation marks that should ordinarily surround that name: "By definition and decision, God, if he must be thought, can meet no theoretical space to his measure [*mesure*], because his measure exerts itself in our eyes as an excessiveness [*démesure*]" (p. 45). To think God outside of Being—to receive in thanks that which is more than what is—is to risk thinking the nothing that is the event of the gift.[15]

Although Marion boldly thinks through the naming of God according to the dynamic of giving, his main concerns remain ontological. He is intent to demonstrate the ways in which giving subverts and frustrates the mechanics of metaphysics. Metaphysics is the absolute idolatry because it places the truth of Being anterior to the question of God and thus reduces the status of God to the merely ontic, making God a being among beings, something to be manipulated or denied. Theology becomes a regional science, subordinated to philosophy's attempt to understand the Being of all beings, including the Being of God. Marion's nonontotheological theology—"a theology that dispenses, as the ultimate in idolatry, with the notion that God has being"[16]—is indifferent to the difference between Being and beings because it attends to a more original difference, that between God and Being, within which the question of the being of God disappears. God, like the gift, is not, yet God's giving creates what is.

In his rush to contrast giving and being, however, Marion is also indifferent to the differences in giving itself. He pushes God's excess so far that the gift analogy is stretched out of recognizable shape: "Love does not suffer from the unthinkable or from the absence of conditions, but is reinforced by them. For what is peculiar to love consists in the fact that it gives itself. Now, to give itself, the gift does not require that an interlocutor receive it, or that an abode accommodate it, or that a condition assure or confirm it."[17] Instead of saturating phenomena with a graced giving, God's giving obliterates any sign of either a given or a receipt. God's giving is not a process but a singular act that defies our understanding and resists our participation. At best, through gratitude we can glimpse the infinite distance breached by this abundant giving, but we cannot know God's giving through our own giving, which is totally different from and thus unrelated to the divine excess.[18]

Just as giving opposes being, for Marion, excess is unrelated to reciprocity. What cannot be understood can be received but not returned. The emphasis on gratitude, I have argued, reduces the dynamism of the gift to a static relationship, and this is evident in Marion's conservative ecclesiastical agenda. The gift of God, he avers, should be received, not explained. The primary theological virtue, as with Barth, is obedience: "We are infinitely free in theology: we find all already given, available. It only remains to understand, to say, and to celebrate. So much freedom frightens us, deservedly" (p. 158). In fact, the gift without being does not in the end give freedom. The free gift of God becomes highly regimented once it is incorporated into the church, and thus differences in giving return with a vengeance. The eucharist as the given of God is the site of theology, and only the celebrant is fully invested with the person of Christ; thus, "only the bishop merits, in the full sense, the title of theologian" (p. 153). Marion purportedly speaks of a giving without mediation or condition, but we are left with the most massive mediation possible. The gift must be passed down (not along) a hierarchical chain of receivers, and reception is tantamount to submission. Excess quickly gives way to organization and order. Any questioning or protestation risks the disgrace of ingratitude. By strenuously displacing the gift from the reach of metaphysics, Marion ends by giving the gift over to an absolute authority that correlates giving with a docile and humble beholding, not an active return.

Marion helps us understand how the gifting God differs from the God of the philosophers—how, that is, the question of the gift needs to be disentangled from the question of what is—but we need to look further for both the full range of the practical application of God's giving and an account of divine giving that proliferates further giving, along lines that are unpredictable and multiple, not static and hierarchical. We need to know how giving—properly understood and practiced as that which precedes that which is and thus who we are—can free us from the obsessive desire to secure and save our existence at the cost of others, to own ourselves before we give, to place our own being before God's giving. In other words, we still need to know what giving does, or how giving works.

Giving and Saving

M. Douglas Meeks, in *God the Economist,* offers the most systematic attempt to show how God's giving has progressive political consequences.[19] Meeks does not want to argue that there is something called Christian economics or that the Bible can solve technical economic problems. Nevertheless, the Bible does use the idea of the economy of God (*oikonomia tou theou*) in reference to both the Christian community (Col. 1:25; 1 Cor. 9:17; Eph. 3:2, 1 Tim. 1:4) and the whole of creation (Eph. 1:9-10; 3:9-10). For Meeks, God is an economist in the broadest sense of that term; the way in which God organizes the household of creation is relevant for our own acts of appropriation, production, distribution, and consumption. He rejects the traditional division of labor (and mutual disregard) between economics and theology that assigns the former to public, practical matters and relegates the latter to the internal affairs of the heart. The language of the Bible is, after all, thoroughly economic: "In both fields one regularly hears such words as trust, fidelity, fiduciary, promissory, confidence, debt, redemption, saving, security, futures, bond, and so on" (p. 29). Meeks wants us to worry more about church-market relations than about church-state relations.

Economics, too, uses theology, but it is an unacknowledged debt. Economists have truncated and protected their discipline by effectively transferring the immutability of God to human nature in an attempt to portray economics as an ahistorical science based on the calculations of aggregate human needs and desires. Since goods are scarce and desires are infinite, every choice has a cost, and human agency is equated with the economizing of costs and benefits, which, in turn, can be automatically and mechanistically harnessed by the market and measured and manipulated by the economist. Consequently, human behavior is reduced to the model of exchange. Exchange is justified as the only way of taking seriously the sin of greed. As a result, greed itself is legitimated as natural, inevitable, and incorrigible.

Such a portrait of human nature seems to leave no room for God, but God does not disappear. Somehow, the forces of the market are orchestrated by a providential plan, which leads short-term sin to long-term success, sacrificing the inefficient for the prosperity (or salvation) of the whole.[20] The market thus performs the function of theodicy, "justifying the ways of God to men" by saving humans through and not in spite of their sin. Meeks admits that at one time removing God from the economic sphere could have had the advantage of eliminating this powerful term frequently used to support coercive and oppressive social arrangements.[21] Domination, though, persists in all modern, godless economies. The concentration of capital limits access to the means of livelihood. In fact, economics is insistently faced with the dilemma of defending liberty or maximizing justice. The market creates winners and losers, but to distribute goods in any other way substitutes coercion for freedom. The trade-off between these two agendas means that one usually impinges on the other.

By denying the historical and social construction of economics, economists disconnect material pursuits from the power of external forces to reshape human motivation and alter social systems. Generosity becomes a way of supplementing an economic system, not transforming it.[22] Stewardship is "the voluntary giving of left-over money and time."[23] Surplus is generated in order to increase wealth for those who already control access to the market. Political economy thus eliminates any operation of influence for Christian charity. Giving personalizes exchange, permitting individual freedom, but the laws of the market cannot be violated in the public sphere. On a public, institutional level, reinvestment is the responsibility of surplus. "What characterizes surplus in a market society is that wealth is used not as an end in itself but as a means for gaining more wealth" (p. 59). Goods are given up or sacrificed in order to increase one's savings. Indeed, money is to be saved from expenditures that do not serve to satisfy present desires or increase the ability to satisfy those desires in the future. Generosity, characterized by compassion and unpredictability, cannot be reconciled with the rigorous and agonistic rules of exchange.

Meeks wants a conception of God that would make the goal of justice internal to the pursuit of liberty. To achieve this, he must turn to the Trinity to show how God's own economy is both social and individual. The God reflected by the traditional market is a God who is free to choose; he is also self-sufficient and all-powerful, able to dispose of his property however he wishes. His freedom is a form of owning. The God of the Trinity, Meeks argues, is a God who shares abundantly who God is: "God owns by giving" (p. 115). More specifically, "God is not a self-possessor. God is rather a community, a community of persons united in giving themselves to each other and to the world" (p. 111). God saves us not through prudence but generosity. If we practice God's righteousness, Meeks suggests, we will be satisfied both spiritually and materially. Our freedom will be found in justice.

An ambiguity arises because it is not clear if Meeks is juxtaposing God and economics or fusing the two. Meeks does not simply oppose the rhetoric of divine benevolence to the logic of the marketplace. He is not against the market per se but its pretensions to completeness, which privatize and sentimentalize Christian giving. He wants a critical correlation between God and economy. One does not produce the other—each has its own sphere, and so some tension between the two is inevitable—yet one cannot be consistently understood without the other. How are they to be related? Meeks wants to name God with economics in order to alter the way we think about economics, but by capitalizing on their similarity he also sanctifies the activities of the market. Creation is the distribution of God's righteousness, he argues. Love is God's labor. To know God is to participate in God's work.

This mingling of rhetorics raises a question: Is the claim that God is an economist metaphorical or literal? If God *is* an economist, then the idea of God has been subjected to the definition and rhetoric of an extrinsic framework. If God's economy is similar to but different from the economies of modern, Western states, then it is important to show that even as they overlap and intermingle they are also irreducibly and fundamentally different, so different, perhaps, that one does not deserve the name of the other. Indeed, it is arguable that the economy (salvation) of God can be illuminated only in contrast to human economizing (saving). To think them apart, it is necessary to think them together.

At his best, this is what Meeks accomplishes: in the process of bringing theology and economics together, he actually separates them. He reads economics through a theological translation. He knows, for example, that the ancient world put a higher value on politics than on economics, and he wants to embrace the lowliness that economics once implied: "Already in antiquity it was thoroughly problematic to refer to God as Economist, since the *homo economicus* was qualitatively inferior to the *homo politicus*. In short, an 'economist' was a household servant, one who was by definition unfree. An economist was what our culture has termed a 'steward' " (p. 76). Politics is about ruling, and economics is about working. God's economy involves the lowly labor of service and its attendant humiliations and frustrations. God gives up the power of politics—the freedom of rhetoric unhindered by social reality—in order to labor modestly for the good of the whole. The problem is that today economics, more than politics, represents power, and to conceive of God as an economist is to grant God enormous cunning in the way that God handles the world's household. "God saves" is both a theological and an economic proposition because saving involves sacrifice, and thus it is necessary to understand how God spends, what God gives up, and what God wants back.

Meeks best distinguishes God's economy from economics proper when he talks not about economics but about giving. If economics has its own logic, then it should not be transferred to the logic of God's grace. Indeed, as Meeks recognizes, the logic of grace is constituted by the illogic of hyperbole, which befits the extravagant giving of gifts:

> The righteousness of God brings manna in the wilderness; there is enough. The pretense of scarcity is not tolerated as the starting point for economics. The righteousness of God creates justice, which enables five thousand people to share five loaves and two fish; there is enough. No, the story ends with marvelous semitic hyperbole, there is more than enough. (p. 175)

Meeks even uses the word *gifting* to describe the activity that God engenders: "By gifting what one has, one becomes free for the new life of the kingdom and the discipleship of Jesus. Radical freedom for gifting is possible because of God's radical provision of God's righteousness" (p. 119). He often refers to the New Testament term *pleroma*,[24] which means the fullness or satisfaction that comes from God's blessings and the gifts of the Holy Spirit. God gives more than enough to enable us to live together as strong givers, in the Nietzschean sense: "To be human and to live abundantly is exclusively the gift of God's grace, of which there is no scarcity, no lack."[25] The gifts of God cannot be exchanged because they are abundant and because their value lies only in their freely being given on, not kept and owned.

At times, Meeks can still lapse into economic jargon as he explains the implications of God's giving. Indeed, this is the risk or danger of any theorization of God's activity. In a defense of the dignity of work, Meeks argues that "the 'more than enough' value of the messianic hope results in added effort, self-denial, and self-giving" (p. 153). In other words, the excessive gift is so obliging that it generates strenuous and efficient giving (labor) in the givees. At other times, though, Meeks remains true to the dynamic of giving itself:

> The peculiar reality of gifting is that when the gift is used, it is not used up. A commodity is truly consumed when it is sold because nothing about the exchange assures its return. The gift that is passed along remains abundant. In fact, a gift multiplies. Gifts that remain gifts can support an affluence of satisfaction, even without numerical abundance. Those who share are satisfied. (p. 179)

The antieconomy of God is predicated on an abundance that yields not the bloated satiety that comes with narcissistic consumption but the liberating satisfaction that stems from sharing. Aiding in the construction of a gifting community can help us reshape the notion of scarcity that governs much of modern thinking and acting. Through gifting, the feeling of emptiness that compels the frantic competition for scarce goods is filled with a sense of connectedness and mutuality.

I want to extend this direction in Meeks's work, with the emphasis on the idea that God is a giver, not an economist, so that we need to keep in mind the complex relationship between giving and exchange before we talk about what kind of antieconomy God embodies. Just as it is important to resist the temptation of making God relevant (that is, productive) by procuring the language of economics in order to identify God, it is not enough simply to oppose giving to exchange, as play is often contrasted to work. The influential North American theologian Horace Bushnell utilized this strategy, arguing that history shows religion evolving from the labor of the law to the spontaneity of play.[26] Work, he thought, designates conscious, intended effort, whereas play is carefree and formless, and he was glad that religion, in his day, was moving into its proper sphere in the impulsive free play of the human spirit liberated from the oppressively goal-driven constraints of labor. I argued in chapter 1, however, that simply opposing excess to exchange can serve to marginalize the former and reinforce the latter. If work and play are defined relationally, as a binary compound, then assigning religion to the realm of play can only either discharge it as a frivolous but redundant leisure activity or employ it as a necessary but hardly transformative release to its serious and strenuous counterpart. Religion as play or gift is thus drained of any social value: in a word, it does not work. I want to argue that the gift does work, and not in a magical way; the gift does the labor that we give to it, by passing it along. Nonetheless, this work of the gift does not reduce the play of excess to the productivity of labor. Our culture increasingly finds work to be meaningless, so it is tempting to make play more rigorous, specialized, and profitable. Nevertheless, the play of giving has its own drama that does not merely mirror the toil of exchange. The dynamic of gifting challenges and transforms the law of economics based on scarcity and competition.

I argued in the first chapter that we need narratives that end elsewhere than they begin and thus broaden, not constrict, the possibilities of giving. Now more than ever, we need a pattern for giving that does not repeat what is usual and expected, a nonontotheological theoeconomics that can empower, direct, and consummate our giving without reproducing the current ideologies of giving as either mere excess or exchange alone. Against the cynicism of contemporary culture, perfectly captured by deconstructionism's celebration of impotence and deferral, Christianity should promote the idea that in giving resides a liberating power. One of the broadest stories of giving is the Christian framework of gratuity and gratitude. Traditionally, however, that framework polarizes the giver from the givee, turning the gift process into a static event of revelation and obedience. I have tried to suggest how a theory of gifting can preserve the exuberance of the transcendent Giver while at the same time encapsulate the involvement of that Giver in the destiny of the given, its reception by the givees, and its ultimate return. To conclude this chapter, I want to return in more detail to the coordinates of the triadic theory of gifting that Christianity provides. I do not offer a simple or magical formula for giving because giving is beyond our control and thus resists our knowing, yet we can try to glimpse the various stages of the gift, and by receiving the mystery of God, we can have some sense of the gift as a whole. I organize my comments along the trinitarian pattern of the Giver, the Given, and the Giving, in order to discern the "house rules" of the reign of God (*basileia*) that Jesus preached.

God the Giver

Being clear about how God gives is of the utmost importance. As Marvin Olasky asserts, "Cultures build systems of charity in the image of the God they worship, whether distant deist, bumbling bon vivant, or 'whatever goes' gopher."[27] Olasky is afraid that an emphasis on the largesse of God's love leads to an anything-goes attitude, in which giving is flippant, permissive, and anarchic, not correlated with obligations and responsibilities. He would have us retreat from the notion of God's generosity to the idea of God as a scrupulous manager, frugal, efficient, and prudent. For Olasky, God's love is not laborless; instead, it is careful and calculated, rewarding those who conserve rather than spend.

His concerns deserve serious reflection. Excessive giving can disregard the crucial question of the return of the gift. Yet the problems of excess should not lead to exchange as an answer. The end point of gifting—a community that responds to giving with further giving, creating relationships of obligation and responsibility—should not be read into the beginning of the process. God does want us to give, so that God does not give for no purpose, but God wants us to give—not save or consume—as God gives, excessively. Olasky treats giving as a form of conservation, not expenditure. He polarizes generosity and responsibility, love and labor, so that he is forced to choose one over the other. The starkness of the alternative is false. Excess and exchange need to be conceived, in a Chalcedonian manner, as separate and yet one, different but cohering aspects of one dynamic, threefold process.

For Christians, God's giving is initially hyperbolic, or, in other words, it is excessive because it initiates all of our own giving. The Christian paradigm suggests that giving always begins not with some heroic act or erotic profusion but with a prior giving ("Give us this day our daily bread"). The gift always precedes the act of passing it along. Such excess, however, is not unrelated to mutuality. Primordial giving does not originate according to the logic of a free act of the will but follows the desire that is embedded in the act of giving. In the words of Pseudo-Dionysius, God is "yearning on the move."[28] God is an abundant, transcendent, and intrusive giver who nevertheless is implicated in the full range of the gift-giving dynamic. God's gifting is not random or reckless, even though it is wanton and prolific. Its extravagance does not paralyze us into acts of ineffective gratitude. Instead, it allows us to give without arrogance or anxiety. Paul asks the gifted congregation at Corinth: "What do you possess that was not given you? If then you really received it all as a gift, why take the credit to yourself?" (1 Cor. 4:8).[29] The end of the gift is more gifting. Everyone can give because what we give is really our own, and yet nobody has the right to be proud of what they give because it has been given to us precisely in order to be passed along.

To say that giving is born of excess is to acknowledge God as the one who creates our giving. To talk about the gift demands a rhetoric capable of delineating the height from which it comes. Christianity has always given to excess the name of love or, to put it in other words, has always spoken of love in a hyperbolic voice. Grace, hyperbolically construed as an action that receives healing by going too far in the name of that which is too much, gains its most elegant articulation in the simple Johannine declaration that "God is love" (1 John 4:8). This formulaic proclamation actually condenses in the most compact fashion an explosive fusion of two names, both of which are unimaginable. The impact is neither a conceptual clarification, in which what we know is replaced by more general and therefore useful terms, nor a metaphorical image, in which our knowledge is increased by coupling the known with the unknown. The effect is an identification that pushes each term outward toward the other in an absolute intermingling, the seductive copula signifying a venture in which love is heightened and raised to the more vertically powerful term, *God,* and God is widened and stretched to include the more horizontally effective term, *love.* "God is love" is a call for outrageous action that will find in love the desire for God and in God always and only the desire of love.

A hyperbolic imagination would open our myopic visions to God's unbounded love, the impossible priority of the other, and the unreal hope in ultimate redemption. For Christianity, excess is not the occasional spilling of constrained emotions that comes at the end of a hard day. Excess is not an aesthetic amplification or a dangerous vitiation of the moral realm. Indeed, Christian excess is not simply at odds with ethics but implies or, better, is itself an ethics. To go too far in the name of the other is to wager that hyperbole makes sense, that too much, sometimes, is just right. The strange logic of this rhetoric of giving enables us to solicit excess not as an intoxicating experience or as a means to a moderate ethics of neighborliness but as a conjunction of style and praxis that conjures and creates the bold and vigorous desire that finds the self in the other.

As the starting point for theology, God's initiative gives theology its own, distinctive rhetoric. To give/squander/love—to put into play a poetics of the impossible—is to resist the qualifications and moderations that inevitably tend to attenuate the excessive by relocating it within the fastidious talk about the proper and the prudent, the pragmatic limitations of responsibility—a prose of the probable.[30] A hyperbolic imagination of God's giving sees the world as it really is, but in addition sees it as it most certainly is not—that is, as what it can become and therefore was meant to be.[31] There are many discourses—ethics and economics chief among them—that traverse the same ground that theology tries to occupy; not all of them are hostile to religion, but they are all overly eager to diminish the good news to a frail whisper or a somber mumble by belaboring—that is, exaggerating—its difficulties, its irrationality, its unreality. Theology has the task of staging a style appropriate to its own peculiar mission. Theological rhetoric must be personal, acknowledging the lack of any neutral standpoint. It also must be practical, recognizing the political, even the sociological, matrix of every communicative exchange. More than anything else, though, theological rhetoric must seek to promote the impossible. A desire for the other overfunded by the reckless giving of the Ultimate Other is a point worth trying to make, even as that very point unmakes and confounds all of our attempts to grasp what we can never reach and to speak what we can never know.

God the Given

For Karl Barth, God's giving in Jesus Christ makes sense of all of God's other gifts; this gift, then, orders and organizes God's giving. It is the paradigmatic gift. It shows that the gift of creation is good, even when life does not seem so. This must be true, of course, for any Christian, yet I want to argue that this gift does not show that God's giving is intentional, orderly, purposeful, and teleological alone. This giving also shows just how much all of God's giving is excessive. As Paul Ricoeur notes, the abundance of God's grace in Jesus Christ follows the logic of "how much more" or "more than that" (Rom. 8:34). This " 'how much more,' which overturns the 'as . . . so also,' gives to the movement from the first to the second Adam its tension and its temporal impulsion; it excludes the possibility that the 'gift' should be a simple restoration of the order that prevailed before the 'fault'; the gift is the establishment of a new creation."[32] Every gift is unique, an event in itself. The gift of Jesus looks forward to more giving, not backward to a lost sense of order. This gift does not reveal what was disguised, conserving what was once wasted, replacing or clarifying something that was hidden or obscured; instead, it initiates something new.

Hence, in Jesus Christ we have a Christian version of squandering, a lavishing that both shocks and consoles. As the Apostle Paul writes, God "did not spare his own Son, but gave him up for us all; and with this gift how can he fail to lavish upon us all that he has to give?" (Rom. 8:32). Paul is drawn to the hyperlogic of superabundance as the only way of describing the excessive giving of God.[33] Although it is impossible to clarify the conceptuality of this giving, its contours can be followed narratively in that most passionate story of squandering—the life, death, and resurrection of Jesus Christ. The singular unity of God and humanity is an excessive configuration startling us into multiple possibilities that otherwise could only remain remote and indifferent. This Godperson, however, goes even further. Indeed, Jesus Christ's splendid squandering on the cross is an expenditure that we can never expect to recuperate and thus redeem. This endowment of suffering generosity, which exceeds the boundaries of our understanding, subsidizes all of our attempts to contribute to others without accommodating the relentless pursuit of profit and interest. The squandered Christ is a gift that calls us to spend in kind, a demanding opportunity that we too frequently squander, in the pejorative sense, by trying to order, secure, and conserve that which goes further than we dare try to follow.

We come to Jesus like the woman who, having spent all she had without profit, now seeks the benefits that money cannot buy (Mark 5:26). Jesus, in turn, gives us more than we think we want. As Ched Myers observes, images of more than enough, often connected to food, proliferate the Markan narrative (see Mark 4:8; 6:44; 7:19; 8:8, 19; 10:30).[34] For example, in Mark's first feeding story (chapter 6), the disciples want Jesus to let the hungry crowds go to the surrounding farms and villages to buy food. Jesus rejects this economic solution to the problem of scarcity and tells the disciples to give the people food themselves. The result of this process of sharing is a "more than enough" that leaves everyone full and content. As Ched Myers notes, "The disciples can imagine only market scarcity in the dominant economy. Against this, Jesus keeps referring them to their own resources, challenging them to forge an alternative economics" (p. 442). Myers suggests that many of Jesus' teachings and actions have subversive economic significance. Mark's Jesus rejects the consolidation of economic and political power in the temple. He also rejects asceticism and purity laws as the privileged practice of the wealthy, not the hungry. Instead, he advocates a cooperative sharing that has radical consequences. When Jesus sends his disciples out, he demands that they depend on hospitality (Mark 6:8). Through an inclusive table fellowship, he practices a solidarity with outcasts that invites everyone to the bounty of God. He even encourages not just sharing but extravagance: Jesus accepts the gratuitous anointing of the costly perfume against his disciples' justifiable objections ("Why this waste?" Mark 14:4). Jesus shows how God's household is both excessive and reciprocal, putting into circulation all that we are able to give in order to give to all who need.[35]

What God gives is excessive compared to what we need, even if not relative to our desires. We can transform our desires, though, and satisfy our needs by passing on the given to others. The given is not a burden but a task of abundance that draws giving from us as an appropriate response of stewardship to the riches that precede us.[36] This is sufficiently clear from the complexity of the natural world, which endows us with all that we are and all that we need when it is approached with gratitude and thanksgiving, not greed and anxiety. The gift, however, is transacted not only out of an initial abundance (the Father) but also across the multiple divides separating givers and receivers that can be crossed only through shared suffering and moments of despair (the Son). The gift is not only the givenness of the world but also the movement that draws us into the world, bridging and intersecting, and thus taking the form of the cross. It is appropriate, then, that Jesus' death has come to signify the ultimate act of giving. Giving is a kind of relinquishing or undoing that prepares us for death, a letting go or giving up that enables us to give in to our finitude with hope and courage.[37] Every gift is both a death and a rebirth, simultaneously the loss and return of the self.

In a way, it is unfortunate that "grace" has come to signify smoothness and ease because the acts through which we are able to reach out and love each other more often involve awkwardness, stuttering, anxiety, and anguish. The communication of the gift is not polished speech or purple prose but heartfelt stammering. To give is to lose control, not to display prowess and skill. Christian squandering is not heroic in the Nietzschean sense. It is also not cheerful in a naive, innocent way. Instead, the given of Jesus Christ reveals that all giving is sacrifice, failure, ruin, and even disaster.[38] This is due not just to the idea that the something given was wanted or needed and, therefore, difficult to give but also because giving occurs in and through loss, the wound, the wasted, suffering. The economy of gifting is born from a blessed bankruptcy, an acknowledgment that we have nothing of our own to give, a poverty that liberates us to share in the lives of others and to pass along all of God's riches.

Although the cross connects giving to losing, it does not suggest that squandering is a fruitless self-denial aimed at some otherworldly reward. Nor is it connected to an ideology of self-hate. Certainly, such giving/losing is not a prudent show of sociability seeking admiration and respect, or the compulsive desire to maximize one's investments. Instead, this lavishing stems from an inner strength, a spiritual richness that suggests that we give because we already have been given too much. This is the Christological dimension of giving. Jesus Christ preserves both the futility and the fecundity of the gift. In Jesus Christ, the giving of God is both sacrificed and revealed, hidden and made manifest, squandered and returned, denied and reborn. The gift is shown to be both excessive and mutual in that the gift must be forsaken for it to be effective. Jesus is "the Good as goodness that infinitely forgets itself."[39] We can give this gift because the giver has all but disappeared into it, leaving us free to do with it what we will. There is no reward for such a fortuitous gesture, but there is an insinuation or revelation of something that is more than real. The hope of giving is that a renewed self is what remains of the otherwise wasteful acts of an antieconomical generosity. Giving is not always impotent, frustrated, incomplete. Sometimes giving gives birth to a rejuvenated subjectivity that finds itself in the transformative space of a healing loss.

In order to rethink the connection between gaining and losing in giving, we need to recover a sense of the prodigious by welcoming again the return of the prodigal. The return of the prodigal is the recognition—through that classic parable (Luke 15:11–32)—that giving is a force that breaks boundaries, supersedes limitations, and thwarts expectations. In Marion's insightful commentary on this story, the son's request for his share of the father's possessions (the Greek word is *ousia*) constitutes an attempt to convert the dynamic of the gift into the logic of property. According to the traditional doctrine of the Trinity, the *ousia* of God exists as three hypostases; that is, God's *ousia* is dynamic and ever circulating. For the prodigal, who already enjoyed the goods that he wanted to own, an economy in which property is continuously shared was not enough. In Marion's words: "He asks that one grant that he no longer have to receive any gift: he asks to possess it, dispose of it, enjoy it without passing through the gift and the reception of the gift. The son wants to owe nothing to his father, and above all not to owe him a gift; he asks to have a father no longer—the ousia without the father or the gift"; he wants to turn the ground that the family shares into "liquid money, which, by definition, seeps and trickles between the fingers."[40] The cost of the gift for the father is forgiveness; the expense of property for the son is the loss of his humanity. The gift is abandoned, it is squandered, but, nonetheless, the donee is pardoned, and the giver continues to give. Nothing has changed: what the father has is still the son's (Luke 15:31), but the son has come to find his being (*ousia*) in the giving of the father and not in his own taking and spending. When we claim our share of the world for ourselves, removing it from the dynamic of the gift to the structure of what we can understand and control, we cut ourselves off from the capacity to both give and receive, in response and responsibility.[41]

Sin, it is important to note, should not be equated simply with the existence of private property. After all, gifts are really given, and possession is one of the key moments of the gifting process. The pleasure of having is a necessary component of the infusion of power that enables giving. Nonetheless, ownership is not an end in itself but a means to further giving. Sin is the denial of the essential mobility of all goods, what Lewis Hyde has called the erotic life of property. Too often the theological tradition has defined sin as the striving for pleasure, especially sexual pleasure. Theology should instead contrast the pleasure of giving with the greed of keeping.[42] Note, for example, Paul Tillich's definition of concupiscence as "the unlimited desire to draw the whole of reality into one's self," the temptation of "reaching unlimited abundance" in which the self denies all limits.[43] The sinner tries to find abundance within the self, not in the relation between self and others. This is a false and illusory excess that actually creates borders and restrictions on the flow of goods and the enlargement of the self. We resist God most when we anxiously want our share of things, patrolling the excess that gives and taxing the mutuality of the return.

As the story of the prodigal demonstrates, the rhetoric of gifting does justice to the illogic of abundance that operates in the parables of Jesus, in which love is offered over and above the moderate and reasonable concerns of self-interest and self-preservation. The parables, significantly, do not merely illustrate moral principles. They demonstrate the inherently rhetorical features of any language of love, as well as the particular characteristics of this fundamental stratum of Christian discourse. In the Gospel parables, a poetics of praise—an encomium celebrating the apparently impossible but the miraculously necessary— unfolds as an ethical discourse in which the other is situated above (in terms of priority) and in front of (in terms of accessibility) the self, demanding and deserving recognition. This ethical discourse, however, is not a prosaic reflection on the need for justice, the careful demands of fairness and equivalency. Instead, this hyperethics is disclosed through the poetics—the poetry establishes an appealing imperative—by a compact and tense account of an action that makes sense because it is narratable, but demands existential verification because it is extravagant. The parables themselves, the excessive stories of Jesus, become, then, an avenue of grace: they open a way toward a giving in which, no matter how much we resist, we can find the empowerment that permits us to give in—the end to which is our own beginning.

God the Giving

Gratitude as it is usually understood and practiced presents two problems. First, it can be a substitute for action, and thus it displays an anxious paralysis in the face of the gift. A gift is burdensome when we do not know what to do with it, when we cannot give it back in some way, or when we are not permitted to pass it along. We are reduced to abject declarations of utter dependence, to repeating over and over again that we cannot do anything with the gift except to say how little we deserve it and how it really belongs to the giver alone. This kind of gratitude is most appropriate in an economy based on scarcity, with not enough goods to go around, so that we must demonstrate our surprise and relief when we finally get our share. In such an environment, we are forced to consume the gift in private, to make it an emblem of our own proper identity as conceived by the giver. Second, gratitude can also be an attempt to nullify the gift by responding in a proportionate manner. Gratitude is a kind of repayment, the labor that converts the gift into exchange by creating the semblance of equality. Gratitude thus aims at balance; as Meeks explains, "The exchange of commodities aims at stasis or equilibrium."[49] Gratitude inevitably reduces the idiosyncrasy of excess to the flatness of exchange.

I have argued that the gratuitous God of Christianity does not summon gratitude as either dependence or exchange; instead, the divine giver begets further giving, the obligation to continue the gift, not to substitute giving with the attitude of thanksgiving. The antieconomy of gifting is dynamic, inclusive, and expansive. Giving is itself the most potent form of praise (2 Cor. 9:11–12). Our gifts are not to be buried in the ground for safekeeping (Matt. 25:14–20) but increased by distributing them to others. Passing the gift along transforms the static and ambiguous obligation of gratitude into a joyous participation in the life of the gift. What we can most give to others is to help them discover, develop, and deploy what they have to give, and sometimes this means that we must give up our own gifts, as did Jesus Christ, and learn how to receive.

If every gift is a new event, gifts are also essentially repeatable; in fact, the process of repetition makes community possible. Repetition also means that there is no single shape of the gift; giving is always multiple. Even if Christians find the structure and content of God's giving in Jesus Christ, the gift can always be named otherwise; in a way, giving never has a simple beginning or a single conclusion because giving goes on and on. Christian theologians often depict an isolated and independent God at the beginning of history and a well-organized society of dutiful worshipers at the end of history, but from the gifting perspective there is reason to think not only that God has always given but also that God will continue to grow and change along with the gift and share in its various expressions and manifold destinations. Perhaps the most significant challenge for Christian theology in this regard is to articulate an understanding of giving that learns from instead of usurps the giving that constitutes Judaism. There is no question here of dividing God's covenant into two in order to perpetuate the terribly unfair and historically inaccurate charge that Judaism operates out of an economy of labor while Christianity exists in an antieconomy of grace. Any covenant is always subjected to the temptations of exchange, of turning grace into profit, and this is equally true for Christian practice as for Jewish. Moreover, no community can claim ownership over God's giving.

Indeed, Christians are in debt not just to God but also and especially to the faith of Judaism. What Christians receive is the surplus of God's giving to the Jews, a gift that does not take back prior gifts. Jesus is the gift to the church from both the God of Israel and the Israel of God.[45] Of course, gifts change as they are passed along, and what is given is no longer under the control of the giver, but one giver can give different gifts, all with the same intention (thus, grace can take different forms while still remaining one grace). God's giving is equally excessive (and thus always varied) for all people, just as the struggle to articulate the duality of the gift—its gratuity and its demand—is also constant (and thus different) across the religions. That God gives excessively means that God follows through the gift to the very end; one gift does not displace the other, even if there is a complex relationship of repetition and innovation. God gives more than enough for all, which means that the gift is always different, thus capable of creating ever new communities of responsive givers.

In any case, the excess of God's grace does not dissipate in the act of its giving; such excess inevitably takes shape in the lives of the people who choose to respond to it, and this response is community. It is even important to say that community makes giving possible; without its continuation, the gift perishes. When we give, God honors our gifts with the grace of discovery and solidarity. Indeed, giving is grace (the Greek *charis* means both gift and grace[46]); giving is the paramount activity of strength and hope. In this giving, the self does not suffer in self-denial and humiliation but instead discovers itself in and through the other. In the words of Mark, "What does a man gain by winning the whole world at the cost of his true self? What can he give to buy that self back?" (Mark 8:36–37). In Ched Myers's interpretation, this passage is an explicit attack on economic rationality. To renounce Jesus is a "bad investment" because even if it shows a return of the whole world it does not represent a profit but rather a complete loss.[47] Jesus is not naming his price but insisting that he has no price; the decision to follow him can be subjected to economic analysis only by negating those very terms, turning profit into loss just as Paul paradoxically reverses strength and weakness.

All gifts, as Derrida argues, create time. They also create space. The church can be defined as the place where excess meets excess, where, that is, the proportionate response to the disproportionate grace of God marks the site of the process (the continuing event) of the gift. This can occur in actual churches, but it can also occur wherever people acknowledge giving with further giving. Paul Tournier observes that "we cannot give that which we have not received."[48] If giving always begins with an excessive intrusion, then we need to cultivate and support with every available means (through both the government and the market) the whole range of third-sector organizations that take our gifts and pass them along. Certainly, these organizations function to meet specific needs and promote political programs, but they can also unleash the unpredictable power of giving itself, thus empowering individuals to continue to give. What the church illustrates is that giving is really for giving itself, that it is in giving that excess is discovered and increased. In this community, excess takes the form of mutuality, which is a dynamic form without structure or limit. Only in a community that gives everything back to giving can excess take shape without being diminished. All organized giving, then, anticipates or approximates the formless form of what is called the church.

For Lewis Hyde, the community giving creates is the elite community of the gifted, those who are able to recognize and take advantage of the special gifts of others. For many people, the gift is a vote of confidence in both a prior surplus and the community's ability to properly invest that surplus. "The act of donation is an affirmation of goodwill."[49] Robert Wuthnow also notes the connection between giving and the affirmation of the social order; "Sharing makes sense because we have faith in the future. And our faith in the future is heightened by our capacity to share. We feel stronger because we are joining forces with other human beings."[50] For Wuthnow, however, giving does not merely affirm the status quo; it also stretches the imagination toward something better. The expansive action of giving broadens our thinking. Giving can express what people seek or desire as well as what they already have; "Helping others may not lead to a better society, but it allows us to *envision* a better society" (p. 234). Compassion functions as a standard, a goal, and an ideal by which we can measure ourselves and our society. Wuthnow understands the symbolic value of giving, that giving is not simply for the eradication of needs. Needs will always be there, and under the pressure of the market they seem to multiply endlessly; moreover, our deepest needs are basic and thus constant. However, giving is more than symbolic in that it does meet the need for giving itself. Indeed, giving is for the galvanization of the gift and the creation of giving in others. It has a ripple effect that creates what it intends. Gifting creates its own disorder, a community of givers that empowers others to give and give again. The goal is not simply the redistribution of goods or the creation of an elite group but the growth of God's "presence" (through the divine withdrawal in Jesus Christ) in graceful acts of sharing that expand participation along egalitarian and mutual lines.

A good gift circulates with the quiet power of a leisurely return, making community possible, but, even so, Derrida is right to insist that the return of the gift makes the thinking of giving problematic. The Christian horizon for the return of giving, however, does not negate the extravagance of giving. On Christological grounds, I have suggested that excessive kindness does not form a closed circle; it is incomplete, and that is why it involves pain and suffering. Yet, the hope of generosity is that it will, eventually, create an inclusive circle, an encompassing sphere of mutuality and reciprocity. This is the meaning of Christian eschatology. God's gifts create an eschatological time in which their ultimate return can be only the mutuality and harmony of sharing, living in and for and with the other. The return of the gift is not an exchange, as if nothing was really given. It is the circulation of empowerment by which equality and solidarity are created. The end of giving is not literally a place where giving is no more but where the more of giving becomes what really is. We know this place only through hope, but such hope makes the ordinary calculations of economics seem provisional, temporary, and already overcome, even while it does not deny the overwhelming presence of exchange. The gifting community, then, serves as a sign of the return of the Gift, the eschatological embodiment of God's excesses within a completely reciprocal community, where giving begets itself in mutuality, integrity, and harmony. Such a community would be possible not as a place where self-interests perfectly coincide with each other, allowing compassion as a by-product of selfishness, but as a place where excess begets reciprocity, which, in turn, empowers further excess, so that giving gives the power of giving.[51] Jesus captures this dynamic, open-ended, inclusive process in the image of the eschatological feast, where the joy of abundance is experienced in the reigning of the Messiah (Luke 14:16–24). Gifting advances toward that point where excess and mutuality meet, not obliterating differences but creating them, in a community ruled not by prudence and moderation but by the idiosyncrasies of various excesses, all directed toward the hope that all will be able to give, so that gifting itself becomes the sign of the eternal presence (or present) of God.

To borrow a phrase from William Corlett, gifting creates a community without unity: "Gift-giving is communitarian in the sense that it is never solitary: one becomes fully implicated in the play of differences between arbitrary signifiers that are arranged and rearranged to make sense. Because this sense of community without unity is accidental and free, a politics of extravagance is necessarily incomplete."[52] For Corlett, gift giving assures mutuality without imposing on society a set of common beliefs and values. It also introduces into a community an element of chance and randomness, the surprising connections that result from extravagant risks and reckless endeavors. The gift, which is a wager against the probability of exchange, gives infinite possibilities that everyday tensions and constraints conceal. When a gift is given, its origin cannot be easily named, and its destination cannot be predicted. To give extravagantly is to enter into relationships that are not regulated by the binary oppositions of served and servant, privileged and needy, insider and outsider. Excess directed toward mutuality undermines hierarchy. As Paul writes, "Thanks [*charis*] be to God for his gift beyond words!" (2 Cor. 9:15). The hypertrophic gift bursts boundaries before it creates new visions of cohesion. Pseudo-Dionysius writes:

> Think of how it is with our sun. It exercises no rational process, no act of choice, and yet by the very fact of its existence it gives light to whatever is able to partake of its light, in its own way. So it is with the Good. Existing far above the sun, an archetype far superior to its dull image, it sends the rays of its undivided goodness to everything with the capacity, such as this may be, to receive it.[53]

In describing such giving, geometrical images break down. As Pseudo-Dionysius notes, God's gifting is linear, circular, and a spiral all at once (p. 78). Giving takes multiple forms even as it disrupts old formations.

The early Christian community was grounded in sharing, as demonstrated in the famous description of how they had all things in common in Acts 4:32–35. Acts 2:42 calls this community *koinonia*, which means "fellowship." It also means "partnership," the idea that the members of the group are related in a common venture. Justo L. Gonzalez argues against commentaries that try to spiritualize the early Christian community's practice of sharing; the distribution of material goods was the necessary precondition for other expressions of solidarity and support.[54] This communal life was grounded in the regular sharing of meals, a practical and yet symbolic exercise in giving. The communion ritual in this context was not an acknowledgment of a preexisting state of unity and harmony (such an acknowledgment would be both premature and nostalgic) but a celebration of the space for a giving that would empower mutually beneficial differences. Such eucharistic thanksgiving looks to the future more than the past.[55] The communion meal that looks forward to the Messianic banquet makes giving not only concrete but also festive. Giving occurs not only through suffering but also joy. The eros of giving is the way in which it drives outward, in search of the gathering rhythms of God's encompassing love.

The combination of the spiritual and the material in giving is nowhere more evident than in Paul's second letter to the Corinthians, where he requests an offering for the poor of the Jerusalem church. This sensitive and practical subject is intermingled with rhetoric about God's own generosity and the need for the Corinthian church to maintain a loving and mutual fellowship. Gifts should overflow from the church, just as God's grace has overflowed in Jesus Christ. Paul makes clear that these gifts should be voluntary, a bounty and not an extortion (2 Cor. 9:5). He praises the Macedonians who have been through hard times and yet "have been so exuberantly happy that from the depths of their poverty they have shown themselves lavishly open-handed" (8:2). What they gave, significantly, was themselves, and thus "their giving surpassed our expectations" (8:5). This self-giving is modeled on Jesus: "For you know how generous [*charin*] our Lord Jesus Christ has been: he was rich, yet for your sake he became poor, so that through his poverty you might become rich" (8:9). The exchange of Christ's sufferings generates a new economy that can liberate resources for justice and compassion. As Paul states: "Penniless, we own the world" (6:10). The mutual support of the churches reflects and aims at the glory of God:

> There is no question of relieving others at the cost of hardship to your-selves; it is a question of equality. At the moment your surplus meets their need, but one day your need may be met from their surplus. The aim is equality; as Scripture has it, "The man who got much had no more than enough, and the man who got little did not go short." (8:13–15)

The languages of giving, justice, and grace are one and the same.

Paul borrows from but also subverts the theory and practice of generosity in his own day. He uses economic metaphors for God, calling the gospel a priceless treasure and the Spirit the "downpayment" or "deposit" (1:22) of God's grace. The economic metaphors function to emphasize differences as well as similarities between grace and exchange. As Frances Young and David F. Ford explain in their study of this letter, Corinth was a booming commercial center, and Paul was a craftsman who integrated his work with his ministry, so the employment of economic language is not surprising.[56] What Paul emphasizes is our need to collaborate with God's abundant grace. Paul wrote to an audience that lived in a subsistence economy in which economic growth and the distribution of goods were severely limited. Most people worked in agriculture and were bound through inheritance to the place of their family in society, aided by relationships based on reciprocity. Benevolence was possible only for the wealthy, and it was institutionalized in patron-client relationships. Gratitude, though a recognition of submission and dependence, was also supposed to be active and concrete, a continuation of the gift. As Young and Ford note, "In Greek giving and receiving, grace and thanksgiving are intimately connected in a way that is not true in English" (p. 97). Paul accepts the Greek idea that gifts beget more giving, but he resists the idea that giving is a part of an institutional hierarchy.

For Paul, God's grace is overwhelmingly different from the economy of scarcity. As Young and Ford argue;

> Vis-à-vis Hellenistic reciprocity, what seems to have happened is that the inexhaustible generosity of God places everyone in the position of his clients and therefore owing him thanks; but among the clients themselves there is no basis for anything other than equality or uncalculating generosity, and so all patron-client relationships are relativized. (p. 179)

Paul's theology combines debt, obligation, and dependence with freedom, mutuality, and community. Our indebtedness enables us to spend freely. We are all clients of God, and thus our patronage to each other is made possible but also deprived of any power and prestige.

Grace is a light freely distributed, driven by a dynamic of proliferation and fecundity. Such abundance, however, also makes its own demands and creates special tasks. The grace of God, our thanks to God, and the generosity we thus give each other are all forms of *charis,* are all interrelated. The foundation of this economy is an exchange in which God gives us God's own self in order to generate spiritual wealth and power for us. Giving is the currency of the new creation inaugurated by Christ. As Young and Ford state: "To have the Spirit is to spend oneself" (p. 175). Jesus gave his life so that we can have more life. Cost benefit analysis breaks down, and earthly values are relativized. "In the face of what this God gives," Young and Ford suggest, "calculations of reciprocity are pointless: one simply gives freely in the spirit of the God who does likewise" (p. 198). The relief work for the Jerusalem church is both material and spiritual; it spirals toward God by overflowing to others. Giving is a gracious task, a joy made possible by God's gifts. Giving, in fact, is a gift, one of the primary blessings of God. Grace is a gift, given equally to all, that can be received without enslavement or resentment and returned without thought of repayment or interest. This is the lesson of God the receiver.

God the Giving is what I am calling the Holy Spirit. The Holy Spirit is traditionally depicted not as the historical unfolding of God's activity but as the unity of God, the mutual love of the Father and the Son that also includes our love for God.[57] This reduces the Spirit to the static and closed idea of an already completed love, an economy of reserve, not extravagance. Thomas Aquinas demonstrates both the strengths and the weaknesses of the traditional position in a fascinating discussion that brings together the Spirit and the Gift.[58] Although Aquinas focuses on the Spirit as the love between the Father and the Son, rather than the love that involves God in the return of that which is sent, his comments are moving and instructive. The Father and the Son, although not the same, are equal in dignity and honor, and the Spirit is the evidence of that mutual love. The Spirit is love simultaneously excessive (he defines the Spirit as love proceeding, the outflowing energy of God) and reciprocal (*mutuus amor*, not between a superior and an inferior). There is biblical warrant for thinking of this love in terms of the gift; as Paul writes, "God's love has flooded our inmost heart through the Holy Spirit he has given us" (Rom. 5:5; also see Acts 2:37–38; 10:44–46; 11:15–17).

Lamenting "the poverty of our vocabulary" about the Spirit, Aquinas is willing to carefully appropriate the rhetoric of giving in terms of the activity of the Spirit. At first, he hesitates to identify together Spirit and Gift because the latter "imports relation to the creature, and it thus seems to be said of God in time." Aquinas is aware of the relations of obligation and dependence created by giving, and so he must define God's giving in a special way in order to maintain God's eternity and independence. Consequently, he argues that the "gift imports an aptitude for being given." The gift has to do with the potential exercise of a power, not actual and risky involvement in a perpetual process. He thus connects the gift to freedom, decision, and the will, rather than to desire, vulnerability, and need. Moreover, Aquinas further connects the gift to ownership and property. God can be said to give because "a gift must belong in a way to the giver." God is not, then, subjected to anything external to God. The Holy Spirit is Gift only to the extent that God is always able to give, regardless of how such giving actually takes place. Nevertheless, even though Aquinas has to alter the meaning of giving in order to protect God's immutability, he still wants to claim that the Gift is, indeed, the proper name of the Holy Spirit. In an eloquent passage, he suggests that the divine gratuity is spent for the advancement of love:

> A gift is properly an unreturnable giving . . . a thing which is not given with the intention of a return—and it thus contains the idea of a gratuitous donation. Now, the reason of the donation being gratuitous is love; since therefore do we give something to anyone gratuitously forasmuch as we wish him well. So what we first give him is the love whereby we wish him well. Hence it is manifest that love has the nature of a first gift, through which all free gifts are given.

Aquinas is reaching toward the idea that God is the First Giver, not in the sense of causing all other giving but in the sense that God gives the love that is the action of the gift. Love motivates the continuation of the gift, propelled by a spirit that is both free and binding.

Although Aquinas risks connecting the Holy Spirit to the Gift, more frequently the Spirit has been only vaguely conceived in Christian theology. The Spirit is often portrayed as that which circulates in mysterious ways, not only between the Father and the Son but also among us. It makes no sense to contrast this circulation with the rest of the Godhead, as if the Spirit were the dynamic aspect of an essentially static and unchanging divinity. What the Spirit does cannot be different from what God does. What the Spirit accomplishes is made possible by God's total involvement with what God has given and what we return. To inquire into the economy of the Spirit's inflationary circulation, therefore, is to make clear God's own stake in the vicissitudes of history.

The Spirit is of God and ourselves, belonging only to the dissemination that is grace. The nature of the Spirit's movement is usually ascribed to the personal and private realm of human emotion, which, in turn, exposes the Spirit to all those psychological methodologies that analyze human development and expression. From the perspective of gifting, however, the vagueness of the Spirit's power makes it a more public activity than a private one. A splurged gift can never be controlled; thus, the gift always transgresses the intention of the giver and cannot be confined to psychological explanation. The gift does not say who we are but who we wish to become. Whatever you give your all to, that is who you are and where you are going. Even more important, the gift does not speak with the "I" at all but says more than what we can say alone, and so it resists the explanations and methodologies of all psychologies and anthropologies. In a way, the gift is always given by more than one person, just as it is always given to more than a single individual; behind and in front of the gift is a "we" that is always coming into being on the basis of giving itself. Gifting always involves at least three people, not two, because the givee is motivated to continue what the giver has begun. As a result, the ways in which God participates and directs our giving cannot be specified in terms of our own plans and purposes. The antieconomical covenant of the gifting community is based on luck, chance, and accident, which are terms that, under the hermeneutics of the gift, are other names for grace. The Spirit is the vehicle that is self-effacing, leading us further toward the perfect relationship of excess and mutuality in God.

The Spirit is not absolutely faceless; rather, the shape of this face comes into focus only in the community that enables God to receive as well as give. We do not worship the Holy Spirit in itself because it is the power of giving that God provides by sustaining and organizing our giving along the lines of a harmonious community. This power is, in a significant way, in our hands, so that it can be said that the Spirit is cocreated by our sharing; the Holy Spirit is the potential for sharing as that is actualized in the gifting community. Our giving adds to God's movement by enlarging God's active involvement in the destiny of God's gift. God's giving would not be complete without our return of the gift, and our return enables God to give even more. Donald W. Hinze has suggested that giving is a sacrament, one of the visible signs of God's grace.[59] For many congregations, the offering is something to be hurried through, while organ music quietly plays in the background, letting us pretend that nothing is happening. The offering, instead, could be seen as the completion of the worship service. In baptism and the eucharist, symbolized by the bowl or fount and the communion ware, we take from God, but in the offering, symbolized by the empty plate, we give to God, by giving to others. The empty plate is God's gift to us of our ability and opportunity to give.

Following Hegel, I am arguing that God's trinitarian agency is thoroughly implicated in the developments of history. God's giving puts God's being at risk in the destiny of the gift. If the Son loves the Father through the Spirit, then the gifting community is the way in which God comes to be God. We, in turn, enter the love of God not through an emotional state or cognitive decision but when we give to others what has been given to us. After all, the gifts of the Holy Spirit (what Paul calls in Greek the *charismata*) are for the common good (1 Cor. 12:7). They are given to us so that we can give for others. The Spirit gives not for intoxication or for individual reward but for the broadest vision of the good, building up the body of Christ. The Holy Spirit is the life (Hebrew *ruach* and Greek *pneuma*, meaning breath, air, wind, or soul) of the gift, the way in which it moves and proliferates beyond anyone's ability to control it. The Spirit animates and vivifies exchange with a life that resurrects our gestures of generosity from the inert calculation of bartering, luring our giving from futility to fecundity, even in the midst of frustration and despair.

Giving does not deny frustration; it seeks out the other in spite of the impossibility of the gift arriving at its designated destination. When we say, after we have given, that "it was nothing," we are suggesting more than a (false or otherwise) modesty. Giving, to the extent that it actually breaks with the logic of equivalence and exchange, is necessarily counted, as Derrida insists, as nothing, as surplus and waste. Nonetheless, giving is a way of doing nothing that does a lot; giving thus names, as Marion suggests, that which is more than what is, the good that is beyond being (which Plato discusses in the *Republic*), the love that is not exchange, the more that is yet enough. In tortuous prose, Levinas captures this doubleness of the good that is both useless and worthy: "To be good is a deficit, waste and foolishness in a being; to be good is excellence and elevation beyond being."[60] Giving is both less and more than being; it is both something else and something more. The gift marks the site where the good is born, contrary to our expectations and calculations. Is this gift a temporary interruption, always fated to fade into its opposite, or is it capable of more permanent articulations, of provoking and challenging the usual and the everyday? The gift survives only in its nonidentical repetition; as long as we give, there will be more giving, the more that really is, as well as the more that is not. We give in order to make something out of nothing, to make that which is not (yet) real. Again and again we give, in a never ending gesture of longing and hope, a protest against what is and a hope for what is not. That we can give is enough for us to be able to name what we still do not know, but for which we expectantly wait, the return of the Gift, when giving will be all in all.

In sum, the Christian conception of generosity connects gifting to an antieconomy of surplus, not scarcity, displacing strife and competition with sharing and mutuality. As the Lord told Paul, who was caught up in the "third heaven" of ecstasy, "My grace [*charis*] is sufficient for you" (2 Cor. 12:9): the excess that is grace/gratuity is the more that is enough, the too much that is just right. To give is to exercise a sovereign freedom to spend the gift of life. We can inhabit in gifting that dimension in which the gift is already there, restlessly circulating, no matter how it is utilized or spent, through the calculative mazes of our careful plans and agendas. The true gift replenishes itself even as it is passed along. "These are gifts which however widely they are shared by all," explains Pseudo-Dionysius in *The Divine Names*, "remain nevertheless undiminished and possess the same super-fullness. They are not lessened by being partaken. Indeed, they pour out all the more generously."[61] The gifting process is not anxious; we cannot repay the original gift of God's love, but this gift does not paralyze us with the infinite burden of gratitude. The Christian countergift is neither an excessive display of gratitude that does not affect the giver (praise) nor an equivalent exchange that satisfies the giver's demand for reimbursement (sacrifice).

Certainly, praise is an appropriate response to such gratuitous giving, but the momentum of the gift solicits a praise that leads into action, not just attitude.[62]

By giving into the ultimate priority of giving itself, we discover, by means of the rash and ardent, the irreducible givenness of the gift that has already been given before. This original foregift, a splendid insolvency that makes possible all of our subsequent giving, is forgiveness—the acceptance that releases, the holding that frees, the embrace that restores. To accept forgiveness and to forgive the other ("Forgive us our debts as we forgive our debtors") is not to receive the gift in spite of who we are (the gift as a compensation for our guilt and unworthiness) but to put into play the gift we always already are, an abundance that produces a shared debt redeemable only by repeatedly passing it along. By giving ourselves, we pledge our participation in the communion of excess that creates solidarity without constraint, a community without fixed shape, held together by the eccentric unity of an indiscriminate giving that makes room for every gift by perpetuating the power of giving itself.

Giving, in the end, is both rhetoric and act; it literally refigures exchange and accomplishes the communication of efficacy.[63] The model of giving I develop here is therefore based neither on self-punishment nor on investment. Our culture seems stuck, imagining the gift as either pain or reward; we are unable to overcome or synthesize this polarization. Certainly, giving does involve loss; it occurs through shared wounds that erase boundaries and give us a felt, tactile sense of the other. Nevertheless, self-sacrifice is a necessary but not sufficient condition for the gift, and it is definitely not the aim or criterion of effective giving. Likewise, giving does result in reward and benefit, but it is a gain that is diffuse, incalculable, even as it draws people together in a community of gratitude and further giving. Thus, the guarantee, often heard among televangelists, that equates giving with profit is deceptive and destructive. Gifting is a process that combines elements of risky and disruptive excess with anticipated and gradual mutuality in a circle (to modify Lewis Hyde's comment) that never ends where it begins but keeps spiraling outward in increasingly inclusive loops of expansion and consolidation, movement and rest. Our consolation is found in the recognition that our giving is beyond our control—indeed, that gifting itself is out of control, even as it is guided by the excesses of God: God the Giver who gives us life, God the Given who gives the self in total abandonment, and God the Giving who receives our gifts, which is also God's giving again.

Notes

Introduction

1. Walter Lowe, *Theology and Difference: The Wound of Reason* (Bloomington: Indiana University Press, 1993), p. 3.
2. Paul Piccone, "The Changing Function of Critical Theory," *New German Critique* 12 (1977): 29–37.

Chapter 1

1. For a historical overview, see Robert H. Bremner, *Giving, Charity and Philanthropy in History* (New Brunswick, N.J.: Transaction, 1994). For a survey of philosophical theories of giving, see Lester H. Hunt, "Generosity," *American Philosophical Quarterly* 12 (July 1975): 235–44. For a survey of sociological theories of gift giving, see David Cheal, *The Gift Economy* (London and New York: Routledge, 1988). Social scientists often argue that exchange is the real (and the only observable) basis of giving. They assume that balance and calculation are predicates of all relationships. For an early discussion along these lines, see Alvin Gouldner, "The Norm of Reciprocity: A Preliminary Statement," *American Sociological Review* 25 (1960): 161–78. Gouldner argues that people feel compelled to rectify the imbalance the gift giving creates. Also see the comprehensive treatment in Paul F. Camenisch, "Gift and Gratitude in Ethics," *Journal of Religious Ethics* 9 (spring 1981): 1–34. Camenisch tries to articulate gift giving as a moral relationship that establishes trust and commitment in the midst of protecting each person's autonomy: "In terms of their moral dimensions, gifts exist somewhere between windfall and contract, and gratitude somewhere between whimsy and obligation" (p. 4). In my terms, gift giving lies "somewhere between" excess and exchange.
2. Put another way, theology must deconstruct the tendency (inherent in extreme polarizations) of collapsing one term in this binary pair into the other—without synthesizing the two terms into some organic whole, compartmentalizing them in an attempt to preserve the purity of each, or replacing them with a middle or mediating term.
3. Michael Walzer, *Spheres of Justice: A Defense of Pluralism and Equality* (New York: Basic Books, 1983), pp. 123, 128.

4. Michael Ignatieff, *The Needs of Strangers* (New York: Penguin, 1985), p. 16.

5. Indeed, the language of rights seems to be, to some extent, inimical to the language of giving: "No gift can bring joy to the one who has a right to everything" (Paul Tournier, *The Meaning of Gifts,* trans. John S. Gilmour [Richmond: John Knox Press, 1970], p. 32).

6. Barry Schwartz, "The Social Psychology of the Gift," *American Journal of Sociology* 73 (1967): 1. Not only does the gift say what we want the other to think about us, but it also says what we think about the other. Schwartz perceptively points out that although sometimes the presentation of the gift coincides with a descriptive statement about the recipient, frequently we give a gift to exaggerate a worthy or conspicuous characteristic of the recipient. Further, the exchange of objects functions to support identity on both a personal and a social level. As Sut Jhally (*The Codes of Advertising* [New York: St. Martin's Press, 1982]) has argued, the exchange of objects is the way in which we communicate today, and advertising is our common discourse about such transactions. Advertising is the symbolic interpretation of the circulation of commodities that is increasingly meaningless and therefore ever in need of more interpretation. If all transactions are subjected to the symbolics of advertising, then distinguishing between gift giving and commerce is both increasingly difficult and crucial.

7. Ignatieff, *Needs of Strangers,* p. 17.

8. Susan A. Ostrander and Paul G. Schervish, "Giving and Getting: Philanthropy as a Social Relation," in *Critical Issues in Philanthropy: Strengthening Theory and Practice,* ed. Jon Van Til (San Francisco: Jossey-Bass, 1990), pp. 67–97. For a discussion of theology and the third sector, see William Dean, *The Religious Critic in American Culture* (Albany: SUNY Press, 1994), ch. 9. Dean argues that theologians should find their psychological home and develop their public voice in the third sector, since universities are increasingly devoted to professional activities that have little to do with public involvement or the common good.

9. Teresa Odendahl, *Charity Begins at Home: Generosity and Self-Interest among the Philanthropic Elite* (New York: Basic Books, 1990), p. 234.

10. Robert Wuthnow, *Acts of Compassion* (Princeton: Princeton University Press, 1991). Also see Stephen Hart, *What Does the Lord Require? How Americans Think about Economic Justice* (New York: Oxford University Press, 1992).

11. For a history of cynicism in the modern period and the argument that cynicism can be overcome only through a process of intensification and acceleration, see Peter Sloterdijk, *Critique of Cynical Reason,* trans. Michael Eldred (Minneapolis: University of Minnesota Press, 1987).

12. Wuthnow, *Acts of Compassion,* 292.

13. For a critique of the economic portrait of self-interested humanity, see Amartya K. Sen, "Rational Fools: A Critique of Behavioral Foundations of Economic Theory," in *Beyond Self-Interest,* ed. Jane J. Mansbridge (Chicago: University of Chicago Press, 1990). Sen states: "The *purely* economic man is indeed close to being a social moron" (p. 37). No matter how statisti-

cally successful the economic reduction of motivation to self-interest is, it results in an impoverished view of human nature, shortchanging our self-understandings by isolating only those factors that are easily measured and manipulated. (I am grateful to Frank Howland of Wabash College for this and several other citations related to economics.)

14. For an exploration of excess in modern culture, see Alphonso Lingis, *Excesses: Eros and Culture* (Albany: SUNY Press, 1983). Lingis celebrates the excessive, which he interprets as the expression of pure eroticism finally breaking through a phallocentric, patriarchal, and repressive past. The only common language we have today, he argues, is the language of bodily energy, the way in which energy is resisted, blocked, rechanneled, and discharged in a fusion of the sublime and the carnal. Like Freud, Lingis thinks of desire as a reservoir of pressurized energy seeking an outlet. Modern economies, both material and cultural, are organized in order to imitate, represent, and exploit this rhythm of sexual energy. While it is true that generosity has a biological dimension—how we give is related to bodily wants and needs—Lingis ironically seems dangerously close to reproducing the widespread prejudice that male sexuality is the master trope of contemporary culture. Much of Lingis's work follows the more convoluted program of Jean-François Lyotard, *Libidinal Economy,* trans. Iain Hamilton Grant (Bloomington: Indiana University Press, 1993; orig. pub. 1974).

15. Wuthnow, *Acts of Compassion,* p. 105.

16. As Charles Taylor explains, "From the very beginning of the human story religion, our link with the highest, has been recurrently associated with sacrifice, even mutilation, as though something of us has to be torn away or immolated if we are to please the gods" (*Sources of the Self: The Making of the Modern Identity* [Cambridge: Harvard University Press, 1989], p. 519).

17. See Lori D. Ginzberg, *Women and the Work of Benevolence* (New Haven: Yale University Press, 1990). For a positive reading of women and the gift, note the following: "She doesn't 'know' what she's giving, she doesn't measure it; she gives, though, neither a counterfeit impression nor something she hasn't got. She gives more, with no assurance that she'll get back even some unexpected profit from what she puts out. She gives that there may be life, thought, transformation. This is an 'economy' that can no longer be put in economic terms" (Hélène Cixous, "The Laugh of Medusa," trans. Keith Cohen and Paula Cohen, in *New French Feminisms,* ed. Elaine Marks and Isabelle de Courtivron [New York: Schocken, 1981], p. 264).

18. For the sake of logical simplicity and clarity, I have emphasized two different discourses on giving in Christianity. The reality is obviously much more complex. Garth L. Hallett (*Christian Neighbor-Love* [Washington, D.C.: Georgetown University Press, 1989]), discusses six rival norms: self-preference, parity, other preference, self-subordination, self-forgetfulness, and self-denial. The last three basically correspond to what I am calling sacrifice; the first two are complementary components of generosity. For another treatment of these

issues, see Stephen G. Post, *Christian Love and Self-Denial* (Lanham, Md.: University Press of America, 1987). Post provides historical background to my twofold distinction. What I am calling the language of generosity is rooted in the Augustinian-Thomistic tradition, which is basically an extension of Aristotle. This tradition argues that all people seek happiness, and the virtue of generosity does not fundamentally contradict that search. In fact, the Christian framework unifies self-love and the love of God because God is the ultimate source of human happiness. The alternative tradition, the language of sacrifice, argues that the only true love is pure and disinterested. This tradition is rooted in Abelard, Duns Scotus, Luther, and Eckhart. Happiness must be renounced in order to turn toward the other, whether divine or human.

19. Notice this representative comment about Christian generosity by Albert Schweitzer: "In the history of ethics there is a downright fear of what cannot be subjected to rules and regulations. Again and again thinkers have undertaken to define altruism in such a way that it remains rational. This, however, is never done except at the cost of the naturalness and living quality of ethics" ("He That Loses His Life Shall Find It," in *Moral Principles of Action: Man's Ethical Imperative*, ed. R. Anshen [New York: Harper, 1952], p. 678).

20. Note this example from St. Gregory Nazianzen's funeral eulogy for St. Basil: "Basil rendered service freely, relieving the dearth of food without drawing any profit therefrom. He had in view only one object: to win mercy by being merciful, and to acquire heavenly blessings by his distribution of grain here below" (*Funeral Orations*, trans. L. McCauley et al. [New York: Fathers of the Church, 1953], pp. 58–59). Both this and the Schweitzer quotation are from Hallett, *Christian Neighbor-Love*.

21. David Heyd, *Supererogation* (Cambridge: Cambridge University Press, 1982).

22. Gregory Mellema, *Beyond the Call of Duty: Supererogation, Obligation, and Offence* (Albany: SUNY Press, 1991).

23. Hunt, "Generosity," p. 239.

24. For a full account of Aristotle's views, see Stephen A. White, *Sovereign Virtue: Aristotle on the Relation between Happiness and Prosperity* (Stanford: Stanford University Press, 1992), ch. 4.

25. Aristotle, *Nicomachean Ethics*, trans. Martin Ostwald (New York: Macmillan, 1962), Book IV: "He [the generous man] will give to the right people, the right amount, at the right time, and do everything else that is implied in correct giving. Moreover, it will give him pleasure to do so, or (at least) no pain; for to act in conformity with virtue is pleasant or painless, but certainly not painful" (p. 84). Aristotle does distinguish between generosity and magnificence; the latter, though, is not extravagant because it is the virtue of those who have much to give. "A magnificent man is like a skilled artist: he has the capacity to observe what is suitable and to spend large sums with good taste" (p. 90). For a wonderful study of the Greek word *eleutheros*, see C. S. Lewis, *Studies in Words* (Cambridge: Cambridge University Press, 1960), ch. 5. The

word means "free," in contrast to slave. *Eleutherios* is an adjective referring to the behavior or qualities appropriate to a free person. For the Greeks, only the free person (someone who owns property and possesses a certain degree of autonomy) is capable of generosity. A similar connection appears with the Latin *liber* and *liberalis*.

26. Marcel Mauss, *The Gift*, trans. Ian Cunnison (1925; reprint, New York: Norton, 1967). Mauss (1872–1950) was Émile Durkheim's nephew and principal intellectual heir.

27. "The thing given is not inert. It is alive and often personified, and strives to bring to its original clan and homeland some equivalent to take its place" (ibid., p. 10).

28. Raymond Firth accuses Mauss of mystifying the process of exchange. He argues that gifts must be returned in Maori culture because there are social sanctions that punish, through witchcraft, the refusal of exchange. Giving in primordial cultures, then, is not spontaneous but carefully regulated. See Firth, *Economies of the New Zealand Maori*, 2nd ed. (Wellington: R. E. Owen, 1959).

29. Blake Leland, "Voodoo Economics: Sticking Pins in Eros," *Diacritics* 18 (summer 1988): 39.

30. Mauss, *The Gift*, pp. 33, 35.

31. Claude Lévi-Strauss, *The Elementary Structures of Kinship*, trans. James Harle Bell, John Richard von Sturmer, and Rodney Needham (Boston: Beacon Press, 1969), ch. 5. Lévi-Strauss actually rejects any dimension of excess in giving. He argues that modern-day gifts may appear to be excessive in order to be differentiated from exchange, but gifts function as exchange carried on by other means. Indeed, his own structuralist approach to anthropology universalizes the principle of reciprocal exchange to explain all aspects of human culture. The prohibition of incest, for example, is based on the rules of exchange, "for I will give up my daughter or my sister only on condition that my neighbour does the same" (p. 62). For Lévi-Strauss on Mauss, see his "Introduction à l'oeuvre de Marcel Mauss," in M. Mauss, *Sociologie et anthropologie* (Paris: Presses Universitaires de France, 1966).

32. Bronislaw Malinowski, *Argonauts of the Western Pacific* (London: Routledge, 1922).

33. Malinowski argues that it is the passage of objects, their durability, that gives them value: "However ugly, useless, and—according to current standards—valueless an object may be, if it has figured in historical scenes and passed through the hands of historic persons, and is therefore an unfailing vehicle of important sentimental associations, it cannot but be precious to us" (ibid., p. 89).

34. "A man who owns a thing is naturally expected to share it, to distribute it, to be its trustee and dispenser. And the higher the rank the greater the obligation" (ibid., p. 97). "Meanness, indeed, is the most despised vice, and the only thing about which the natives have strong moral views, while generosity is the essence of goodness" (ibid., p. 97).

35. Marshall Sahlins, *Stone Age Economics* (Chicago: Aldine, 1972).

36. For a critique of the lack of an adequate notion of satisfaction (and thus joy) in both modern economic theory and behavior, see Tibor Scitovsky, *The Joyless Economy: An Inquiry into Human Satisfaction and Consumer Dissatisfaction* (New York: Oxford University Press, 1976).

37. Sahlins, *Stone Age Economics*, p. 37.

38. For the argument that scarcity is axiomatic, see Jean-Paul Sartre, *Critique of Dialectical Reason*, trans. Alan Sheridan-Smith (London: NLB, 1970), ch. 3. Scarcity is what makes history possible. It is the essence of humanity's relation to the environment.

39. For the classic study, see David M. Potter, *People of Plenty: Economic Abundance and the American Character* (Chicago: University of Chicago Press, 1954). Also see Kenneth Boulding et al., *From Abundance to Scarcity: Implications for the American Tradition* (Columbus: Ohio State University Press, 1978).

40. Pierre Bourdieu, *Outline of a Theory of Practice*, trans. Richard Nice (Cambridge: Cambridge University Press, 1977).

41. Richard M. Titmus, *The Gift Relationship* (London: George Allen and Unwin, 1970).

42. Kenneth J. Arrow, "Gifts and Exchange," *Philosophy and Public Affairs* 1 (summer 1972): 360. This essay also challenges the empirical data and assumptions of Titmus's work.

43. Lewis Hyde, *The Gift: Imagination and the Erotic Life of Property* (New York: Vintage, 1979), p. xi.

44. Leland, "Voodoo Economics," p. 40.

Chapter 2

1. It is also interesting that the noun *thank* originally meant "thought"; to thank meant to think well of somebody or something, to have good will or gratitude. Thinking and thanking are both responses to something that is given. See the relevant entries in John Ayto, *Dictionary of Word Origins* (New York: Arcade, 1990).

2. For a discussion of this Latin phrase as illuminating one possible origin of sacrificial rituals, see G. van der Leeuw, *Religion in Essence and Manifestation*, trans. J. E. Turner (New York: Harper & Row, 1963), 2:350–60. I have been influenced by van der Leeuw's connection of giving and community: "For the principal feature is not that someone or other should receive something, but that the stream of life should continue to flow. From this point of view, therefore, not only are gift and communion sacrifices not antitheses but, still further, the sacrifice is transplanted into the very midst of life itself. It is no *opus supererogatorium*, but the working power of life itself. And thus instead of the rationalistic *do-ut-des*, we must say: *do ut possis dare*—'I give in order that thou mayest be able to give': I give thee power that thou mayest have power, and that life may not stagnate because of any lack of potency" (p. 354). Van der Leeuw locates generosity in the organic fecundity of life itself.

3. For a careful analytic overview, see Terrance McConnell, *Gratitude* (Philadelphia: Temple University Press, 1993). Also see Fred Berger, "Gratitude," *Ethics* 85 (1974–75): 298–309.

4. From Streng's introduction to *Spoken and Unspoken Thanks: Some Comparative Soundings,* ed. John B. Carmen and Frederick J. Streng (Harvard: Center for the Study of World Religions, 1989), p. 5.

5. Indeed, Kant in *Lectures on Ethics* (trans. Louis Infield and ed. Lewis White Beck [New York: Harper & Row, 1963]), describes ingratitude as one of the three vices that "are the essence of vileness and wickedness" (p. 218). "It is inhuman to hate and persecute one from whom we have reaped a benefit, and if such conduct were the rule it would cause untold harm. Men would then be afraid to do good to anyone lest they should receive evil in return for their good" (p. 219). Kant is here worried about the social consequences of ingratitude. He admits that noble-minded men might "refuse to accept favors in order not to put themselves under an obligation" (p. 218).

6. Arjun Appadurai, "Gratitude in a Social Mode in South India," in Carmen and Streng, *Spoken and Unspoken Thanks,* p. 14.

7. Notice the wishful thinking of Paul Tournier on this point: "The best businessmen, those who illustrate most truly the business mind, are men who like to give, who like to please the customer. They always feel as if they were bestowing a gift with their merchandise, adding again a kind word and a beautiful smile. They also feel that they are recipients of a gift when people pay them" (*The Meaning of Gifts,* trans. John S. Gilmour [Richmond: John Knox Press, 1970], p. 32). What he gets at is the way in which the marketplace uses the accoutrements of giving in order to better sell exchange.

8. See Gilbert C. Meilaender, *The Theory and Practice of Virtue* (Notre Dame, Ind.: University of Notre Dame Press, 1984), p. 164.

9. From Kurt H. Wolff, ed., *The Sociology of Georg Simmel* (New York: Free Press, 1950), p. 387. Simmel (1858–1918) taught sociology and philosophy at the University of Berlin for most of his life. Although lesser known than some of his contemporaries, his work can be compared to that of Weber and Durkheim. For a fuller expression of his views on the philosophy of economics, see his *The Philosophy of Money,* ed. David Frisby, trans. Tom Bottomore and David Frisby (New York: Routledge, 1990).

10. On the relationship between gratitude and political loyalty, see A. D. M. Walker, "Political Obligation and the Argument from Gratitude," *Philosophy and Public Affairs* 17 (summer 1988): 191–211. Walker observes, "The argument from gratitude has never enjoyed philosophical popularity" (p. 192).

11. For a wonderful analysis of sullenness, see Albert Borgmann, *Crossing the Postmodern Divide* (Chicago: University of Chicago Press, 1992), pp. 6–12.

12. For a full examination of this relationship, see George J. Stack, *Nietzsche and Emerson: An Elective Affinity* (Athens: Ohio University Press, 1992). Stack does not systematically compare these two thinkers on gift giving, but he does make other relevant comparisons. See especially pp. 280–87 and 333–35.

13. Harold Bloom, *Agon: Towards a Theory of Revisionism* (New York: Oxford University Press, 1982), p. 145. This claim is repeated in Bloom's *The American Religion* (New York: Touchstone, 1992).

14. Ralph Waldo Emerson, *Essays: First and Second Series*, intro. Douglas Crase (New York: Vintage, 1990), p. 241.

15. See, for example, Michael T. Gilmore, *American Romanticism and the Marketplace* (Chicago: University of Chicago Press, 1985), pp. 18–34.

16. Cornel West, *The American Evasion of Philosophy: A Genealogy of Pragmatism* (Madison: University of Wisconsin Press, 1989), p. 27.

17. Emerson, *Essays*, p. 184.

18. Friedrich Nietzsche, *Ecce Homo*, trans. R. J. Hollingdale (New York: Penguin, 1979), p. 35.

19. For a reading of Nietzsche as a hyperbolic author that sheds much light on this trope, see Bernd Magnus, Stanley Stewart and Jean-Pierre Mileur, *Nietzsche's Case* (New York: Routledge, 1993): "Hyperbole is, of course, inflated language, and since what goes up must come down, it follows from this, deflated language as well. But hyperbole is not just the language of heights aspired to and depths fallen to, it is also the language of detours, of errancy, extravagance, and even errantry" (p. 139). For my own connection of hyperbole and Nietzsche, see Webb, *Re-Figuring Theology: The Rhetoric of Karl Barth* (Albany: SUNY Press, 1991), ch. 4. For a warning about Nietzsche's hyperbole, note this comment by Alan White: "Even the Nietzscheans among us — as opposed to the Nazis and fascists — must avoid the rhetorical excesses of Nietzschean thunder and fireworks: we have seen, as Nietzsche had not, how dangerous they can be" (*Nietzsche's Labyrinth* [New York: Routledge, 1990], p. 6).

20. Henry Staten, *Nietzsche's Voice* (Ithaca, N.Y.: Cornell University Press, 1990), p. 34. Staten's book isolates the libidinal economy of Nietzsche's works, the dialectic between logic and libido that drives Nietzsche's rhetoric in often contradictory ways.

21. Friedrich Nietzsche, *Thus Spoke Zarathustra*, trans. Walter Kaufmann (New York: Penguin, 1978), p. 10. I have kept Nietzsche's language, as well as some of my commentary, male specific because I think that his account of generosity reflects a masculine perspective. Nietzsche thought that philosophers and theologians were "castrated" (*beschnitten*, which can also mean circumcised), that is, feminine, and much of his critique of Christian generosity is an attempt to return giving to a masculine sphere. To give for another without a calculated plan for a richer return is to act like a woman, Nietzsche thought. The Christian understanding of sacrifice is essentially feminine because such giving seeks to create life, while squandering, an infertile, irresponsible, and wasteful act, is the provenance of the male.

22. See, for example, the way Derrida plays with the ambiguity of the word *pharmakon* in Plato's *Phaedrus*, a word that can mean both remedy and poison, in *Dissemination*, trans. Barbara Johnson (Chicago: University of Chicago Press, 1981).

23. Nietzsche, *Zarathustra*, p. 57.

24. Compare to Paul Tournier's observation: "Generally speaking, those who do not enjoy giving are those who are unsure of themselves. They are always afraid lest their choice will not be appreciated. They are afraid of being reproached for too little originality or else for too great familiarity. Such hesitations turn gift giving into a burden and betray the failure in affirming oneself, the lack of courage in being oneself" (*Meaning of Gifts*, p. 42).

25. Nietzsche, *Zarathustra*, p. 62.

26. Zarathustra's relationship to his disciples is illustrative of his theory of giving. As Gary Shapiro notes, "Is this not also a squandering of his disciples, a willingness to let them be dispersed and disseminated rather than identified as his intellectual property?" *Alcyone: Nietzsche on Gifts, Noise, and Women* (Albany: SUNY Press, 1991), p. 36. Shapiro also observes the enclosed circuitry of Nietzsche's giving: "One way in which one could be both giver and receiver, sun and darkest night, would be to give to oneself" (p. 38).

27. Nietzsche, *Zarathustra*, p. 74.

28. Staten, *Nietzsche's Voice*, p. 12.

29. In opposition to my line of argument, Leslie Paul Thiele interprets Dionysian excess in terms of a mystical kind of ecstasy: "In the Dionysian feast man loses his sense of identity, entering into the mystical frenzy wherein the distinction between creator and created, pain and ecstasy, man and man, disappears" (*Friedrich Nietzsche and the Politics of the Soul: A Study of Heroic Individualism* [Princeton: Princeton University Press, 1990], p. 140). "This transformation of suffering and strife into affirmation, into an experience of the holy, is the foundation of Nietzsche's piety and his self-projection as saint" (p. 142).

30. Nietzsche, *Zarathustra*, p. 264.

31. Some of Nietzsche's most explicit comments about the cost of squandering are contained in his notes posthumously gathered and organized in *The Will to Power*, trans. Walter Kaufmann and R. J. Hollingdale (New York: Vintage, 1968). First, he criticizes Christianity for exaggerating the self-control necessary for expenditure: "In fact, the Christian proves himself to be an exaggerated form of self-control; in order to restrain his desires he seems to find it necessary to extirpate or crucify them" (p. 132). Then he blames Christianity for promoting solidarity: "What is 'virtue' and 'charity' in Christianity if not just this mutual preservation, this solidarity of the weak, this hampering of selection? What is Christian altruism if not the mass-egoism of the weak, which divines that if all care for one another each individual will be preserved as long as possible?" (p. 142). By contrast, Nietzsche argues that "genuine charity demands sacrifice for the good of the species" (p. 142). Nietzsche is transforming classical economic theory into supply-side ethics. For a true profit, there must be a loss. Moreover, wealth or power inevitably tends to accumulate in hierarchical and concentrated patterns. If the wealth is redistributed—if the power is leveled flat by an allocation based on Christian principles—then the species has lost its pyramidal shape, and without a point of convergence it cannot penetrate the future and

move forward. Nietzsche can also praise efficiency as an end in itself: "That which constitutes growth in life is an ever more thrifty and more far-seeing economy, which achieves more and more with less and less force—as an ideal, the principle of the smallest expenditure" (p. 341).

32. Staten, *Nietzsche's Voice*, p. 42.

33. For a similar criticism of Nietzsche, note this comment: "My reading is constrained by the observation that Nietzsche evaluated culture, nations, and epochs in terms of their 'highest' products, an evaluation that allows the misery of many not to be entered into the ledger, but one that counts only the items of greatest value. This seems to me to be wrong, and hence I am not a Nietzschean" (Robert John Ackermann, *Nietzsche: A Frenzied Look* [Amherst: University of Massachusetts Press, 1990], p. xi). As Staten argues, "the grand economy is not afraid to squander, and what it squanders is individuals" (p. 11).

34. As Staten (*Nietzsche's Voice*) argues: "Nietzsche thus takes cover from the vast, senseless, irrecuperable squandering of the grand economy in the image of the vast, well-formed, self-augmenting squandering of the great men" (p. 138). Moreover, "the orgasm of the great man is not into the future, not an emptying of the self outward but a kind of self-consumption, a using up of the accumulation from the past for which others have been sacrificed, countless others, so that all they accumulated is now his, he is the terminus, the grand conclusion" (p. 144). The genius alone bestows meaning to life; all others are instruments of his will.

35. For a survey of theories of giving in contemporary philosophy, see Julian Pefanis, *Heterology and the Postmodern* (Durham, N.C.: Duke University Press, 1991).

36. For my reading of Bataille, see *Blessed Excess: Religion and the Hyperbolic Imagination* (Albany: SUNY Press, 1993), ch. 3. For Bataille's own work, see *Erotism, Death and Sensuality*, trans. Mary Dalwood (San Francisco: City Lights, 1986). For Bataille's homage to Nietzsche, see his *On Nietzsche*, trans. Bruce Boone, intro. Sylvere Lotringer (New York: Paragon House, 1992). For an analysis of the politics of excess that Bataille develops in his fiction, see Leo Bersani, *The Culture of Redemption* (Cambridge: Harvard University Press, 1990). For comprehensive commentary, see Michele H. Richman, *Reading Georges Bataille: Beyond the Gift* (Baltimore: Johns Hopkins University Press, 1982). Richman explains that Bataille is trying to recover excess from modern attempts at compartmentalization: "The forms of *dépense* are neutralized within the sanctioned grace period of adolescence, conceived as a rite of passage between the childhood and adulthood when sexual energies are sufficiently squandered such that the adult, equated with the worker, will be more willing to assume the necessity of entering a work force dedicated to production and accumulation" (p. 34). Although Bataille celebrates the death of God, he is not an easygoing atheist. The elimination of the absolute outer limit collapses and obliterates the notion of subjectivity, which must always be correlated to something objective. The result is an interior experience of infinite depth, a vertigo of possible

impossibilities in which something like mysticism results from the fall of the self into the void. God's death is a catastrophic withdrawal, which we can restore by venturing into and surpassing this empty space. Richman notes "the disturbing persistence of a Christian terminology" in Bataille's vision of excess (p. 110).

37. Norman O. Brown, *Life against Death* (New York: Vintage, 1959), especially parts 5 and 6. Also see Brown's *Love's Body* (Berkeley: University of California Press, 1966). For Brown's acknowledgment of his debt to Bataille, see *Apocalypse and/or Metamorphosis* (Berkeley: University of California Press, 1991): "In Bataille's Heraclitean vision we are suffering not from some repressed longing for death but from excess of life – the Dionysian principle of excess, Blake's principle of exuberance. . . . There is a built-in need for toomuchness, for flamboyance (flaming), for exaggeration" (p. 183). Brown also notes Bataille's roots in Christianity: "Bataille himself could never free himself from the need for Christian pedagogy toward the sado-masochistic truth, the Suffering Servant" (p. 198).

38. Staten, *Nietzsche's Voice*, p. 107.

39. Jean-Paul Sartre, in *Being and Nothingness* (trans. Hazel E. Barnes [New York: Philosophical Library, 1956]), develops a phenomenological portrait of the kind of giving that I sense in Nietzsche: "The craze for giving which sometimes seizes certain people is first and foremost a craze to destroy; it is equivalent to an attitude of madness, a 'love' which accompanies the shattering objects. But the craze to destroy which is at the bottom of generosity is nothing else than a craze to possess. All which I abandon, all which I give, I enjoy in a higher manner through the fact that I give it away; giving is a keen, brief enjoyment, almost sexual. . . . But at the same time the gift casts a spell over the recipient; it obliges him to recreate, to maintain in being by a continuous creation this bit of myself which I no longer want, which I have just possessed up to its annihilation, and which finally remains only as an image. To give is to enslave" (p. 594).

40. For example, see Jacques Derrida, *Glas*, trans. John P. Leavey Jr. and Richard Rand (Lincoln: University of Nebraska Press, 1986), pp. 242–45. "But when *someone* gives *something* to *someone*, one is already long within calculating dialectics and speculative idealization" (p. 243). For Derrida's most positive account of the gift, see "Women in the Beehive: A Seminar with Jacques Derrida" in *Men in Feminism*, ed. Alice Jardine and Paul Smith (New York: Methuen, 1987). Here Derrida argues that the gift creates difference, not opposition; the subversive and free-floating nature of the gift could serve as a model for a new sexuality, with the emphasis on undecidability, plurality, and multiplicity. But Derrida also continues, in this seminar, the theme that gift giving is possibly impossible. There is no guarantee that a gift has ever really been given. The gift is thus related more to chance than intentionality. Note some other fascinating passages: "Just as there is no such thing then as Being or an essence of *the* woman or the sexual difference, there is also no such thing as an essence of the *es gibt* in the *es gibt Sein*, that is, of Being's giving and gift" (*Spurs, Nietzsche's Styles*, trans. Barbara Harlow [Chicago: University of Chicago Press,

1978], p. 121). "A text, I believe, does not come back. I have insisted a lot on this theme, and I am doing it once more: I have tried to write texts that don't return and don't allow for retranslation" ("Roundtable on Translation," trans. Peggy Kamuf, in *The Ear of the Other*, ed. Christie McDonald [Lincoln: University of Nebraska Press, 1988], p. 157). "Needless to say, these unthoughts may well be mine and mine alone. And what would be more serious, more drily serious, they may well *give* nothing" (*Of Spirit, Heidegger and the Question*, [trans. Geoffrey Bennington and Rachel Bowlby [Chicago: University of Chicago Press, 1989], p. 13). Derrida also talks about "knowing whether *to give* is something other than *to waste*— that is, whether 'to give one's life by sharing it' is in sum something other than 'wasting one's time.' Wasting one's time would amount to wasting the only good of which one has the *right* to be avaricious and jealous, the unique and property itself, the unique property that 'one would take pride in guarding jealously.' What is therefore in question is to think the very principle of jealousy as the primitive passion for property and as the concern for the proper, for the proper possibility, in question for everyone, of his existence" (*Aporias*, trans. Thomas Dutoit [Stanford: Stanford University Press, 1993], p. 3). Finally, in his most recent work on giving, he connects giving to secrecy, responsibility, and death: "Secrecy is the last word of the gift which is the last word of the secret" (*The Gift of Death*, trans. David Wills [Chicago: University of Chicago Press, 1995], p. 30). The gift from the other that makes us responsible also announces our own singularity, and thus the gift is in the end our acknowledgment of our death, which we must give to ourselves (that is, following Heidegger, no one can die for us). "On what condition does goodness exist beyond all calculation? On the condition that goodness forget itself, that the movement be a movement of the gift that renounces itself, hence a movement of infinite love. Only infinite love can renounce itself and, in order to *become finite*, become incarnated in order to love the other, to love the other as a finite other. This gift of infinite love comes from someone and is addressed to someone; responsibility demands irreplaceable singularity. Yet only death or rather the apprehension of death can give this irreplaceability" (pp. 50–51).

41. Jacques Derrida, *Given Time: 1. Counterfeit Money*, trans. Peggy Kamuf (Chicago: University of Chicago Press, 1992).

42. Note this remarkable comment: "It is necessary to be forgiven for appearing to give" (Derrida, *Memoires, for Paul de Man*, trans. Cecile Lindsay, Jonathan Culler, and Eduardo Cadava [New York: Columbia University Press, 1986], p. 149). If forgiveness is an assurance freely given, then it is hard to know how forgiveness could be given to one who appears to give, without leading to an infinite regression of forgiveness.

43. Derrida, *Given Time*, p. 14.

44. He plays with (subverts or suspends?) this possibility in a brilliant reading in *Given Time* of a story of gift giving, Baudelaire's tale "La fausse monnaie" ("Counterfeit Money").

45. Derrida's comments about silence are suggestive. Think of the ways in which some religious traditions, like Quakers or Trappists, use silence in excessive ways in order to interrupt the demands for explanation and reciprocation. To enter into silence is to leave behind the give and take of conversation and to join a communal space where what is given is received without the need for counting and balancing. Put simply, silence suggests that all questions do not need to be answered. In this way, it could be argued that silence is to conversation as the gift is to exchange. To pause in silence before the gift is not to ignore it but to give it the only response that can be given in kind. Nevertheless, silence is only possible for those who speak, just as giving gains its power in contrast to exchange. The silence appropriate to giving should empower new modes of communication, rather than appear as an end for its own sake. In the end, if we cannot say anything appropriate to the gift, then Derrida is right in implying that the gift cannot even be given, that the gift must be ignored or denied (which are very different reactions from silence) in order to be received.

46. Derrida, *Given Time*, p. 119.

47. What Derrida most attends to in Mauss is his confusion of the two dimensions of excess and reciprocity: "On the one hand, Mauss reminds us that there is no gift without bond, without obligation or ligature; but on the other hand, there is no gift that does not have to untie itself from obligation, from debt, contract, exchange, and thus from the bond" (ibid., p. 27).

48. Derrida, *Given Time*, p. 63.

49. For Martin Heidegger's most powerful statement on Being as giving, note the following: "To think Being itself explicitly requires disregarding Being to the extent that it is only grounded and interpreted in terms of beings and for beings as their ground, as in all metaphysics. To think Being explicitly requires us to relinquish Being as the ground of beings in favor of the giving which prevails concealed in unconcealment, that is, in favor of the It gives. As the gift of this It gives, Being belongs to giving" (*On Time and Being*, trans. Joan Stambaugh [San Francisco: Harper & Row, 1972], p. 6). Thinking is thus a form of thanking. For the relationship between Heidegger's gift of Being and the Christian notion of love, see John Macquarrie, *Heidegger and Christianity* (New York: Continuum, 1994), pp. 98–100. Also see the insightful commentary by John Milbank, "Can a Gift Be Given? Prolegomena to a Future Trinitarian Metaphysic," in *Rethinking Metaphysics*, ed. L. Gregory Jones and Stephen E. Fowl (Cambridge: Blackwell, 1995), pp. 119–61.

50. Derrida, *Given Time*, p. 24.

51. Gary Shapiro contrasts Heidegger's nostalgic longing for authentic gift giving with Nietzsche's embrace of squandering: "There perhaps is a desire here to preserve the authenticity and distance of such thinking from a vulgarized culture of the market. But might Heidegger have concluded too hastily that all economies, whether in the common or metaphysical sense, must be founded on the alienation of goods and the conventions of private property? If that is so, it might help to account for the common feeling that there is

something vague and empty in Heidegger's talk of *es gibt*. This giving in which there is no subject, no circulation, and no articulation of a structure in which gifts might be exchanged comes to appear as a determined flight from the modern market. If Heidegger sometimes opposed to the world of commodified exchange a certain appeal to preindustrial conditions of peasant agriculture and handicraft, we could ask why his range of cultural options is so narrow, and why the peasant life on the land that he evokes is still implicitly committed to an economy of private ownership" (*Alcyone*, p. 6).

52. See Susan A. Handelman, *Fragments of Redemption: Jewish Thought and Literary Theory in Benjamin, Scholem, and Levinas* (Bloomington: Indiana University Press, 1991).

53. Emmanuel Levinas, *Totality and Infinity*, trans. Alphonso Lingis (Pittsburgh: Duquesne University Press, 1969). For Derrida, the other who begins generosity is the beggar, who requests our giving in direct, immediate ways. "The beggar represents a purely receptive, expending, and consuming agency, an *apparently* useless mouth. One must indeed say, as always, apparently, for in fact he can play a role of symbolic mediation in a sacrificial structure and thereby assure an indispensable efficacity" (Derrida, *Given Time*, p. 134).

54. For a reading of Levinas's use of hyperbole in his conception of the height of the other, see Paul Ricoeur, *Oneself as Another*, trans. Kathleen Blamey (Chicago: University of Chicago Press, 1992), pp. 335–41. In Levinas's other great work, *Otherwise Than Being, or Beyond Essence*, trans. Alphonso Lingis (The Hague: Martinus Nijhoff, 1981), the hyperbolic proclamation of otherness is intensified. He equates the metaphysical quest for essence with "interest" in the fullest sense of that word, where "nothing is gratuitous" (p. 5). In contrast to metaphysics, he defends what he calls "saying," a sensuous and disinterested reception of the other that precedes the thematization of the "said." The result is a "sacrifice without reserve" (p. 15), "a hyperbolic passivity" (p. 49) in which "the debt [to the other] increases in the measures that it is paid" (p. 12). Subjectivity is comprised of radical vulnerability and exposure, "a passivity more passive still than the passivity of matter" (p. 180). I must be willing to substitute myself for the other (to die the other's death, in contrast to Heidegger), even to the point of giving the bread out of my own mouth. The language of verticality continues in this book, even though Levinas now emphasizes proximity as well: "Height is heaven. The kingdom of heaven is ethical. This hyperbole, this excellence, is but the for-the-other in its interestedness" (p. 183). For Levinas, the good literally does not count, in the sense that it does not calculate, and thus it is not valued by the interests of this world: "Freedom in the genuine sense can be only a contestation of this book-keeping by a gratuity" (p. 125), "the gratuity of sacrifice" (p. 120).

55. Derrida, *Given Time*, p. 30.

56. Jacques Derrida, "At This Very Moment in This Work Here I Am," trans. Ruben Berezdivin, in *Re-Reading Levinas*, ed. Robert Bernasconi and Simon Critchley (Bloomington: Indiana University Press, 1991), p. 13.

57. Simon Critchley, *The Ethics of Deconstruction: Derrida and Levinas* (Oxford: Blackwell, 1992), p. 137.

58. Derrida, *Given Time*, pp. 80–81.

59. "One must give without knowing, without knowledge or recognition, without *thanks [remerciement]:* without anything, or at least without any object." Derrida, *The Gift of Death*, p. 112.

60. For Derrida's commentary on this and other passages from Matthew, see ch. 4 of *The Gift of Death*. He suggests that the economy of abundance (grace) is not only bought by God's promise of heavenly treasure ("Through the law of the father economy reappropriates the *an*economy of the gift as the gift of life or, what amounts to the same thing, a gift of death" [p. 97]) but also inevitably divides the world into two groups, those with whom the believer shares this surplus and those who remain outside the economy the surplus creates, thus limiting the very responsibility such giving was meant to initiate. In the last chapter I talk about the church as the site of God's giving, a location that is not self-enclosed but rather expansive, mobile and fluid, thus capable of receiving grace but also giving beyond the limits that necessarily circumscribe our sense of responsibility and duty. The question is: Can we return a gift indirectly, by giving to others as a way of being responsible for what was given to us?

61. Derrida, *Given Time*, p. 91.

62. Derrida is trying to give us something new concerning gift giving, but how that newness can be sustained is a difficult question. When deconstruction becomes an *ism*— that is, when it is repeated and systematized—the event Derrida stages loses its novelty. One of the thrills of reading Derrida is in being surprised (and to the extent that a real surprise is not what one expected, reading Derrida is also frustrating), but can we keep surprising each other in deconstructive improvisations if we are all expecting nothing but surprise? Can surprise be repeated? The question of the repetition of the gift is the question of community, and I address that in some detail at the end of chapter 4.

63. Derrida, *Given Time*, p. 137. "But an infinite calculation supersedes the finite calculating that has been renounced. God the Father, who sees in secret, will pay back your salary, and on an infinitely greater scale" (*Gift of Death*, p. 107).

64. Derrida, *Given Time*, p. 30.

Chapter 3

1. In the conclusion to John Carman and Frederick J. Streng, eds., *Spoken and Unspoken Thanks* (Cambridge: Harvard, Center for the Study of World Religions, 1989), Carman distinguishes several types of giving in the world religions. In the Hindu temple, the cycle of gifts between the gods and people sustains the workings of the universe. Gift exchange is the primary form of worship; reciprocity is the most basic attitude one can have toward the divine. Gift giving is the language in which the gods and humans speak to each other. In opposition to this form of dualism are the monistic religions like Buddhism or

some forms of Hinduism in which the divine and the human are so closely connected that gift giving no longer makes sense. Giving becomes a metaphor for the way in which we should recognize the unity of all things; the actual practice of giving is itself illusory. What I want to do is to heighten the sense of reciprocity that already exists in Christian teaching about God without reducing that relationship to a strict form of exchange. Christianity teaches that God is involved in our givings—but as the excessive initiator of all that we are able to give and thus not according to the rules of exchange. Christian teaching also cannot accept the idea that giving is illusory; giving is really possible because it is the way in which we can best relate to others as well as to God, as manifest in God's ultimate giving in Jesus Christ.

2. *Economy* is the traditional theological term that integrates the diverse and complex ways in which God is involved in the world. For Irenaeus, for example, creation, fall, redemption, and eschatology all form an interrelated whole, demonstrating God's consistent and yet rich participation in history. For the development of this term by the Cappadocians, see Jaroslav Pelikan, *Christianity and Classical Culture* (New Haven: Yale University Press, 1993), ch. 17. For a general discussion of the use of this term in theology, see Colin E. Gunton, *The One, the Three and the Many* (Cambridge: Cambridge University Press, 1993), pp. 157–62. My intention is to portray God's "economy" while criticizing economic (in the modern sense of that term) interpretations of the divine.

3. Geoffrey Wainwright, *Doxology: The Praise of God in Worship, Doctrine, and Life* (New York: Oxford University Press, 1980), p. 27. For a similar analysis that emphasizes the exuberance of praise and the way in which excess is contagious, see Daniel Hardy and David Ford, *Praising and Knowing God* (Philadelphia: Westminster, 1985).

4. Langdon Gilkey, *Maker of Heaven and Earth: The Christian Doctrine of Creation in the Light of Modern Knowledge* (1959; reprint, Lanham, Md.: University Press of America, 1985).

5. Augustine, for example, defends the voluntary nature of creation in opposition to the argument that creation is necessary and therefore eternal. His problem is how to resolve the difficulty of relating the constancy of God's eternity to the novelty of the creative act. How can creation, which is a specific act in time, occur in God at one time but not another, if God is always doing what God always does? In his haste to deny any change in God, as well as to affirm God's independence from need or want, Augustine is forced to dwell on the superfluity of creation: "In this way perhaps he shows, in a wonderful manner, to those who can see such things, that he did not stand in need of his creation, but produced his creatures out of pure disinterested goodness, since he had continued in no less felicity without them from all eternity without beginning" (*City of God*, trans. Henry Bettenson [New York: Penguin, 1972], p. 496 [XII, 18]). Although propagation is a duty, divinely commanded, for humans, God seems to propagate only mysteriously, arbitrarily, with reticence and even reluctance.

6. For a historical survey of the development of the theme of plenitude in Western thought, see Arthur O. Lovejoy, *The Great Chain of Being* (Cambridge: Harvard University Press, 1964). The idea of a fecund, overflowing God is in stark contrast to the idea of the self-sufficiency of God. Although I am drawn to Neoplatonic images of emanation, this position is not easy to reconcile with the idea of God's freedom. Moreover, the principle of plenitude states that the world of ideas is exhaustively manifested in the world as we know it; if every level and kind of being is good, to the extent that it partakes of existence, and if God naturally wills the good into being, then all possible types of being exist out of necessity. As Lovejoy points out, this position is easily conflated with the optimistic theodicy that this world is the best of all possible worlds; that is, that all things are good because they are necessary constituents of a good whole.

7. E. L. Mascall, *He Who Is,* quoted in Paul S. Fiddes, *The Creative Suffering of God* (Oxford: Clarendon, 1988), p. 65. Fiddes quotes one theologian, Keith Ward in *Holding Fast to God,* who takes the traditional relationship between transcendence and giving to an unfortunate extreme: "God on his own cannot be self-giving love; for there is nothing to give himself to" (p. 102). Many theologians try to make giving an inessential or contingent attribute of God because otherwise God and the world appear to be codependent. If God must give, then the world must exist in order for God to have something to give to. The problem is that God's involvement in the world is then separated from God's eternal being; the former is revealed in the Bible, and the latter is accessible only by metaphysics. I agree with Fiddes that such codependency, correctly conceived, does not threaten the initiative or the primacy of God's giving, but it does mean abandoning the doctrine of ex nihilo (see Fiddes, pp. 75–76).

8. Quoted in Fiddes, *Creative Suffering of God,* p. 86.

9. From the Proslogion, in *A Scholastic Miscellany,* ed. and trans. Eugene R. Fairweather (Philadelphia: Westminster, 1956), pp. 77–78.

10. For this position from Thomas Aquinas, see the *Summa Theologiae,* I, Q. 19, Art. 10. As a contemporary Thomist puts it, "Creation means the free origination of all from the one God, who gains nothing thereby." David B. Burrell, *Freedom and Creation in Three Traditions* (Notre Dame, Ind.: University of Notre Dame Press, 1993), p. 8.

11. Notice Kant's argument that we cannot give God gratitude because God's giving, according to the traditional notion, does not involve suffering: "We can only establish the degree of good-will in terms of the obstacles it has to surmount. In consequence we cannot comprehend the love and goodness of a being for whom there are no obstacles. If God has been good to me, I am liable to think that after all it has cost God no trouble, and that gratitude to God would be mere fawning on my part." Kant concludes that it is easier, therefore, to fear than to love God. See *Lectures on Ethics,* trans. Louis Infield and ed. Lewis White Beck (New York: Harper & Row, 1963), p. 221.

12. For the argument that the Qur'an promotes the idea that God is thankful, or *Shakara,* see Lamin Sanneh, "Thanksgiving in the Qur'an: The Outlines

of a Theme," in Carman and Streng, *Spoken and Unspoken Thanks*. Thankfulness in Islam is primarily a divine attribute, one of the names by which God is known and acknowledged: "As such it describes in God an attitude by which human beings also may be distinguished. Such a bold assertion brings God and human beings within mutual range, and that significantly moderates any doctrine of stern transcendence" (p. 138). Islamic theologians have also emphasized God's transcendence by denying God's need for any human countergift; in some interpretations of the Qur'an, it is argued that God does not need our thanks but is grateful to us only for our own good. See Muzammil H. Siddiq, "Thankfulness in Islamic Thought," also in Carman and Streng, *Spoken and Unspoken Thanks*.

13. I do not mean to suggest that Christianity can solve the polarization of excess and exchange simply by offering a threefold rather than twofold account of generosity. Doctrines of God that include the Trinity can still emphasize one pole (excess or exchange) over the other. The number 3 does not solve any problems, because it still depends on how each member of the Trinity is understood to operate. All three persons of the Trinity, I am arguing, are involved in the full range of giving, exemplifying both excess and reciprocity, even though each person plays a special role in the process as a whole. Too often the Trinity is used to restrict giving to the Godhead, making generosity eternal, unchanging, and self-enclosed. I am suggesting that giving constitutes the complexity as well as the divinity of God; the creativity of excess makes God who God is. God's identity, then, will be eschatologically consummated in the return of the gift, which cannot occur without our participation.

14. For a discussion of the use of Wittgenstein's notion of rules in theology, see Kathryn Tanner, *God and Creation in Christian Theology* (Oxford: Basil Blackwell, 1988), ch. 1, and George Lindbeck, *The Nature of Doctrine* (Philadelphia: Westminster, 1984).

15. Brian A. Gerrish, *Grace and Gratitude: The Eucharistic Theology of John Calvin* (Minneapolis: Fortress, 1993). For a recent constructive summary of the Reformed position on God's grace as gift giving, see John H. Leith, *Basic Christian Doctrine* (Louisville: Westminster/John Knox Press, 1993), chs. 5 and 17.

16. Gerrish, *Grace and Gratitude*, p. 31.

17. Gerrish notes that Calvin uses *gratia* to denote both God's favor and God's gifts. In the former sense, it is linked with *gratitus* (free) and *gratis* (for nothing) and thus connected to forgiveness. God's favor is thus the free gift of Christ (see ibid., p. 69, n. 83).

18. Gerrish refers to a passage from Luther that concisely states the reformers' disagreements with medieval piety: "When we ought to be grateful for benefits received, we come arrogantly to give that which we ought to take. With unheard-of perversity we mock the mercy of the giver by giving as a work the thing we receive as a gift, so that the testator, instead of being a dispenser of his own goods, becomes the recipient of ours. Woe to such sacrilege!" (*The*

Babylonian Captivity of the Church, trans. A. T. W. Steinhauser, revised by Frederick C. Ahrens and Abdel Ross Wentz, in *Three Treatises* [Philadelphia: Fortress, 1970], p. 167; quoted in Gerrish, p. 147). For a discussion of how Luther separates grace (the external, transcendent imputation of righteousness that is the product purely of God's forensic judgment) from gifts (of which there are two kinds: common gifts given to all, but not appreciated except from the perspective of faith, and the special gifts of the Holy Spirit, which, in contrast to grace, belong to the Christian and are the mechanism of sanctification), see Kyle A. Pasewark, *A Theology of Power: Being beyond Domination* (Minneapolis: Fortress, 1993), ch. 3.

19. Gerrish, *Grace and Gratitude,* p. 155.

20. Dom Gregory Dix, *The Shape of the Liturgy* (Westminster: Dacre Press, 1945), pp. xviii–xix, quoted in Gerrish, *Grace and Gratitude,* p. 50.

21. Calvin, *Institutes of the Christian Religion,* ed. John T. McNeill and trans. Ford Lewis Battles (Philadelphia: Westminster, 1960), 1:772, quoted in Gerrish, *Grace and Gratitude,* p. vi.

22. On the connection of gratitude and guilt, see Joseph Anthony Amato II, *Guilt and Gratitude: A Study of the Origins of Contemporary Conscience* (Westport, Conn.: Greenwood, 1982), pp. 51–55. William J. Bouwsma has argued that Calvin approached the world with a basic sense of anxiety, bothered by experiences of disorder and insecurity. Order and prudence are thus central themes in his thought. See *John Calvin: A Sixteenth Century Portrait* (New York: Oxford University Press, 1988), especially ch. 2 and p. 193. Anxiety turns gratitude into prudence and excess into order.

23. Karl Barth, *Church Dogmatics,* ed. G. W. Bromiley and T. F. Torrance (Edinburgh: T.&T. Clark, 1939–69), II/1, p. 260. George Hunsinger emphasizes this point as one of Barth's main motifs, what he calls *actualism:* "Our active relationship to God is a history of love and freedom; we are capable of it not because it stands at our disposal, but because we who stand at God's disposal are given it" (*How to Read Karl Barth* [New York: Oxford University Press, 1991], p. 31). Notice how Hunsinger connects God's freedom to love with God's independence from any external motivation or necessity: "The being of God in act is a being in love and freedom. God, who does not need us to be the living God, is perfectly complete without us. For God is alive in the active relations of love and freedom which constitute God's being in and for itself" (p. 30). God does not need to give but does so anyway.

24. Barth, *Church Dogmatics,* II/2, p. 10.

25. Ibid., II/1, p. 198.

26. Ibid., IV/1, p. 41.

27. Ibid., II/2, p. 10.

28. Karl Barth, *The Christian Life, Church Dogmatics IV/4, Lecture Fragments,* trans. Geoffrey W. Bromiley (Grand Rapids: Eerdmans, 1981), p. 86. Also note this comment: "To give thanks is to recognize an unobligated and unmerited favor. It is to show that one recognizes the favor as a favor, and as a free one at

that. It is to express this in act and attitude toward the one who does the favor. As a concept that is both formally clear and materially important, standing as it does in excellent relation to man's encounter with God in the covenant of grace, this seems to be fairly exactly the concept we are seeking. . . . We might accept this rich and living concept joyfully and with no reserve" (p. 39).

29. Since I want to comment on the *Church Dogmatics* alone, I analyze in this footnote only Barth's most extensive treatment of gratitude. In the 1928–29 University of Münster lectures on ethics published after his death as *Ethics* (ed. Dietrich Braun and trans. Geoffrey W. Bromiley [New York: Seabury, 1981]), Barth discusses our moral response to God in the trinitarian scheme of creation, reconciliation, and redemption. From the standpoint of creation we must recognize God's order, from reconciliation we must be humble, and from redemption we must be grateful. Gratitude answers the question of how we are to act: we must do what God wills gladly, voluntarily, and cheerfully: "Insofar as we are grateful to God, the strangeness of his command and the hostility with which it confronts us drop away" (p. 505). Gratitude is our welcome, even playful response to God's initiative: "If God commands gratitude this means that by my own choice, although wholly in response to his act, he wants to win me for himself" (p. 500). Gratitude is not just obedience; it is our recognition that we obey God for our own ultimate good: "Gratitude cannot be commanded. I must really command it of myself. But how can I issue this command if I do not confront myself as I do when seen from the standpoint of eternity in my divine sonship, in my participation in divine nature? It is in the Holy Spirit, without whom the Word of God would not come to me, that this commanding of self by the self, of the self as the one that has to be commanded here, is an actual event" (p. 501). Barth goes on to describe gratitude as play (release and relaxation), and he amplifies this description with a discussion of humor and art. Although Barth was uncomfortable with some aspects of this lecture course, some of it was utilized in his later work, so if he had lived to finish the *Church Dogmatics* (the completion of volume IV would have discussed the thanksgiving involved with the Lord's Supper, and the last volume would have addressed God the Redeemer), he surely would have written much more about gratitude. For a discussion of the development of Barth's ethics, see Nigel Biggar, *The Hastening That Waits: Karl Barth's Ethics* (Oxford: Clarendon, 1993).

30. Barth, *Christian Life*, p. 106.

31. Barth, *Church Dogmatics*, II/1, p. 217.

32. As Sheila Greeve Davaney explains, "God is capable of obedience and humility in relation to the world because this is first and primarily a mode of relationship within the intertrinitarian life; it is a mode of God's own conscious and willed determination of Godself" (*Divine Power* [Philadelphia: Fortress, 1986], p. 51). Barth tries to combine the idea that God gives as a free decision with the originally Neoplatonic theory of emanations, which connects God's giving with the natural overflow of the good, by arguing that God chooses to be for God's self in a trinitarian or social form: "We must certainly regard this

overflow as itself matching His essence, belonging to His essence. But it is an overflow which is not demanded or presupposed by any necessity, constraint, or obligation, least of all from outside, from our side, or by any law by which God Himself is bound and obliged" (*Church Dogmatics*, II/1, p. 273).

33. Barth, *Church Dogmatics*, II/2, p. 121.

34. Davaney, *Divine Power*, p. 56. Davaney is developing an earlier criticism of Barth by Jürgen Moltmann, who suspects that Barth's emphasis on freedom harbors traces of nominalism. See *The Trinity and the Kingdom*, trans. Margaret Kohl (San Francisco: HarperCollins, 1981), pp. 52–56.

35. Barth, *Church Dogmatics*, II/1, p. 279.

36. Ibid., III/1, p. 331.

37. Ibid., II/1, p. 284.

38. "I believe in Jesus Christ, God's Son our Lord, in order to perceive that God the Almighty, the Father, is the Creator of heaven and earth. If I did not believe the former, I could not perceive and understand the latter" (ibid., III/1, p. 29).

39. Ibid., II/1, p. 669. In a Calvinistic mode, Barth continues on the same page: "Gratitude is to be understood not only as a quality and an activity but as the very being and essence of this creature. It is not merely grateful. It is itself gratitude. It can see itself only as gratitude because in fact it can only exist as this, as pure gratitude towards God. What the creature does in its new creatureliness, which in Jesus Christ has become gratitude to God, is to glorify God."

40. Barth argues that if God's gifts were other than God's own self, then our love "would not really be directed to him as the Giver, but to the goods and gifts appointed for our own consumption, and to himself only to the extent that what is truly desired and valued, i.e., grace and salvation in all these forms would be received and enjoyed, not without him, yet nonetheless only through him" (ibid., IV/3, pp. 595–96, quoted and revised in Hunsinger, *How to Read Karl Barth*, p. 144). Barth is afraid that a gift separated from God would lead us to treat God as an instrument to be used for our own purposes.

41. *Church Dogmatics*, IV/3, p. 656.

42. Barth admits that the problem of double agency is unsolvable in his theology. He wants to avoid any hint of determinism or monism, yet human freedom is only miraculously and mysteriously provided by divine grace: "The difficulty with which we are faced appears to be an insuperable one, and it would be so, and remain so, if we had to consider whether we could give an answer, and if so what, merely within the framework of a general philosophy of God and the world" (ibid., III/3, p. 139). I am arguing that the general framework of gift giving helps us conceptualize God's transcendence along with human freedom and responsibility without reducing the latter to the status of miracle and mystery.

43. Ibid., II/1, p. 586.

44. Ibid., I/1, p. 45.

45. The closest Barth comes to a notion of reciprocity is in a comment about the excess of gratitude that matches God's own excess: "But just as the glory of God itself is the superabundance, the overflowing of the perfection of the divine being, so the glorification of God through the creature is in its own way equally an overflowing, an act of freedom and not of force or of a self-evident course of events" (ibid., II/1, p. 671). It is the momentum of God's overflowing love, however, that the creature is able to direct to God; the gift returns on its own accord, not out of the effort of the givee. Our glorification of God is God's self-glorification. We only know God because and as God knows God's self.

46. Ibid., II/2, p. 28.

47. Alfred North Whitehead, *Process and Reality*, corrected ed. (New York: Macmillan, 1978), p. 18.

48. Charles Hartshorne, *Beyond Humanism* (Lincoln: University of Nebraska Press, 1937), p. 50.

49. "That the human creator always has a given concrete actuality to work with does not of itself establish a difference between him and God, unless it be admitted as made out that there was a first moment of creation. For if not, then God, too, creates each stage of the world as successor to a preceding phase. Only dubious interpretation of an obscure parable, the book of Genesis, stands between us and this view" (Charles Hartshorne, *The Divine Relativity* [New Haven: Yale University Press, 1948], p. 30).

50. Note some of the last words of *Process and Reality*: "What is done in the world is transformed into a reality in heaven, and the reality in heaven passes back into the world. By reason of this reciprocal relation, the love in the world passes back into the love in heaven and floods back again into the world" (p. 351). The language here is that of exchange. God adds to the world by reappropriating what God has given in the first place. Note also this revealing comment by John Cobb: "Divine influence does not restrict that of the world; it supplements it" (*God's Activity in the World*, ed. Owen C. Thomas [Chico, Calif.: Scholars Press, 1983], p. 115). God's own form of exchange with the world embellishes or heightens the ordinary economy of exchange, supplementing it with preservation and persuasion, but it does not challenge or transform exchange itself.

51. Charles Hartshorne, *Man's Vision of God* (Hamden, Conn.: Archon, 1964), p. 161.

52. For more on Hartshorne's attraction to the classical virtue of prudence, see his *Wisdom as Moderation: A Philosophy of the Middle Way* (Albany: SUNY Press, 1987).

53. *Divine Relativity*, p. 47. Hartshorne also argues in the same book: "For if God can be indebted to no one, can receive value from no one, then to speak of serving him is to indulge in equivocation" (p. 58).

54. Davaney raises this objection in a more pointed way: "If the primary good is aesthetic, that is, intensity and harmony of experience, does not the suspicion arise that God might seek or encourage creaturely conflict or suffering as a means of increasing the contrast within God's own experience, thereby

enhancing its aesthetic value at a cost to the nondivine individuals? That is, might God, seeking intensity of experience, sacrifice the experience of God's creatures for God's own ends?" (*Divine Power,* p. 213).

55. Sallie McFague, *Models of God* (Philadelphia: Fortress, 1987).

56. From *Ethics,* 1158b, quoted in ibid., p. 158.

57. For a full treatment of these issues, see Grace Jantzen, *God's World, God's Body* (Philadelphia: Westminster, 1984). Also see Thomas F. Tracy, *God, Action, and Embodiment* (Grand Rapids: Eerdmans, 1984), ch. 6. Tracy criticizes notions of God's embodiment in the world because they limit God's freedom and power. He defends the traditional idea of God's transcendence. I am criticizing McFague from the perspective of God's generosity, not God's omnipotence. For McFague's own development of these issues, see *The Body of God* (Minneapolis: Fortress, 1993). For a vision of nature as not God's body but as the product of God's extravagance—nature as an excessive gift, making our own excessive response to nature problematic but necessary—see Stephen H. Webb, "Nature's Spendthrift Economy: The Extravagance of God in *Pilgrim at Tinker Creek,*" *Soundings* 77 (fall/winter 1994): 429–51.

58. McFague, *Models of God,* p. 184.

59. Mark C. Taylor, *Erring: A Postmodern A/theology* (Chicago: University of Chicago Press, 1984).

60. Altizer reflects this ambiguity in this comment: "Thus the project of *Deconstructing Theology* is not one of actual or literal deconstruction, for that has already long since occurred, but rather one of seeking a passage through the end or death of the primal ground by way of the Western theoretical and theological tradition. This is just the point at which theological thinking is now being reborn, even if reborn in a non-theological form, which is to say a form of thinking that bears no manifest sign of the presence of theology" (Altizer's Foreword to Taylor's *Deconstructing Theology* [New York: Crossroad and Scholar's Press, 1982], p. xi).

61. Mark C. Taylor, *Journeys to Selfhood: Hegel and Kierkegaard* (Berkeley: University of California Press, 1980), p. 146.

62. See Thomas J. J. Altizer, *History as Apocalypse* (Albany: SUNY Press, 1985), and Altizer, *Total Presence* (New York: Seabury, 1980). For an informative reading of Altizer, see Charles E. Winquist, *Epiphanies of Darkness* (Philadelphia: Fortress, 1986), pp. 108–23. For Taylor's critique of Altizer, see *Tears* (Albany: SUNY Press, 1990), chs. 5 and 6. Taylor argues, "What Altizer *cannot* think is a nondialectical other" (p. 69). For Taylor's development of negation as that which must be but cannot be thought, see *Nots* (Chicago: University of Chicago Press, 1993).

63. Jacques Derrida, *Of Grammatology,* trans. Gayatri Chakravorty Spivak (Baltimore: Johns Hopkins University Press, 1974), p. 75 (the italics are Derrida's).

64. Derrida, *Speech and Phenomena* (Evanston, Ill.: Northwestern University Press, 1973), p. 135.

65. Taylor, *Tears,* p. 69.

66. Taylor, *Erring,* p. 29.

67. For Taylor's most recent statement on giving, in which he draws heavily from Derrida's interpretation of the true gift as giving nothing, see "Discrediting God," *Journal of the American Academy of Religion* 62 (summer 1994): 603–23.

68. For a similar criticism, note these comments by Wesley A. Kort: Taylor "posits an undifferentiated plain where distinctions and particularities are dissolved and dismembered. . . . His key word is 'writing,' and he means by it a vast, boundless, leveled terrain of uncentered, mutually canceling, and interdependent meanings from which human life is inseparable and upon which humans hopelessly wander" (*Bound To Differ: The Dynamics of Theological Discourses* [University Park: Pennsylvania State University Press, 1992], p. 39).

69. Taylor, *Erring*, p. 143.

70. He goes on: "Upon the basis of this dialectic the attempt to speak of a necessity to which God himself is supposed to be subject would be radically impossible. But at all events the dialectic in which we ourselves exist, a method which we are ourselves at all times capable of using—this is not the actual dialectic of grace" (Karl Barth, *Protestant Theology in the Nineteenth Century* [London: SCM Press, 1972], p. 420).

71. Peter C. Hodgson, *God in History: Shapes of Freedom* (Nashville: Abingdon, 1989).

72. About Taylor, Hodgson remarks: "God becomes utterly immanent, totally incarnate in worldly inscription, in writing itself" (p. 37). Moreover, "the temptation here is to retreat into intellectual games and hedonistic play, which may very well be a mask for despair, cynicism, nihilism" (p. 40). For his critique of current theories of God's embodiment, see pp. 81–83.

73. Charles Taylor's argument that the introduction of necessity into God's being deprives God of the freedom to give should serve as a warning to any attempt to connect Hegel's God to an emphasis on generosity: "In Hegel's system, God cannot *give* to man—neither in creation, nor in revelation, nor in salvation through sending his Son. To see these acts of God is to see them in the medium of *Vorstellung,* and what makes them acts is just what belongs to the inadequate narrative medium, which we transcend in philosophy. For to see them aright is to see them as emanations of a necessity which is no more God's than it is man's" (*Hegel* [Cambridge: Cambridge University Press, 1975], p. 493).

74. Hodgson, *God in History,* p. 208.

75. Hodgson quotes from Hegel's *Lectures on the Philosophy of Religion:* "To recognize the actual existence of what is substantive in the idea . . . involves hard labor *(harte Arbeit):* in order to pluck reason, the rose in the cross of the present, one must take up the cross itself" (pp. 277–78, n. 83).

76. Hodgson, *God in History,* p. 19.

Chapter 4

1. See especially Reinhold Niebuhr, *An Interpretation of Christian Ethics* (1935; reprint, New York: Seabury, 1979). Niebuhr amplifies the rigor of Christlike love and exaggerates the selfishness of humanity, pushing both to such

opposite extremes that he is forced to bring them together only in an eschatological, prophetic manner: "The ethic of Jesus does not deal at all with the
immediate moral problem of every human life—the problem of arranging some
kind of armistice between the various contending factions and forces. It has
nothing to say about the relativities of politics and economics, nor of the
necessary balances of power which exist and must exist in even the most
intimate social relationships. The absolutism and perfectionism of Jesus' love
ethic sets itself uncompromisingly not only against the natural self-regarding
impulses, but against the necessary prudent defences of the self, required
because of the egoism of others. . . . It has only a vertical dimension between
the loving will of God and the will of man" (pp. 23–24). The strength of
Niebuhr's position is evident in the way that he is able to argue that human
generosity is never pure (excess is never completely free from exchange).
Nevertheless, Niebuhr is also forced to argue that generosity never transforms
social structures: "Voluntary acts of kindness which exceed the requirements of
coercive justice are never substitutes for, but additions to, the coercive system of
social relationships through which alone a basic justice can be guaranteed" (p.
112). The excess of giving supplements but does not basically challenge the
order of justice. For Niebuhr's critique of gratitude as a sufficient basis for
morality, see p. 91. For a later statement on giving from Niebuhr, see "Man's
Selfhood in Self-Seeking and Self-Giving," in his *Man's Nature and His Communities* (London: Geoffrey Bles, 1966), where he illuminates the paradox of the
intimate connection between self-seeking and self-giving: "Consistent self-
seeking is bound to be self-defeating; on the other hand, self-giving is bound to
contribute ultimately to self-realisation" (p. 81).

2. Kathryn Tanner, *The Politics of God* (Minneapolis: Fortress, 1992). Especially see pp. 155 and 192.

3. I do not mean to imply that there was a time when religion was totally
separate from economics. Nevertheless, in this century, religious groups have
become especially eager to adapt the Christian message to the mechanics of the
market. See R. Laurence Moore, *Selling God: American Religion in the Marketplace
of Culture* (New York: Oxford University Press, 1994). The question is whether
there can be a Christianization of the market, since it is obvious that capitalism
can infiltrate and control Christian rhetoric.

4. Catherine Mowry LaCugna, *God for Us: The Trinity and Christian Life* (San
Francisco: HarperCollins, 1991). LaCugna's concerns are both political and
feminist. Note this perceptive comment: "Classical metaphysics, the effort to
ascertain what something is 'in itself,' is perhaps the ultimate projection of
masculinity" (p. 398). For an influential account of the social conception of the
Trinity, the idea that God is more like an inclusive society than an individual, or
set of individuals, who must enter into relationships subsequent to that individuality, see Jürgen Moltmann, *The Trinity and the Kingdom* (San Francisco: Harper
& Row, 1981). The society of the Trinity is politically relevant because it is
nonhierarchical and nonmonarchical.

5. See Karl Rahner, *The Trinity* (New York: Herder & Herder, 1970).

6. LaCugna, *God for Us*, pp. 210–11.

7. Jean-Luc Marion, *God without Being*, trans. Thomas A. Carlson and foreword by David Tracy (Chicago: University of Chicago Press, 1991). A comment by Abraham Heschel is appropriate here: "The statement 'God is' is an understatement" (*God in Search of Man* [New York: Harper & Row, 1965], p. 121).

8. Marion, *God without Being*, p. 3.

9. Notice how Pseudo-Dionysius places the good before being by drawing from the idea of the gift: "The first gift therefore of the absolutely transcendent Goodness is the gift of being, and that Goodness is praised from those that first and principally have a share of being" (*The Divine Names*, in *The Complete Works*, trans. Colm Luibheid [New York: Paulist Press, 1987], p. 99).

10. See Kevin Hart, *The Trespass of the Sign* (Cambridge: Cambridge University Press, 1989), p. 202.

11. Marion, *God without Being*, p. 75.

12. "Ontotheology when taken to affective excess demands mediating performance and thus an ethics. Love can only be known in loving and being loved" (Anthony J. Godzieba, "Ontotheology to Excess: Imagining God without Being," *Theological Studies* 56 [1995]:19).

13. Marion, *God without Being*, p. 48.

14. "In the idol, the gaze of man is frozen in its mirror; in the icon, the gaze of man is lost in the invisible gaze that visibly envisages him" (ibid., p. 20).

15. "God can give himself to be thought without idolatry only starting from himself alone: to give himself to be thought as love, hence as gift; to give himself to be thought as a thought of the gift. Or better, as a gift for thought, as a gift that gives itself to be thought. But a gift, which gives itself forever, can be thought only by a thought that gives itself to the gift to be thought. Only a thought that gives itself can devote itself to a gift for thought. But, for thought, what is it to give itself, if not to love?" (ibid., p. 47).

16. Rodolphe Gasché, *Inventions of Difference: On Jacques Derrida* (Cambridge: Harvard University Press, 1994), p. 99.

17. Marion, *God without Being*, p. 47.

18. Marion does talk about returning the gift, but only in terms of the discourse of praise: "To return the gift, to play redundantly the unthinkable donation, this is not said but done. Love is not spoken, in the end, it is made. Only then can discourse be reborn, but as an enjoyment, a jubilation, a praise" (ibid., p. 107).

19. M. Douglas Meeks, *God the Economist: The Doctrine of God and Political Economy* (Minneapolis: Fortress, 1989).

20. "Neoclassical economists speak of these forces as religious people speak of the numinous, for these mostly unexamined premises entail a 'transcendent' destination of capital not of its own making" (ibid., p. 65).

21. The historical question, however, about the influence of theology on economics is complex. For one of the best historical treatments of this issue, see

Boyd Hinton, *The Age of Atonement: The Influence of Evangelicalism on Social and Economic Thought, 1785–1865* (Oxford: Clarendon, 1988).

22. John Milbank summarizes Adam Smith's understanding of the relationship between sympathy and self-interest: " 'Pure benevolence,' he avers, is suited only to a non-dependent being, namely God, whereas human beings must take account of the more self-interested virtues of 'propriety,' which entail habits of economy, industry and discretion, the judicious spending of our own resources" (*Theology and Social Theory: Beyond Secular Reason* [Oxford: Blackwell, 1990], p. 31). God can afford to do what we cannot.

23. Meeks, *God the Economist*, p. 21.

24. This word later comes to play an important role in Gnostic thought; it denotes the fullness of the heavens, where the Aeons assemble, glorifying God, freed from the impediment of matter. See Hans Jonas, *The Gnostic Religion* (Boston: Beacon, 1958), ch. 8.

25. Meeks, *God the Economist*, p. 172.

26. Horace Bushnell, *Work and Play* (New York: Charles Scribner, 1881). For a thorough treatment of the ways both preindustrial and modern societies envision work and play, see Victor Turner, *From Ritual to Theater: The Human Seriousness of Play* (New York: PAJ, 1982).

27. Marvin Olasky, *The Tragedy of American Compassion* (Wheaton, Ill.: Crossway, 1992), p. 8.

28. From *The Divine Names* in *The Complete Works*, pp. 82–83.

29. All scripture quotations are from *The New English Bible* (New York: Oxford University Press, 1976).

30. In my thoughts on the poetics of excess, I have been greatly influenced by a brief essay by Paul Ricoeur, "Love and Justice," in *Radical Pluralism and Truth: David Tracy and the Hermeneutics of Religion,* ed. Werner Jeanrond and Jennifer Rike (New York: Crossroad, 1991). Ricoeur addresses the relationship between giving and justice. In fact, one of the key issues of politics concerns the question of who is able to give. Ricoeur suggests that it is not enough to establish rules that protect the equality of individuals entering into relationships of exchange: "The highest point the ideal of justice can envision is that of a society in which the feeling of mutual dependence—even of mutual indebtedness—remains subordinate to the idea of mutual disinterest" (p. 196). For Ricoeur, the poetics of love exercises a dialectical pull on the prose of justice. The commandment to love one's enemy, for example, cannot be simply translated into the judicial implementation of justice, and yet its power cannot be denied to raise our expectations higher than equivalency allows. The law of love is "the hyperethical expression of a broader economy of the gift" (p. 197) that forces justice to a higher standard, and yet Ricoeur also suggests, following Niebuhr, that love needs to be subjected to the practicalities of justice. The two complement and correct each other. Justice mediates between the verticality of love and the horizontality of ordinary social practices: "To disorient without reorienting is, in Kierkegaardian terms, to suspend the ethical. In one sense,

the commandment to love, as hyperethical, is a way of suspending the ethical, which is reoriented only at the price of the reprise and a rectification of the rule of justice that runs counter to its utilitarian tendency" (p. 202). Ricoeur wants to preserve the "secret discordance" (p. 202) between the two logics of excess and exchange. On a personal level, we need to be "touched and secretly guarded by the poetics of love" (p. 201), while on a social level we need "the tenacious incorporation, step by step, of a supplementary degree of compassion and generosity in all of our codes" (p. 202).

31. Note the hyperbole in Pseudo-Dionysius's description of God: "God is called great because of that characteristic greatness of his which gives of itself to everything great, is poured out on all greatness and indeed reaches far beyond it. His greatness takes in all space, surpasses all number, moves far beyond infinity in abundance, in the overflowing of its great works and in the gifts welling up from it" (*The Divine Names*, in *The Complete Works*, p. 115).

32. Paul Ricoeur, *The Symbolism of Evil*, trans. Emerson Buchanan (Boston: Beacon, 1969), p. 272.

33. Notice Paul's use of superabundance *(hyperballōn, hyperbolē)* in 2 Cor. 3:10; 4:7, 17; 9:14; 11:23; Eph. 1:19; 2:7; 3:19. There are other uses of the *hyper* compound in 2 Thess. 1:3; Eph. 3:20; 1 Thess. 3:10; 5:13; Phil. 3:8; 4:7; Rom. 5:20; 2 Cor. 7:4; 1 Tim. 1:14.

34. Ched Myers, *Binding the Strong Man: A Political Reading of Mark's Story of Jesus* (Maryknoll, N.Y.: Orbis, 1988).

35. In a culture that obsessively focuses on thinness as the goal of ascetic discipline and the paradigm for all affirmative bodily values, this theological message of abundance should have radical and transformative consequences.

36. Note this wonderful comment by Hans Urs von Balthasar: "In the mystery of the Trinity, the creature can affirm itself as an act of thanksgiving to God. Receiving itself, freely identifying with itself—and here the gift of God separates itself from God as the fruit separates itself from the tree—it really performs the perfect act of thanksgiving, accepting precisely what God wishes to give" (*Theo-Drama, Theological Dramatic Theory*, vol. 2; *Dramatis Personae: Man in God*, trans. Graham Harrison [San Francisco: Ignatius, 1990], p. 288).

37. "Would the specter of death be as disturbing if we could begin the practice of relinquishing something of ourselves daily? If we have the opportunity to be aware of our final moments of life, perhaps we could then let go in glad and reckless abandon. We could see death not as taking life from us but as something to which we *give* our lives in joyous liberation" (Donald W. Hinze, *To Give and Give Again* [New York: Pilgrim, 1990], p. 14).

38. As Donald W. Hinze reminds us, "It is important to note that it is not out of abundance that God gave, there being only one self to give, but God gave God's *only* self" (ibid., p. 38). I would say that giving from abundance is not antithetical to giving up all that one is, especially when such giving is done joyfully, as a way of increasing the giving of others.

39. Jacques Derrida, *The Gift of Death*, trans. David Wills (Chicago: University of Chicago Press, 1995), p. 49.

40. Marion, *God without Being*, pp. 97–98.

41. Mark Taylor often uses the story of the prodigal son to illustrate the type of economy that his own version of excess seeks to disrupt and escape. In a passage critical of the circularity of the Hegelian system, Taylor writes: "Though rarely recognized, this closed circle, whose roundness smooths rough edges and softens rigid angularity, is actually an extension of Hegel's family circle. [Taylor makes much of the fact that Hegel never reconciled with his illegitimate son, an excess that the economy of his own family life could not accommodate.] The philosopher is not a nomadic wanderer who, never settling down, has no place to lay his head. [Deconstructionists often talk about philosophy in the desert—that is, in perpetual exile.] To the contrary, the philosopher is the prodigal son who faithfully returns to the home of the father. Within this father's house, the son who saves rather than the son who spends is rewarded" (*Altarity* [Chicago: University of Chicago Press, 1987], pp. 31–32). What is interesting is that Taylor (intentionally?) misreads the parable. The son who spends is rewarded, not the older brother. Moreover, the son who spends does not represent true excess; he leaves the household because he does not want to share. Rather, he wants to own, possess, and control. The only real figure of excess in the story is the father, who loves both sons unconditionally, having already given away what each of them, in their own way, wants to gain.

42. I do not mean by these comments to justify sexual promiscuity. Indeed, marriage can serve as a paradigm for all relationships because lifelong partnership must balance both excess and exchange, holding them together in tense and creative ways.

43. Paul Tillich, *Systematic Theology* (Chicago: University of Chicago Press, 1957), 2:52.

44. Meeks, *God the Economist*, p. 118.

45. On the idea that Jesus is the gift from Israel to the church, see Paul M. van Buren, *A Theology of the Jewish-Christian Reality, Part III: Christ in Context* (San Francisco: Harper & Row, 1988), pp. 73–78, and Clark M. Williamson, *A Guest in the House of Israel: Post-Holocaust Church Theology* (Louisville: Westminster/John Knox, 1993), ch. 7, esp. pp. 200–201.

46. For a full discussion of *charis*, see Stephen J. Duffy, *The Dynamics of Grace* (Collegeville, Minn.: Liturgical, 1993), pp. 29–36.

47. Myers, *Binding the Strong Man*, p. 247.

48. Paul Tournier, *The Meaning of Gifts*, trans. John S. Gilmour (Richmond: John Knox, 1970), p. 27.

49. Hyde, *The Gift*, p. 35.

50. Robert Wuthnow, *Acts of Compassion* (Princeton: Princeton University Press, 1991), p. 225.

51. Nicholas Rescher argues that we should act to promote a social order in which prudential self-interest coincides with the common good. For Rescher,

this is not a morally superlative order but rather an adequate moral economy: "The thesis that if one acts so as to advance the general welfare of the social group, one thereby furthers one's personal welfare-interests is simply not a descriptive truth—it is not a statement of actual facts. But if the thesis of reciprocal coordination of personal and social advantage is not an inescapable fact (and it is not), it is at any rate a regulative ideal. It is not actually so, but it *ought* to be. In an ideal state of affairs, it would surely be in the firsthand interest of people to promote the general good: someone who exerts himself for the welfare of his fellows ought not to find his own abridged thereby, and someone who consults his own best interests ought to find that in serving them he advances those of others as well" (Nicholas Rescher, *The Role of Vicarious Affects in Moral Philosophy and Social Theory* [Pittsburgh: University of Pittsburgh Press, 1975], p. 102). I am suggesting that such an idealized harmony of giving and receiving is only possible within a theological horizon that does not make selfishness and other-regard magically coincide but encourages excessive acts that create the bonds of mutuality by empowering further giving.

52. William Corlett, *Community without Unity: A Politics of Derridian Extravagance* (Durham, N.C.: Duke University Press, 1989), p. 212. Corlett distinguishes a politics of extravagance from a politics of reassurance; the former is a necessary supplement to the latter: "Free gift-giving stands beside the reassuring forces of shared oneness and reciprocity in an accidental, silent, extravagant way that strikes with force and irruption until silence is again broken by discourse" (p. 202). "Perhaps the mutual service of community is possible without the unity of sharing anything in common" (p. 203). I have learned much from Corlett's reflections on the kind of community that giving gives, but I disagree with his connection of extravagant giving to Derridean deconstructionism. Derrida, I argued in chapter 2, undermines the hyperbole of the gift with the irony of suspicion. Corlett is closer to Bataille, who defines *community* as "the aggressive and gratuitous gift of oneself to the future—in opposition to chauvinistic avarice, bound to the past" (quoted in Steven Shaviro, *Passion and Excess: Blanchot, Bataille and Literary Theory* [Tallahassee: Florida State University Press, 1990], p. 98). Also note the reflections of Bataille, Maurice Blanchot, and Jean-Luc Nancy on the community that is *désoeuvré*, that is, unworking, idle, unoccupied. See Maurice Blanchot, *The Unavowable Community*, trans. Pierre Joris (Barrytown, N.Y.: Station Hill, 1988). For a community to work, it must be, in a way, workless, unproductive; otherwise, the law of exchange creates a homogeneity of isolated individuals. Nevertheless, waste is also utilized by modern societies in cunning ways: "Waste is part of the rigorous administration of things which requires a certain slack. It is no longer a sign of failure, but a form of use whereby utility preserves itself by accommodating what is apparently of no use" (Maurice Blanchot, *The Writing of the Disaster*, trans. Ann Smock [Lincoln: University of Nebraska Press, 1986], p. 88). Only giving allows for a kind of work that is not really work, a work that will become increasingly important, incidentally, as market- and government-created jobs continue to shrink.

53. Pseudo-Dionysius, *Complete Works*, p. 72.
54. Justo L. Gonzalez, *Faith and Wealth: A History of Early Christian Ideas on the Origin, Significance, and Use of Money* (San Francisco: HarperCollins, 1990), ch. 4. Also see Christopher J. Berry, *The Idea of Luxury: A Conceptual and Historical Investigation* (Cambridge: Cambridge University Press, 1994).
55. See Geoffrey Wainwright, *Eucharist and Eschatology* (London: Epworth, 1971).
56. Frances Young and David F. Ford, *Meaning and Truth in 2 Corinthians* (Grand Rapids: Eerdmans, 1988). Also see Stephen Charles Mott, *Biblical Ethics and Social Change* (New York: Oxford University Press, 1982), pp. 30–34.
57. Augustine explains the Holy Spirit as the principle of reciprocity in *On the Trinity*. For criticism, see David Coffey, "The Holy Spirit as the Mutual Love of the Father and the Son," *Theological Studies* 51 (1990): 193–229.
58. In this and the next paragraph, all quotations are from *Summa Theologica*, the Benziger edition translated by the Fathers of the English Dominican Province, I, Q. 37 and 38. For Aquinas's fascinating discussion of prodigality, where he at least considers the possibility that "marks of prodigality are lavishness in spending and the absence of anxiety about riches. This is above all the mark of the spiritually perfect," see 2a2ae Q. 119.
59. See Hinze, *To Give and Give Again*, p. 62.
60. "God and Philosophy," trans. Richard A. Cohen, in *The Levinas Reader*, ed. Sean Hand (Oxford: Basil Blackwell, 1989), p. 179.
61. Pseudo-Dionysius, *Divine Names*, p. 115.
62. LaCugna emphasizes praise as the response to grace, but she portrays praise as a dynamic movement outward toward the other, not the static announcement of unworthiness and inability: "Praise is the creature's mode of ecstasis, its own self-transcendence, its disinclination to remain self-contained. The creature's doxology is evoked by God's ecstasis, God's glorification in the economy. Praise is the mode of return, 'matching' God's movement of exodus. God creates out of glory, for glory. The return is part of the rhythm of life from God to God. In that communion of love is gathered all religious endeavor. In that rhythm of movement all economic and political life is caught up in a vast communion of shared life, shared goods, shared pain, and shared hope" (*God for Us*, pp. 350–51). For a detailed discussion of praising that distinguishes it from thanking, see Claus Westermann, *Praise and Lament in the Psalms*, trans. Keith R. Crim and Richard N. Soulen (Atlanta: John Knox, 1981). He argues that thanking is a secondary and derivative development of praising; praising is the more comprehensive as well as the older term: "Thanking presupposes that the community is no longer primary and no longer self-evident. It presupposes that the community is no longer prior to the individual" (p. 28).
63. I borrow the phrase "communication of efficacy" from Kyle Pasewark's definition of divine power in *A Theology of Power: Being beyond Domination* (Minneapolis: Fortress, 1993).

Index